Subhas Chandra Bose and the Bengal Revolutionaries

Subhas Chandra Bose
and the
Bengal Revolutionaries

Roma Banerjee

New Delhi-110 002

Subhas Chandra Bose and the Bengal Revolutionaries

Copyright © by Roma Banerjee

All rights reserved. No part of this book may be reproduced in any form or by any electronic or mechanical means including information storage and retrieval systems without permission in writing from the publisher, except by a reviewer, who may quote brief passages in a review.

ISBN: 978-81-8405-057-8

Rs.875/-

First Published 2010

Published by:
Reference Press
4831/24, Ansari Road,
Darya Ganj,
New Delhi-110 002.
INDIA
Phones: 23260807, 41563444
Fax: 41563334
E-mail: info@essessreference.com
www.essessreference.com

Printed and bound in India at Salasar Imaging Systems.

DEDICATED TO

Pratima Banerjee
&
Dr. H.K.Banerjee

Forever and always, my parents, you have my endless gratitude for this precious gift of life...

the gift of your enduring love.

Foreword

Indian national movement had two divergent paths of action one was nonviolent non-co-operation movement led by M.K. Gandhi and the other, armed struggle led by revolutionaries and Subhas Chandra Bose and his INA. Both had tremendous impact on the British Indian government shaken by the two world wars and both finally contributed to our winning of independence. It is fatuous to argue which had greater contribution to make.

The alternative path of armed revolution was paved by the patriotic revolutionaries who sacrificed their lives for the cause in Bengal, Punjab and Maharashtra. Martyrdom was a monument to ultimate victory. The role of revolutionaries and their link with Netaji had not so far been properly delineated. Dr. Roma Banerjee has successfully forged their link in her odyssey into the subject. Now Netaji is properly focused in context. In bold stroke of pen, she has inked the subject with grace and poise. This will surely attract the attention of the reading public mainly interested in a public figure like Netaji at a time when patriotism has vanished and the country is taken for a joyride by scheming politicians and tycoons. Netaji was patriotism personified. He has now got a pedestal reared by the blood and sweat of martyrs.

Dr. Chittabrata Palit

PREFACE

To fill the research gap in documented literature on the relation between Subhas Chandra Bose and the Bengal revolutionaries was the prime motive in attempting this work. Archival materials have been consulted on Home (Political) in the National Archives of India, State Archives in Kolkata (at Bhabani Dutta Lane, Writers' Buildings and Shakespeare Sarani). The documents in the archives of the IB and the Special Branch of Kolkata Police at Lord Sinha Road, and the documents in the Justice Mukherjee Commission of Inquiry have also been consulted. Various reference materials have been consulted at the National Library; West Bengal Secretariat Library, Home (Political) Department, Writers' Buildings, Kolkata; Calcutta University Central Library; Bhabani Sen Pathagar; Kranti Press Library; Ballygunge Institute Library; Netaji Institute of Asian Studies; Institute of Historical Studies; Mahajati Sadan Library; Ramakrishna Mission Institute of Culture; British Council; General Douglas MacArthur Archives, Norfolk, Virginia, USA; Indian Embassy Library, Moscow and the University of Minnesota Library, USA.

The surviving ex-revolutionaries of Bengal, a number of political personalities who worked with Bose and a few scholars have been personally interviewed.

The introduction spells out in brief, what this work is all about. The chapters that follow describe and analyze Bose's relationship with the revolutionaries, and the secret societies particularly of Bengal. To be precise, this book is not a biography of Subhas Chandra Bose and hence his entire public life has not been covered here.

I would like to express my gratitude (the long list of acknowledgements notwithstanding) to Dr. Asok Kumar Mukhopadhyay, formerly Netaji Subhas Chandra Bose Chair Professor, Department of Political Science, Calcutta University, for his help and guidance. His advice proved immensely beneficial in preparing this work.

I am specially grateful to Mr. Sumit Sethi of the Reference Press for helping me admirably through the whole process of getting this work published.

In course of my research, I had the opportunity of coming into contact with some remarkable personalities who fought for the nation but subsequently went into oblivion as the unsung heroes and heroines of our freedom movement. I was fortunate enough to meet them, talk to them and hear from them narratives about their own experience in the freedom struggle. This work of mine is a humble tribute to Subhas Chandra Bose and those revolutionaries who sacrificed their youth, their career, their entire being for the liberation of the motherland.

- *Roma Banerjee*

Acknowledgements

While completing my final proof, I was confronted with the thought that the acknowledgements might turn out to be a full-length chapter by itself because I owe so much to so many. As a result, I decided to give only a skeletal presentation of acknowledgements and I am confident about the fact that all those who helped me know how much I value their support and cooperation.

I am thankful to Professor Asok Kumar Mukhopadhyay, my research supervisor. When he suggested that I work on Subhas Chandra Bose and the revolutionaries of Bengal, I did not know why he considered me qualified to undertake such an uphill task. Ultimately I decided to devote myself to the task of finding out the hitherto unknown facts about Bose and his relationship, both overt as well as clandestine, with the revolutionaries. I had no financial support or endowment from any quarters, but this lack of monetary support was compensated by the unforgettable help and encouragement I received from my well-wishers without which it would not have been possible for me to go ahead with this difficult task.

I am very much grateful to Mrs. Sevati Mitra, Mrs. Sushil Kutti, Dr. Mrs. Krishna Chatterjee, all ex-Principals of Rani Birla Girls' College and Dr.Smarajit Chakraborty, former President of the Governing Body of the College for their overwhelming support and constant encouragement. Among the many who provided me with information and source materials, mention must be made of Dr. Purabi Roy of Jadavpore University, Dr.Chittabrata Palit, Emeritus Professor of Modern History at the Jadavpore University, Dr.Chitra Ghosh, Mrs. Geeta Biswas, daughters of Mr.Sarat Chandra Bose, the elder brother of Subhas Chandra Bose, and Sj. Ashok Ghosh of the All-India Forward Bloc.

Dr.Nandita Chowdhuri, Department of Education, Rani Birla Girls' College and Dr. Minati Chattopadhyay of the Institute of Historical Studies were a constant source of encouragement for me; I owe a lot to them.

I am thankful to Mr. Amiya Kumar Samanta, former DG, West Bengal State Police, Mr. Sujoy Chakraborty, former Commissioner of Kolkata Police, Dr. Pramod Mehra of the National Archives of India, the staff members of the State Archives, Intelligence Bureau, Special Branch of Kolkata Police, National Library, and Netaji Institute of Asian Studies. I thank Mr.Girish Maity, a renowned scholar, Mr. Sukumar Bhattacharya, former Director of the Institute of Historical Studies, Mrs Bela Dutta Gupta of Calcutta University for their invaluable advice and support.

I would particularly like to thank the late Bengal Revolutionaries Mr. Amalendu Ghosh, Mr.Amar Chatterjee and Mrs. Helena Dutta, who not only helped me in various ways for my research, also treated me like a family member and a friend whenever I visited them.

A special mention should be made here, in this context, of the name of late Mr. Abinash Dasgupta of Kranti Press (RSP) for helping me by providing a cozy corner in the Press and lots of study materials for my research always with a friendly countenance. I express my heartfelt gratitude to the late Mr. Dasgupta.

I really have no words to express adequately my gratitude for my family, particularly *Partho* and *Goldy* for the incredible, never-ending cooperation, help and encouragement that I received from them.

- Roma Banerjee

Contents

Foreword .... *(vii)*

Preface .... *(ix)*

Acknowledgement .... *(xi)*

1   Introduction 1

2   The Rebel in the Making (1921-1928) 5

3   "The Dare-all Bengal Patriot" (1928-1933) 32

4   The Years of Exile (1933-1938) 96

5   The Uncompromising Loner (1938-1941) 187

6   Conclusion 264

Bibliography 294

Appendices 308

Index 324

1
INTRODUCTION

Subhas Chandra Bose, the legendary hero of the Indian freedom struggle, is a unique phenomenon of Indian politics during the first half of the 20th century. The British government levelled serious allegations against Bose as a 'dangerous' revolutionary and an active consort of the terrorists.

From Intelligence records procured from different archives, numerous instances of these allegations have been found which were not always without base. All through his eventful political career, Bose maintained close contact with the revolutionaries of Bengal and their organizations such as 'Jugantar', 'Anushilan Samity', 'Bengal Volunteers' and a few others.

The heroic saga of the Bengal revolutionaries and their collaboration with Bose during the period from 1921 to 1941 has largely remained untold till today. Even after six decades since Independence, there is still no organized academic and authentic account of Bose's relation with the Bengal revolutionaries. Except a few autobiographical accounts written by some revolutionaries and a few prison memoirs, there is hardly anything that can be called a systematic, properly documented history of Bose's involvement in the revolutionary activities in Bengal. Till date, no objective assessment has been made in this particular area.

The Western historians, especially those who have worked on the Indian freedom struggle, have generally overlooked the contribution of Bose because they cannot forget the 'unpardonable offence' Bose committed by fighting the British with the help of soldiers from the British Army itself. In the Cambridge University, Jawaharlal Nehru is an honoured celebrity name, and Lincoln's Inn of London has brought back the name of Mohandas Karam Chand Gandhi with much adulation, the name that was deleted from its student list in the past. But in the Fitzwilliam College in Cambridge, the name of Bose is still not in existence. In the colonial eyes of England, Bose is still blacklisted as a renegade and hence subject to disrespect. Only in the writings of Hugh Toye and Leonard Gordon, a different outlook can be noticed. Toye brushed aside the Fascist tag that goes along with the name of Bose and said in unequivocal terms that Bose was a great patriot who was ready to do anything that was necessary for achieving his country's freedom.

Strangely enough, in the east while Soviet Union, very few people familiar with the name of Subhas Chandra Bose, although Gandhi, Tilak, Bhagat Singh, Jawaharlal Nehru, Indira Gandhi and other leaders, heroes and martyrs of the Indian freedom movement were well-known to them. Surprisingly, for a long time, Soviet historians and Indologists were not allowed even to mention his name in any of their writings or verbal presentations. Glasnost however, has been removing many blank spaces in Soviet history and in the USSR's relations with foreign countries and establishing the truth about various events and personalities. Researchers in that country are now revising their attitudes towards Subhas Chandra Bose. The periodical called "Soviet Land" edited by L.V. Mitrokhin, honestly confessed it in its December 1990 issue. (See Appendix IV).

Leonid Mitrokhin himself wrote a book called "Lenin and Indian Freedom Fighters" published by Panchsheel Publishers, New Delhi in 1988 in which the name of Subhas Chandra Bose was conspicuous by its absence throughout the work.

Introduction

In all the official or semi-official history of the Indian freedom struggle, the Indian political stage seems to be dominated by the Indian National Congress. Since the advent of Gandhi on the national scenario in the early 1920s, the history of the freedom struggle is said to have consisted of nothing but Congress-led mass movements—the non-violent non-cooperation, Satyagraha, Civil Disobedience, Quit India Movement—all conducted under Gandhi's leadership. As a matter of fact, incessant propaganda has been carried on by some historians with the purpose of influencing public mind that India won freedom in an unprecedented manner by non-violent means under Gandhi's leadership. A half-hearted recognition is sometimes given, in the accounts of these historians, to the part played by Bose after his escape from India in January 1941 and to the organized armed attack that he launched from outside. These activities of Subhas Chandra Bose or his escape from the country with a definite mission to accomplish, have never been considered in the proper historical perspective depicting his close political and personal links with the Bengal revolutionaries in the preceding years in India and abroad.

The reason may be the fact that his alliance with the Axis powers to fight against the British imperialism seems to be unacceptable to some historians till today. As a result, none of his efforts for the achievement of the country's freedom have been appreciated by them. But any evaluation of historical facts needs to be made in their proper historical perspective and in an objective manner. Bose challenged the Gandhian leadership risking his own political career. He offered an alternative leadership parallel to Gandhi's and made enormous contribution to India's struggle for freedom. There is a distinct research gap in this respect. The fact that Bose was a staunch supporter of the line of armed resistance against imperialism and had close contact with the established underground revolutionary organizations in the country, particularly in Bengal as well as abroad, deserves careful scrutiny.

There are scattered writings on this subject but serious research work in this area is not that many.

A thorough study of the available literature reveals that these writings did not go into the details of Bose's direct involvement with the revolutionaries. No comprehensive documentation has as yet been made in this area of our freedom movement. While some of these books focus their attention on particular revolutionary groups and their secret activities, others deal with either a general description of India's revolutionary freedom struggle or Bose's contribution to India's independence in a nutshell. Even the works that directly approached the subject of militant nationalism in Bengal did not delve deep into the extent of Bose's connection with the revolutionaries. Many questions, therefore, remain unanswered and the present thesis tries to explore these unknown areas with a full-length study on the basis of mainly primary sources.

2
THE REBEL IN THE MAKING (1921-1928)

Subhas Chandra Bose, effectively destroyed the allegiance of the armed forces of India and of the people in general to the British Raj by his Azad Hind Fauj (Indian National Army) towards the close of the Second World War.[1] All through his eventful political career, Bose maintained close relationship with the revolutionaries, particularly of Bengal. The Bengal revolutionaries wanted to have a nationwide upheaval against the British Raj through their various organizations with single-minded devotion.

It is true that there were incidents of violence by rebellious groups against the Raj in many other parts of India but it was the undivided Bengal that nurtured an ideology of *"Revolutionism"*, a belief in the concept of armed resistance against British Imperialism. The spirit of militant nationalism was generated in Bengal since the last decade of the 19th Century and had its overwhelming impact on the rest of India. In Maharashtra and Punjab, the politics of extremism manifested itself in a sporadic manner. Leaders like Balgangadhar Tilak were not devotees of non-violence, nor did they believe in the methods of prayer and petitions. But a well-conceived ideology of *"Revolutionism"* was non-existent outside Bengal.

Bengal took to *revolutionism* long before the Swadeshi movement which began as a political movement against the partition of Bengal in 1905. The ground was initially prepared by the educated upper and middle class Bengali and the spirit of revolutionism spread all over the province gradually in literature, in music and in culture as a whole. Don Society was established in 1902 by Satish Mukhopadhyay, which gave birth to National Education Council with Aurobindo Ghosh as one of its faculty. The Don Society nurtured a feeling of nationalism and spread it all over Bengal through its seminars and group discussions in which Sister Nivedita and Sakharam Ganesh Deuskar participated regularly.

Although Maharashra and Punjab had a history of militant freedom struggle but the characteristics of Bengal revolutionism were unique without any parallel elsewhere because here the revolutionaries internalized it as a creed not just as a technique or device for uprooting alien rule from the country.

Patriotism in Bengal had its basis on the concept of universal brotherhood that reflected itself in the art, literature and music of the province.

The British rulers labeled the revolutionaries "terrorists" and this label they could popularize amongst a section of the middle class who generally preferred to stay loyal to the rulers. (But after getting a fuller idea of their activities, the Government officials could realize that they were not terrorists in the usual sense of the term.) Reports of the conspiracy cases used to describe their offence as a 'war waged against the King established by law'.

The spirit of the revolutionaries remained intact because they had enormous faith in the philosophy of 'revolutionism', which called for readines to suffer and make self-sacrifice. Even when they were on the verge of dealth in a hospital, these revolutionaries refused to give a dying declaration disclosing the names of their compatriots and organizations.

Swami Vivekananda had inspired the youth of Bengal with his fiery speeches and writings in the 1890s. His clarion call to rise above untouchability, casteism and all kinds of slave mentality, to fight against superstitions and cowardice motivated the youngsters for militancy. They realized that without national liberation, progress was not possible on any front. Poverty had to be eradicated, status of women was to be improved and the so-called low castes and outcastes had to be brought within the mainstream of Indian society. They firmly believed that all this could be accomplished in an atmosphere of political freedom which could be achieved only through the mechanism of an armed resistance.

The Bengal revolutionaries had faith in God and to them love for the country was synonymous with love for God. Their aim of life was rendering service to their motherland, and to the people, and sacrificing everything for achieving the political liberation of their country. The urge for the achievement of national independence resulted from their love for humanity and that is why they insisted primarily on character building and not on the weapons of mass killing. The enthusiasm of the Bengalee revolutionary groups did not come to an end after the initial spark because struggle for national liberation was, for them, worship of God. The leaders of these groups moulded the character of the young activists mainly on the model suggested by Bakim Chandra Chattopadhyay in his widely read novel *Anandamath* which contained the battle cry for the revolutionaires *"Bande Mataram"* (Salute to Mother).

The source of inspiration for Subhas Chandra Bose's patriotism was Swami Vivekananda whom he considered his spiritual Guru. The British Government considered Subhas Chandra Bose "a dangerous revolutionary" and "an active consort of the terrorists". It is true that he did not have much faith in the Gandhian doctrine of non-violence. On the contrary, he used to patronize the Bengal revolutionaires who had enormous faith in him. His contacts with the Russian Bolsheviks were also not unknown to the British. In this connection it may be noted that from the 5th November 1922 to 5th December '22, the Fourth Congress of the Comintern was held in Moscow. This was the last Congress in the lifetime of Lenin who attended it in spite of ill health. The leaders of the Comintern, on the advice of Lenin, congratulated the Indian National Congress, then having a conference in Gaya. They expressed their sympathy and support for the Indian freedom struggle.[2] In response to that, Deshbandhu Chittaranjan Das, in his Presidential speech delivered at the All Indian Trade Union Congress in 1923, said that he wanted real Swaraj in the life of at least 98% of the population.[3]

Chinmohan Sehanabish, the well-known commentator on the Indian revolutionaries abroad, wrote that as per information received in the month of May 1970 from the documents of the Institute of Marxism-Leninism in Moscow, four delegates were invited from India to attend the Fourth Congress of the Comintern. But only one of them was present there whose name had not been mentioned anywhere in the said documents. Furthermore, Sir Cecil Kaye stated that the Indian delegates invited to that Congress included Subhas Chandra Bose, Chiraranjan Das (C.R.Das's son), S.A.Dange, a noted Communist leader, and Sachindra Nath Sanyal the well-known revolutionary of U.P.[4] Bose was not allowed by the British Government to visit the erstwhile Soviet Union.

The British administration never deviated from their assessment of Bose, although they did not have sufficient evidence to prove his involvement with the Bengal revolutionaries. Hence, Bose had to undergo an endless ordeal in the form of lathi charge, frequent arrests and imprisonments without trial and defamation cases.

During the period of the non-violent non-cooperation movement, in the month of November 1921, the Prince of Wales came to India. It was decided by the Indian National Congress that 17th November, the day the Prince was to reach

The Rebel in the Making (1921-1928)

Bombay, would be observed as a day of protest. with nationwide agitation. Gandhiji issued the call for *'Hartal'* which was most successful in Calcutta compared to the other parts of India with unexpected response from all and sundry, thanks to the high organizational skill of Subbas Chandra Bose. The protest was so successful that next day *The Statesman* and *The Englishman* reported that the city of Calcutta had been taken over by the Congress volunteers. From their reports. it seemed as if the rulers had been almost dislodged from their throne due to popular upsurge. These dailies demanded immediate arrest of the Congress volunteers for causing unrest in the country as a result of which the Bengal Government blacklisted the Congress as a prohibited organization. Bose and his political guru Chittaranjan Das were arrested and thrown into the Alipore jail for six months. Bose was released from jail on the 4th of August 1922. Within a few weeks, he rushed towards North Bengal on a mission of relief to serve the flood-hit people there. The Government did not extend a helping hand towards the victims and this indifference on the part of the Government forced Bose to take responsibility unto himself and organize relief distribution and rescue work with discipline and fortitude. In this work he was inspired by the patriot-scientist Acharya Prafulla Chandra Ray and assisted by the Anushilan Samity members with whom he had an intimate relationship.

Bose was again, arrested on the 24th October, 1924 with quite a few prominent workers of the Swarajya Party, a segment of the Indian National Congress itself, along with some leaders of the Jugantar group under Bengal Regulation III of 1818 and the Bengal Emergency Ordinance issued by the Viceroy. He was at that time, the Chief Executive Officer of the Calcutta Corporation with C. R. Das as the Mayor elected under the liberalized Calcutta Municipal Act of 1923. Surprisingly, the said Ordinance was issued just a few hours before their arrest. These "lawless laws" as C. R. Das described them, were according to Lord Birkenhead, the Secretary of State for India in London and Lord Lytton, the Governor of Bengal (1922-1926), aimed at deterring revolutionary acts involving violence or threat of its outbreak. Although Bose was never given the ground of his detention, it is obvious that the British Government, by 1924, had decided to use all extra-ordinary powers at its disposal against him as though he were the undisputed leader of the Bengal revolutionaries. It is to be noted that Bose was not the first Congress leader to be accused by the British as an active consort of the nationalist revolutionaries whom the British Indian bureaucracy preferred to call "terrorists", Lokmanya Tilak was the first prominent Congress leader to be so branded.

Swarajya Party, however, was launched by C.R. Das and Motilal Nehru within the Congress Party itself in a bid to transform its traditional character. The avowed aim of the Swarajya Party was to extend non-cooperation to the legislature, a game plan not acceptable to the Gandhians i.e. the no-changers. At the Gaya Congress, C.Rajagopalachari and the other Gandhians refused to accept Congress President Das's proposal that the device of non-cooperation could be extended to the legislature since the possibility of a Civil Disobedience Movement had been ruled out for the time being. As the non-cooperation movement was suddenly called off by Gandhi as per the Bardoli decision, Das, while in prison, wanted to give a new direction to non-cooperation. His wife Basanti Devi's presidential address to the Bengal Political Conference of May 1922 at Chittagong, suggesting a reformed Congress strategy in the new situation, clearly showed that C.R.Das preferred an extension of non-cooperation to the legislative councils instead of abstention from them as suggested by the no-changers. In jail, Das spoke on these lines with the other non-cooperator prisoners including Bose. As Bose writes:

"According to Deshbandhu, in a revolutionary fight, the points of vantage should not be left in the hands of the enemy. Therefore all elected seats in the legislatures, as also in all public bodies (namely, municipalities, district boards, etc), should be captured by Congressmen." [5]

C.R.Das resigned the Congress presidency and formed the Swarajya Party with Motilal Nehru, B.N.Sasmal and Chaudhri Khaliq-uzzaman on 1st January 1923. Das wanted modification of the Congress policy that instructed all Congressmen to abstain from all elective positions in the councils and local bodies. It should be mentioned in this connection that the non-cooperation movement of 1920- 21 under the leadership of Gandhi roused vast hopes in the minds of the people regarding independence. Due to the sudden suspension of the movement, several thousand people were left impoverished by the sacrifices made for this movement. The disappointing end of a heroic struggle shocked thousands of young students, who had given up schools and colleges with high hopes. These youngsters wondered whether they staked their career on an utopian promise i.e. "Swaraj within a year", as promised by Gandhi. Vallabhbhai Patel, Rajendra Prasad, Rajagopalachari and the other loyal Gandhians, stuck to the policy of "No Change" which was virtually a policy of immobility. To them, it was an act of faith and a proof of loyalty to the great leader.

C. R. Das led the Swarajya Party and Motilal Nehru who, in the past, never gave importance to Bengal radicalism, joined him. The Swarajist experience, however, in the 1920s when Das and Motilal Nehru led the Congress campaign in the legislature and much later the ministries formed by the Congress under the Government of India Act 1935 proved that the Congress in the legislature, far from weakening the freedom movement, actually strengthened it.

In Bengal, however, the police was proud of its skill in suppressing extremism. Sir Charles Tegart, Calcutta's notorious police commissioner, informed Lord Lytton, the then Governor of Bengal, that the Bengal "terrorists" were getting shelter in the Swarajya Party of C.R.Das and they were planning to revive the terrorist campaign. Lytton then felt the necessity of having a law like the wartime Defence of India Act or the Rowlatt Act of 1919 for Bengal to eradicate the menace of 'terrorism' being encouraged by C.R.Das. As Lytton writes: "Matters went from bad to worse during the cold weather of 1923-24. The revolutionary conspiracy became more widespread and received encouragement from the Swarajists who entered the legislative council after the elections."[6]

Evidently the Government was under the impression that there was a strong undercurrent of rebellious activities throughout Bengal and it was very much perturbed by the resolution passed by the Bengal Provincial Congress Committee praising the patriotism of Gopinath Saha, who was hanged for killing Earnest Day whom he mistook for Charles Tegart in January 1924. The General Secretary of the Provincial Congress at that time was Bose. The Bengal Congress with its Swarajist sect was very much under the influence of Bose and the revolutionaries. The British Intelligence, therefore, believed that Bose was the kingpin in the conspiracy of attempting on the life of Tegart and the subsequent passing of the resolution praising Gopinath Saha. It was also alleged that Bose was planning to blast off the Council-chamber.[7] As a confidential report says: "'there were two main organizations in the past. Both are in existence today. Attack on government has been definitely organized on the (Irish) Sinn Fein lines, Local administration is to be captured and controlled by revolutionary organizations throughout the province and government officials terrorized by campaigns of assassination.

"There is reliable information to the effect that Satyen Mitra and Subhas Bose, at the beginning of 1924 (February) contemplated a spectacular outrage namely an attack on the Governor and his Council in the Council chamber with the object of focusing the attention of the world on Indian unrest. Bipin Ganguly opposed this scheme until after the assassination of Tegart had been effected; his object was to disorganize the police in the first instance so that the revolutionists could then commit crimes with impunity."⁸

Another file reports : "In April 1923, 24 Parganas Police learnt that Swarajya party had agreed to cooperate with the revolutionaries. On one side Deshbandhu and on the other Amar Chatterjee and Upendra Nath Banerjee.

"In the beginning of March 1924, C. R. Das called a meeting at night. Those present were Subhas Bose, S. Mitra, Byomkesh Chakraborty, and also Purna Das of Madaripur revolutionary group. At the meeting the speech of the Secretary of State was discussed, it was decided that little could be expected from the Labour Party. Purna Das then demanded formal sanction to revert to revolutionary crimes, he was supported by Subhas Bose who stated that all progress which India had hitherto made in the direction of self-government, was the result of revolutionary activism in the past. B. Chakraborty expressed his agreement and ultimately Purna Das's proposal was accepted by all present."

The above report was signed by the Superintendent of Police, I.B. C.I.D., Calcutta, dated 6.3.24, the news was communicated by Mr.Crear to the Secretary of State for India on 20th March, 1924.⁹

H. W. Hale, a British Intelligence officer writes: "Several of the important leaders including Subhas Chandra Bose, the Chief Executive Officer of the Calcutta Municipal Corporation, who was believed to have been behind the plot to assassinate Sir Charles Tegart and who had given employment to a large number of Jugantar revolutionaries and ex-detenus under the Calcutta Corporation, were incarcerated under Regulation III of 1818."¹⁰

Although the Bengal revolutionaries were ardent admirers of the Irish revolutionaries, it may be considered as one of the great ironies of the impact of Ireland on Bengal that the acknowledged British expert on "Bengali terrorism", Charles Tegart was in Irishman. Even Sir Michael O'Dwyer who devasteted Punjab on the 13th of April, 1919 through the genocide at Jalianwallabagh, was an Irishman.

However, the Government of India as well as the Government of Bengal became worried as to the growing power and influence of the Swarajya Party. The British Intelligence used to refer to Bose as the chief lieutenant of C.R.Das and they wanted to bring him under control. It was Tegart, in particular, who wanted to give Subhas a lesson after the attempt made on his life by Gopinath Saha. There was yet another incident which infuriated Tegart more. One day, the Corporation workers were sprinkling water as usual, on the roads near Park Street in Central Calcutta in the early morning when shots were fired, and one worker got killed. The news reached Bose at the Corporation office who immediately informed the Police and asked them to find out the culprit. As the Park Street area was inhabited mostly by the British and the other European communities, the Police did not show any interest in the matter. Most of the inhabitants there had licensed firearms and it was difficult for the Police to get a witness who would testify against them. Besides, the person who got killed, was a *"Kala Aadmi"*, (as the native Indians used to be called those days). Bose was adamant that adequate compensation had to be paid to the family of the deceased, and made this demand to the higher authorities as the Chief Executive Officer of the Calcutta Corporation. If his demands were not fulfilled, the Corporation would take stern legal action against the Police and the Government, threatened Bose in a statement issued.[11]

His arrest on October 1924 in a pre-dawn swoop was due to the vindictive nature of the alien rulers, particularly Lytton in collaboration with Tegart. Anil Baran Ray, another trusted colleague of C.R.Das and the general secretary of the Bengal Provincial Congress was detained without trial. These arrests, specially of leaders who were, during those days, busy in legislative politics or with the affairs of the Calcutta Corporation, proved that the targets of Lytton's repressive policy

The Rebel in the Making (1921-1928)

were C. R. Das, as the leader of the Swarajya Party and his 'chief lieutenant' Subhas Chandra Bose, Lytton wanted to destroy the Swarajya Party by any means by taking some repressive measures in 1923-25 against it. He virtually forced Lord Reading the then Viceroy, to grant him special powers under an ordinance by means of which he could deal with the "revival of terrorism" in Bengal.

"The organization of the revolutionary societies was the same as in the pre-war days, the same names – Juguntar (Juguntar) and Anushilan – were employed, the same individuals were at work, the same methods were being applied, but the Government no longer had the same weapons with which to deal with them. We therefore, applied to the Government of India for an ordinance giving to us the powers of the Defence of India Act which had proved so effective in the past."[12] As a result, the Bengal Emergency Ordinance was suddenly promulgated in October 1924 and Lytton made an illegitimate use of this emergency power against a legally valid legislative opposition. In October 1924 the Bengal Government seized as many Bengal leaders and revolutionaries as it could lay its hands on, including Bose in one surprise move.

It is to be noted here that the Swarajists stormed into the Bengal Council as the largest single party headed by C.R.Das. This election under the 1923 Act gave the Swarajya Party complete control of the Calcutta Corporation whose revenue in those days exceeded the total revenues collected by some provinces e.g. the undivided Assam. Das was the elected mayor of Calcutta and he appointed his closest associate Bose, only twenty-seven years of age at that time, the chief executive officer of the Calcutta Corporation.

It is evident, however, that the British bureaucracy was very much scared of the Bengal revolutionaries. According to an I.B. report; "Information has been received constantly, during the period, of plots and talk of plots to carry out assassination of officials, whose removal the revolutionaries considered necessary. But there has been far more talk than actual plotting, and in the main, the intention to put into action, such plots as have come to notice, has been apparently a half-hearted kind. Still the reports show that the idea and the desire to take these reprisals remain undiminished. It is confidence and power of organization that are lacking. Another powerful restraining factor is the certainty that any such provocative overt act would entail further drastic action against the revolutionary organizations — actions which in their present condition would be, they feel, fatal to their continued existence."[13] This report analyzes the extremist activities of Bengal uptill 31st March, 1925, without any mention of Subhas Chandra Bose.

The British Government alleged that Bose as the Chief Executive Officer of the Calcutta Corporation provided employment to the freedom fighters or their family members under the Corporation. The Government condemned this act strongly and considered it an anti- government act which encouraged the terrorists. Bose did not deny the allegations made against him by Tegart in this respect.

A Reuter message, dated London, February 5, 1934 says that Bose, in a lengthy letter to the 'Manchester Guardian' with reference to the allegations made by the Government before the select committee that former terrorists were employed as school – masters by the Calcutta Corporation, said that the number is microscopic.

Regarding the employment of ex-political prisoners, generally, he stated that the Congress Party had always adhered to the view that since political offence did not involve moral, they could not be debarred from Municipal or State service.[13A]

When Bose was arrested under Regulation III of 1818, he was not brought before any court, nor was he informed of the charges against him. The I.B.record says: "simultaneously with these arrests and searches, searches were conducted under Indian Penal Code at numerous other places in Bengal, where

The Rebel in the Making (1921-1928)

it was believed that incriminating articles connected with the revolutionary propaganda would be found. Although the raid yielded nothing in the way of arms, ammunitions and explosives, yet a scrutiny of the results reveals the facts that out of a total of 104 houses, revolutionary literature of different kinds was found in 33."[14]

C. R. Das however was very annoyed on hearing the news of Bose's arrest. As the Mayor of Calcutta Corporation, he gave a speech expressing his deep anguish at this action of the police. He said: "Bose is no more a revolutionary than I am. Why have they not arrested me? I should like to know why? If love of one's country is a crime, then I am a criminal. Not only the Chief Executive Officer of the Corporation, the Mayor of the Corporation is equally guilty. Bose's arrest is sheer brute force on the part of the bureaucracy...... no charge was made against him. No reason was given but he was simply told: We have got brute force and we shall drag you to prison. Is this law? Is this justice?" [15]

The British Government tried to justify its repressive action by saying "The objective was to place under restraint certain persons known to be actively dangerous." The report further said "the immediate object of the raid was undoubtedly fulfilled; the revolutionary organizations and campaigns were for the time being thoroughly dislocated and disorganized".[16]

Three Anglo-Indian newspapers of Calcutta, namely, *The Statesman, Englishman* and *The Catholic Herald* alleged that a number of conspiracies were actually Bose's brainchild. As they could not corroborate their allegations with the help of any concrete evidence, they sought the help of the India Office, London. Unfortunately for them, the India Office too could not supply any documentary proof of the involvement of Bose in the alleged conspiracies. In one Police report, it was alleged that he had been using the Corporation funds for importing arms from abroad and for killing the Police officers. He was labeled a 'Congressee Communist' in the police reports.[17] Had there been any authentic proof in favour of these serious allegations, Charles Tegart would have given him a deadly punishment like deportation, without hesitation.

While in jail, Bose used to go through the Corporation files and papers in the presence of one political officer and one jail official who had a knack of insulting him and his visitors with their derogatory remarks.

Bose's tenure as the Chief Executive Officer of the Calcutta Corporation to which he brought unprecedented dynamism, was cut short abruptly by his unjustifiable detention without trial.

The alien government, however, was alarmed at the way the revolutionary periodicals were being published and circulated all over Bengal with inflammatory articles. As one I. B. record states, after the abolition of the Indian Press Act.

'The mushroom vernacular journal like *Atmashakti, Sarathi, Muktikam, Bijoli* and others began to publish articles having a direct or indirect tendency to incite violent hostility against the British Raj. The commonest type of propaganda was to denounce the economic oppression by the British in India, to extol in mystical, sometimes in poetic language, freedom and self-sacrifice and to publish appreciative articles in praise of the revolutionaries".[18]

Subhas Chandra Bose was associated with some of these periodicals. C. R. Das's *Atmashakti* (Self-Power), a nationalist weekly used to publish regularly articles contributed by Hemanta Kumar Sarkar, Bose's close friend. Anushilan Samity started a Bengali daily called *Shankha* and a pamphlet called *Hak Katha. Forward* was one of the leading nationalist dailies published by C. R. Das, the office of which was not just a newspaper office, but the nucleus of the Swarajist circle. Political leaders, social workers, literary personalities like Sarat Chandra Chattopadhyay and many others paid regular visits here and discussed national issues, After the demise of Das, Satyaranjan

The Rebel in the Making (1921-1928)

Bakshi, another close ally of Bose, became the editor of *Forward*. Satyaranjan happened to be the nephew of the well-known revolutionary Hem Chandra Ghosh, the founder-member of '*Mukti Sangha*' (Dacca) which was an active revolutionary group and later merged with the Bengal Volunteers movement.

The Bengal revolutionaries, however, supported Subhas Chandra Bose in spite of their differences on methods. What appealed to them the most were Bose's militant attitude, his anti-compromise stance, and his youthful exuberance. Many of these revolutionaries joined the Indian National Congress for the purpose of conveying their messages to the mass of the population as the Congress was, in those days, not just a political party, but a common platform for furthering the cause of national liberation. During the 1920's and the 1930's, the Bengal revolutionaries believed that it was possible for them to generate a revolutionary spirit in the Congress movement over a period of time. As a result, with the help of C.R.Das, they devoted themselves to the task of implementing the Congress programmes and also participated in the workers' and youth movements.

When Das expired in June 1925, at a relatively early age of fifty-five, Subhas Chandra Bose was in the Mandalay prison (Burma). Here is an extract from the I.B. weekly report for the week ending 20th June, 1925. The Commissioner of Police, Calcutta reports as follows:

> "the sudden death of Mr. C.R.Das has, of course been the most important event of the week. Incidents in connection with the obsequies of the Bengal leader have been fully reported in the press. The crowd which gathered at the Sealdah station, and then followed the funeral procession, was probably the largest ever seen in Calcutta and the popularity of Mr. C.R.Das amongst all communities may be evidenced from the fact that even

Purdanishin ladies came openly into the streets and attended the Burning Ghat to pay homage. The fact that the European press has, as a whole, paid tributes to the memory of Mr C.R.Das and that hundreds of Europeans were amongst the crowd that watched the procession, is being taken as showing that the European community appreciated the genuineness of Mr Das's utterance at Faridpore.

"It would be idle at present to endeavour to gauge the effect which Mr. Das' s death will have on the political situation. Mr. Gandhi, has, however, invited an All-Party Conference to be held at 148 Russa Road (South) in the near future, if possible. In the meanwhile, the Swaraj Party has convened a meeting to be held on the 28th instant. Since the death of C.R.Das, all sorts of rumours have been afloat. Two of the rumours which have been most widely circulated are as follows:-

"(1) that the death of Mr Das was due to slow poisoning which set in during his incarceration in jail, and (2) that Aurobindo Ghosh will return from Pondicherry and become the leader of Bengal.

"In connection with the latter rumour, it may be mentioned that a telegram was actually sent to Aurobindo Ghosh by Adhar Lashkar, the editor of Karma Bijnan asking him to return to Bengal. The absence of Subhas Bose at this juncture is generally deplored."[19] Bose who was released from jail in 1927, steered into the office of the President of the B.P.C.C. mainly with the effort of the Jugantar group of revolutionaries.[19A]

The revolutionary organizations had been trying to consolidate their strength for an uprising under the captaincy of Bose who was identified by the British Intelligence, as a "Jugantar Revolutionary". In a departmental note Bose was described as the recognized leader of the 'Jugantar Group of Terrorists' and was at the back of the terrorist campaign

The Rebel in the Making (1921-1928)

restarted by the Group in 1924.[20] As a matter of fact, since 1914 onwards, Bose and some of his friends namely Annada Prasad Chowdhury and a few others, were in contact with the Jugantar leaders. Initially, this association was clandestine but later, during the days of non-cooperation and the Swarajist movements, this acquaintance developed into an intimate political as well as personal relationship, particularly with leaders like Jadugopal Mukhopadhyay, Bhupen Dutta, Suren Ghosh, Manoranjan Gupta and Bhupati Majumdar. In the words of Nanda Mukherjee,

"though Subhas had sympathy for the terrorists, for their spirit of courage and sacrifice, never by words or by deeds, he extolled their method." [21]

Having witnessed the fate of the non-cooperation movement and the emptiness of Gandhi's promise of 'Swaraj within a year', Bose realized that without an armed rebellion, freedom would remain a far cry. In his Amarabati speech dated 1st December 1929, he reiterated that what the country needed at that time, was a revolution.

From 1921 onwards, Bose came to be associated more and more with the Anushilan leaders. The two role models available for the Bengal revolutionaries in those days were the mass-based Russian and the extremist Irish revolutionary movements, whom they tried to emulate alternatively. Anushilan and Jugantar groups idolized the Russian and the Irish models respectively for the accomplishment of a revolution in India.[22]

Rash Behari Basu, a noted Anushilanite, tried to organize a revolutionary insurrection during the First World War period. The Anushilan Samity, with the active assistance of the repatriated members of the Ghadar Party set a comprehensive plan for a revolutionary uprising under Rash Behari Basu's leadership. In January 1915, Rash Behari Basu had conferred with the leading Anushilan members in Benaras and it was decided that the uprising would take place on 21st Feb, 1915.

Lala Hardayal, an Indian revolutionary abroad, founded the Ghadar Party in USA with the help of the Indian immigrants there and in Sanfrancisco, formed a group called Jugantar Ashram with the purpose of organizing an armed rebellion against British Imperialism in India. He also published a periodical called Ghadar on a regular basis for moulding public opinion abroad.

In November 1914, V. G. Pingley and Satyabhushan Sen came to India from Germany being instructed by Lala Hardayal and told Rash Behari Basu in Benaras about the possibility of getting arms from Germany for the rebellion. Pingley informed Basu that 4000 Ghadr revolutionaries had already reached Punjab for participating in the armed uprising, 15000 trained militants were waiting in Calcutta and 20000 more were expected to arrive after the outbreak of the rebellion. This encouraged Rash Behari Basu to go ahead with his plans to be implemented in February, 1915.

There was nothing new in the idea of obtaining foreign aid for the country's liberation. Jatindranath Mukherjee tried to establish foreign contacts since 1908 when Kshirod Gopal Mukherjee was sent to Burma and Dhan Gopal Mukherjee to Japan and USA. Bhupati Majumdar was sent to Europe with the same purpose in view. Many others besides these representatives of different revolutionary groups of Bengal, who went abroad for higher studies or in search of employment came into contact with the Indian liberation movement organized outside India. Shyamji Krishnavarma and Madame Bhikhaji Rustom K. R. Cama were the two key figures in the nationalist movement being organized in Europe. Anushilan Samity sent Kedareswar Guha, Taraknath Das, Gopen Chakraborty and Abani Mukherjee abroad for exploring the possibilities of getting arms from outside India.

The year 1911 ushered in a new chapter in the history of the relation between Germany and the Indian revolutionaries, particularly of Bengal. Friedrich von Bernherdi's work *Germany and the Next War* was published in October 1911. In this book, the author indicated the German hope that the Hindu population of India marked by the existence of a strong revolutionary element in it might unite with the Muslims of India and that the joint endeavour on their part might create a very grave danger capable of shaking the foundation of England's high position in the world. He anticipated a wartime entente between Germany and the Indian revolutionaries against Britain. This book was widely acclaimed by the Bengal revolutionaries as a sign of German sympathy towards the revolutionaries of India.[23]

While in Benaras, Rash Behari Basu discussed his plans with Jatin Mukherjee and his associates, namely, Atul Krishna Ghosh and Narendra Bhattacharya of the Jugantar group who had no idea about the plans and preparations of the former for a widespread armed uprising in Northern India. These Jugantar revolutionaries went to Benaras towards the end of 1914 to meet Basu and discuss matters relating to procurement of arms from Germany for an uprising in Bengal. Basu was making preparations for an uprising in Northern India to be synchronized with a rebellion in Bengal as stated earlier. The Jugantar leaders heavily banked on the possibility of arms and ammunitions to come from Germany and Basu insisted on the fact that if Mukherjee and his associates could really get supply of German arms and could start a rebellion in Bengal, the Anushilan Samity would be ready to give them full support and help.

Rash Behari tried mainly to mobilize the soldiers to stage an armed resistance with trained battalions and he also motivated revolutionary workers and villagers in this effort. Contact was established with twenty-six Cantonments including those at Firozepur, Rawalpindi, Jabbalpore, Meerut, Benaras and Allahabad. The Jugantar group, however, was not eager to organize a revolution at that point of time because they felt that before the German arms arrived, their planned uprising in Bengal might not succeed. The German shipment was due to reach India not before June 1915. Basu and his associates of Anushilan Samity did not depend entirely on German arms and they were well aware of the hazards and uncertainties involved in the ambitious plan that they wanted to execute. The entire Anushilan Samity was out to implement this brave plan and Sachindra Nath Sanyal, Nagendra Nath Dutta alias Girija Prasanna and Anukul Chakraborty were assigned the task of working in close cooperation with Basu. Early in 1915 the preparation was complete. The troops garrisoned at various places of Northern India were contacted. The Sedition Committee Report says:

"He (Rash Behari) tried to organize the collection of gangs of villagers to take part in the rebellion. Bombs were prepared; arms were got together; flags were made ready; a declaration of war was drawn up; instruments were collected for destroying the railways and telegraph wires." Revolutionaries were counting days in expectation of the great event taking place as arranged. The Anushilan Samity in Bengal kept its volunteers ready in Eastern India to rise in revolt at a given signal. Semi-military attire for large batches of revolutionary cadets was made ready. Unfortunately the meticulous preparations were frustrated by the treachery of a single man called Kripal Singh who was later found to be an IB spy. Basu had to leave India for Japan on the insistence of his associates, particularly Anukul Chakrabarty, in order that he could obtain arms from a foreign country for a fresh attempt at another uprising during the War period. At that time Japan was making preparations for receiving the great Bengali poet Rabindra Nath Tagore as an honoured guest from India and Basu left Calcutta for Japan with a fake passport in the name of Pramatha Nath Tagore as if to make the necessary arrangements for the visit of the poet to Japan. On 12th of May, 1915, Basu left for Japan by a ship called Sankimaru from the Kidderpore Dock, jetty number 12. Two of his closest

The Rebel in the Making (1921-1928)

revolutionary compatriots, Sachindra Nath Sanyal and Girija Dutta came to see him off at the shipyard. Incidentally, the German arms could not reach the Indian revolutionaries as expected by the Jugantar leaders and hence the apprehension of Basu about the uncertainties in getting arms supply from Germany proved true, and his warning against too much dependence on arms supply from Germany for an Indian revolution revealed his pragmatism and political foresight.

Subhas Chandra Bose was in close contact with the established underground revolutionary organizations in the country since the early 1920's. The well-known Anushilan revolutionary Abani Mukherjee was sent from India to Tokyo to contact Rash Behari Basu in Japan. He accompanied Basu to Shanghai where a meeting was arranged between the German Consul-General and Basu regarding arms supply to India by a German ship. Having received information from Abani Mukherjee about the developments of the Indian situation since his departure from the country, Basu might have thought that there was still some hope of an anti-British uprising in Bengal and tried hard to arrange for a supply of arms and ammunition to the Bengal revolutionaries from abroad. The Sedition Committee Report observes:

"To assist the conspirators in Bengal a Chinaman was sent to Hellferich with 66000 guilders and a letter to be delivered to a Bengali at Penang or to one of the two addressees in Calcutta: he never delivered his message for he was arrested at Singapore with the money on his person. At the same time the Bengali who had accompanied 'Martin' to Batavia was sent to Shanghai to confer with the German Consul General there and to return in the ship destined for Hatia. He reached Shanghai with some difficulty and was arrested there."

The Report does not say anything about the person who sent the Chinese to Hellferich. Presumably it was Rashbihari Basu who organized the whole programme. Abani Mukherjee was Basu's trusted lieutenant as both of them belonged to the Anushilan Samity. It seems that Bhupati Majumdar went to Shanghai having received a call from Rash Behari who was there at that time and in close contact with the German Consul-General. He was referred to as the 'Bengali' who accompanied 'Martin' (the pseudo-name of Narendra Bhattacharya) in the passage quoted above from the Sedition Committee Report. Majumdar was also very close to Basu whose home in Chandannagore was in the neighbourhood of Majumdar's.

In the winter of 1915, on his way back to India, Abani Mukherjee was arrested at Penang with a notebook containing a few names and addresses in cipher. The British police deciphered the names and addresses and found the names of many revolutionaries of East Bengal and the *Sramajibi Samabaya* of Calcutta. Abani was detained at the Singapore Fort, tried by a summary court and was subsequently sentenced to death. Later on, he somehow managed to escape from there and ultimately reached Russia where he turned into a Communist. He even represented India in the Second Congress of the Comintern held in Moscow in 1920.

In March 1922, just after the sitting of the Enlarged Executive Committee of the Comintern, Abani was requested by Brandler, the then member of the Presidium of the Comintern to go to India to study the situation personally. His expenses up to Berlin were given by the Comintern and Brandler sent out requests to the then Party workers in Berlin to help him in his attempt to go to India, which he received.[24]

When Abani reached Calcutta as a run-away convict in the eyes of the British, he went to Dr Suniti Kumar Chattopadhyay asking for a shelter who took him to Dilip Kumar Roy, a classmate and good friend of Subhas Chandra Bose. When Bose realized that the Police had already got the information of Abani's arrival in Calcutta, he deposited him into the custody of Santosh Mitra with the help of the Jugantar revolutionaries. Mitra was himself an absconder at that time.

The Rebel in the Making (1921-1928)

Hence, he contacted his Communist friend Abdur Rajjak Khan as advised by Bose who considered the Communists of those days as reliable comrades in his anti-imperialist struggle. It was, however, not very safe for Abani to stay at one place for a long time. Bose, then, asked his Anushilan friends to extend a helping hand to Abani, as a result of which the latter was shifted to Dacca in the safe custody of the Anushilan workers.[25] Abani stayed also in Bose's Elgin Road residence for quite some time.

Satyen Bose, the renowned Bengali scientist of the Bose-Einstein Statistics fame, had contacts with the Anushilan Samity. The Samity was looking for a reliable person through whom some money could be sent to Abani Mukherjee in Europe. When Satyen Bose was going to Europe in 1924, the Samity requested him to hand over the money to Abani and he obliged.[26]

In a Report dated 22nd August 1924, on the Indian situation, submitted to Petrov, the then Secretary, Eastern Section of the Comintern, Moscow, Abani Mukherjee wrote: "The right hand man of C.R.Das, Mr. S.Bose, being pro-communist and a friend of ours, we have a good influence over the Swarajya Party..."[27] Because of his progressive ideas, Bose was considered by many as pro-communist and Abani Mukherjee and his associates felt that through Bose, the CPSU would be able to control the Swarajya Party.

The Swarajya Party had many revolutionaries as its members who supported the candidature of Bose as the Chief Executive Officer of the Calcutta Corporation. As 'A Brief Note On The Alliance Of Congress With Terrorism In Bengal' states: "The terrorists depended on the financial support of the Swarajya Party. It is thus clear that the Swarajya Party and the terrorists were interdependent and were component parts of the same revolutionary machine. In the Bengal Provincial Congress Committee elections of 1925, the terrorists had a majority of 26."[28]

In 1927, the state prisoners of the Midnapore jail decided

to amalgamate all revolutionary groups and attempted to do so after their release. They also tried to revive the 'Karmi Sangha' with the purpose of having an open organization to work with the Congress as the latter was, during those days, not just a political party, but a common forum for those who wanted to work for national liberation.

According to an I.B.Report,

"Subhas Chandra Bose, Bhupen Dutta, Arun Guha, Purna Das and Suren Ghosh of the Jugantar, and Rabindra Sen, and Pratul Ganguli of the Anushilan, decided that Congress activities were not likely to create an atmosphere in the country necessary for an uprising. Bhupen Dutta accordingly drew up a scheme for a "Workers' League" based on the goal of complete independence. The amalgamated revolutionary party approved the scheme and it was discussed at the Madras session of the Indian National Congress attended by all the important Bengal revolutionaries. The latter persuaded Jawahar Lal Nehru to move the Independence resolution which was subsequently defeated. Jawahar Lal Nehru, Subhas Bose and Srinivas Ayengar then formed the Independence League for India.

"In Bengal, the revolutionary leaders summoned a workers' conference in Calcutta early in 1928 over which Subhas Bose presided. It was decided that Bhupen Dutta's "Workers' League" should be known as the 'Independence League of Bengal.' The revolutionaries then decided to capture the Bengal Provincial Congress Committee in Calcutta and the Mufassal in which by the end of 1928, they had largely succeeded and formed a voluntary corps which was intended to be their fighting force when the rising was brought about."[29]

The Calcutta Congress in 1928 opened a new chapter in the history of India's freedom movement. At this Congress, the members of the Independence League for India dissolved their organization and accepted the Congress resolution of

Dominion Status. Nevertheless the Bengal revolutionaries persuaded Subhas Chandra Bose to move an Independence resolution, which was, however, defeated in face of Gandhi's stiff opposition.

The followers of Bose, particularly Hemchandra Ghosh, a former Jugantar revolutionary, and Dinesh Gupta possessed tremendous organizing power. Ghosh had a secret society of his own in Dacca called *'Mukti Sangha'* that joined the volunteer regiment of Bose at the Calcutta Congress. Bose's regiment was named the Bengal Volunteers with Bose himself as the General Officer Commanding (G.O.C.). It also had a Women's Brigade under the captaincy of Latika Ghosh, the daughter of the well-known poet Manmohan Ghosh, the elder brother of Shri Aurobindo. Surprisingly, women in large numbers joined the volunteer force. The huge procession taken out in honour of the Congress President Motilal Nehru was led by Bose in military uniform, had many patriotic women marching on. In response to the call of Bose, Kalyani Das (Bhattacharya) formed *'Chhatri Sangha'* (female students' organization) in Calcutta. Lila Nag organized a women's forum called *Dipali Sangha* in Dacca, the members of which got themselves associated with the revolutionary movements in course of time. Both Lila Nag (who later became Ray) and her husband Anil Ray subsequently became close associates of Bose, as they, too, did not have any faith in the doctrine of non-violence for the country's liberation. Like Bose, these revolutionaries never looked down upon non-violence as a principle but they also realized that the mighty British would never leave the country by way of prayer and petitions. They hoped, as Bose did, that some day in future, the INC would also realize the futility of the principle as a weapon in their fight for freedom and it is to be pointed out here that twelve years later, Gandhi, the epitome of non-violence, gave the clarion call of *Karenge ya Marenge* (do or die) in the well-known Quit India movement in 1942.

The Calcutta Congress session (1928) was hosted by the Bengal Congress under the personal supervision of Bose whose close confidante Major Satya Gupta took charge of the B. V .Corps which had been militarily trained and disciplined. "The smartness, the uniform, the precision, the military-styled ranks for officers and the performance of the corps. ...impressed all and also raised quite a few eye-brows amongst the orthodox Gandhians."[30]

Bose's eye-catching appearance clad in military uniform left a lasting impression on the delegates as well as on the Calcuttans in general, which in retrospect, was a stage rehearsal, so to say, of his becoming the Supreme Commander of Azad Hind Fauj (the Indian National Army) that he organized fifteen years later in East Asia to drive away the British imperialists from India.

REFERENCES

1. Maiti, Girish Chandra, 'Decisive Role of the INA in India's Freedom', *Asian Studies* (Calcutta), XXI (1 & 2), January-December 2003.
2. Adhikari, Gangadhar, ed. *Documents of the Communist Party of India*, Vol.II, People's Publishing House, New Delhi.
3. Chattopadhyay, Gautam, 'Subhas Chandra O Bharater Communist Andolan', article in *Parichaya* (Bengali periodical), Calcutta, June-July 1996.
4. Sehanabish, Chinmohan, *Roosh Biplab O Prabasi Bharatiya Biplabi* (in Bengali), Manisha Granthalaya, Calcutta, 1973, pp. 324-324. Also Kaye, Cecil, *Communism in India*. (National Archives, New Delhi), 1926, (Indian edition in 1971), p.21.
5. Netaji Collected Works, Vol. II, p.87.
6. Lytton, the Earl of, *Pundits and Elephants*, Peter Davies, London, 1942, pp. 57-67.
7. Bose, Mihir, *The Lost Hero* Quartet Books, London, 1982, pp. 45-46.
8. I.B. File No 379(24), page 41.
9. I.B. FileNo.61 (24) p.5.
10. Hale, H.W., *Terrorism in India 1917-1936*, Compiled in the I.B., Govt. of India Publications Division, 1937, p 17.

The Rebel in the Making (1921-1928)

11. Basu, Nimai Sadhan, *Deshnayak Subhas Chandra*, (in Bengali), Ananda Publishers Pvt. Ltd., Calcutta 1997, pp 83-84.

12. Op cit, Lytton, the Earl of, *Pundits and Elephants*, pp. 57-67.

13. Samanta, Amiya, *Terrorism in Bengal*. (A compilation of documents), Volume 1, Government of West Bengal, 1995, p 450.

13A. *Calcutta Municipal Gazette* (1934), Subhas Chandra Bose Birth Centenary Number, Kranti Press, Calcutta, 1997, p.216.

14. Samanta, A. *Terrorism in Bengal*, Vol.I, op.cit. p 360.

15. Markandeya, Subodh, *Subhas Chandra Bose: Netaii's Passage to Immortality*, New Delhi, Arnold Associates, 1990 p 45.

16. Samanta, Amiya, op.cit. p. 359.

17. Basu, Nimai Sadhan, op. cit. p. 85.

18. Hale, H. W. op.cit. p. 17.

19. I.B.C.W.Bengal, file no.39\25, serial no. 97\1925.

19A. Author's interview with Manohar Mukherjee of Jugantar in Calcutta at his residence, on 1/3/2000.

20. India Office Records, File No. UP & J/7/793, cited in *Subhas Chandra Bose : British Press, Intelligence and Parliament*, by Nanda Mukherjee, Jayasree Prakashan, Calcutta, 1981, p.45.

21. Ibid., Mukherjee Nanda, *Subhas Chandra Bose: British Press,. Intelligence and Parliament*, p.14-15.

22. Mustafi, Ashoke, 'Jugantar, Anushilan O Subhas Chandra', article in *Parichaya* (Bengali periodical), Calcutta, June-July 1996.

23. Sedition Committee Report, Government of India, 1918, Para 107, cited in *Indian Revolutionaries Abroad, 1905-1922*, by A. C. Bose, Bharti Bhawan, Patna, 1971, p. 83.

24. Roy, Vasudevan, Duttagupta (ed.), *Indo-Russian Relations* 1917-1928, Volume I (Asiatic Society, Calcutta), pp. 185-187.

25. Pakrashi, Satish, *Agnidiner Katha* (in Bengali), National Book Agency Ltd., Calcutta, 1947.

26. Chattopadhyay, Enakshi, and Shantiranjan, *Bharatiya Bijnaner Uttaraner Kal*, Cambridge India, Calcutta, 2003, p.93).

27. *Indo-Russian Relations*, op. cit., p.187.

28. Confidential File, No. 26/32. Part I: Introductory, IB, (West Bengal State Archives, Calcutta.

29. Samanta, Amiya, op. cit.

30. Markandeya, Subodh, op. cit. p.65.

3
"THE DARE-ALL BENGAL PATRIOT" (1928-1933)

Those were the days when the revolutionary organizations of the country, particularly of Bengal, were trying to consolidate their strength for a nationwide uprising under the captaincy of Bose who was identified by the British Intelligence, as a Jugantar terrorist. According to Hale, the power exercised over the Congress by the Jugantar Party, had been for many years, one of the outstanding features of the inner history of political agitation in Bengal.

According to a report on the activities of the 'Terrorists' in Bengal, during the period, April to December 1930, prepared by R.E.A.Ray, Special Superintendent, IB, CID, the Congress had connivance with the Jugantar groups. "Before describing the activity of the Jugantar groups in the mufassal, it is convenient at this stage of this report to sketch the development of the Jugantar Party since 1927 and to touch on the intimate relations between the Party and the Congress."

The report spoke of the combined effort of the Bengal revolutionary groups, released in 1927, to revive the Workers' League in Bengal and work with Congress. Bose and the revolutionaries of Jugantar and Anushilan Samity felt the necessity of radicalizing the Indian National Congress for achieving complete independence not just Home Rule. With this purpose in view, they wanted to create in the country an atmosphere necessary for an uprising.[1]

These militant nationalists were determined to drive out the alien rulers from India and they were ready to accept Bose as their undisputed leader. Bose was, in every way, the symbol of uncompromising struggle to these extremist groups who used to confide in him and communicate with one another through him. J.M.Sengupta, Bose's political rival in Bengal politics, was also connected with the Anushilan Samity but his involvement was not so deep-rooted as of Bose.[2]

Jawaharlal Nehru was, at that time, on the side of Bose with all his progressive ideas, which led him to form the Indian Independence League in association with Bose and Srinivas Iyengar about which a mention has already been made.

"At the Calcutta Congress in 1928, the members of the Indian Independence League dissolved their party and accepted the Congress resolution on Dominion Status".[3]

Disappointed, the Bengal revolutionaries lost faith in the Congress, and decided to start a Youth and Students' Movement and openly advocated the method of armed resistance at public meetings.

"At the Lahore Congress of 1929, in order to honour the revolutionaries, who had practically captured the Congress in Bengal and the Punjab, Mahatma Gandhi moved the independence resolution which was adopted."[3A]

The Indian National Congress was the common platform through which the nationalist Indians, with different shades of opinion, sometimes opposed to one another, tried to express their viewpoints in an endeavour to serve the nation. In the Bengal Congress, Bose was probably the most charismatic leader during those days who had a huge following both inside and outside the Party. To the youth and the student community in general, he was a symbol of vivacity, a fighter and hence, a source of inspiration.

In June, 1930, Manoranjan Gupta is reported to have stated that his talks with the leading revolutionaries in Bengal, particularly those of the school of thought of Subhas Chandra Bose, had left him with the impression that there was a strong desire for concerted action on an all-India basis. He felt that the Bengal Provincial Congress Committee had been captured by Subhas Bose and his men who were mostly members of the old Bengal revolutionary party and welcomed Gandhi's movement not because of its non-violent programme, but because it provided the means of disseminating their own ideas, among the masses.

"A confessing revolutionary known as no. 560 said that the leaders of the Jugantar Party regarded Subhas Bose as their public leader and kept him and other Congress leaders informed of the policy of the revolutionary group of the Congress, although not of the details of their terrorist activity. In June, a report of a reliable agent was received to the effect that some district organizers had asked the permission of the Congress leaders to launch a campaign of terrorism all over the country and that Dr. Bidhan Roy had replied that Bengal Provincial Congress Committee, a non-violent body, could scarcely be expected to give express permission for this, but at that critical moment, they should decide their own policy and that those who wanted to start a campaign of violence might do so on their own responsibility, for the Congress creed was not binding on them."[4] The above statement clearly shows that even some of the stalwarts of the Congress did not condemn, in express terms, the campaign of violence against the British Raj. Probably they thought that it was impossible to liberate the country through an unpractical device such as non-violence. The same report goes on to say:

"In July, information was received that the All-India Congress Committee had given a large sum of money to Bhupendra Kumar Dutta for the organization of terrorist outrages as a protest against the Simon Commission Report."[5]

"The Dare-All Bengal Patriot" (1928-1933)

Simon Commission came to India on the 3rd of February 1928 to suggest some reforms on the basis of an assessment of the prevalent political situation and the working of the administrative system under the Government of India Act, 1919. The British Government announced earlier that a commission consisting of seven members of the British Parliament under the leadership of Sir John Simon would visit India soon and on the basis of its report, the Government would decide whether to increase or decrease the participation of the Indians in the country's administration.[6]

Throughout India, popular resentment was evident against the composition of the Commission as there was no Indian representative in it to speak for the Indians. It was decided by all the political parties and the people in general that the said Commission would be protested against and boycotted. Unprecedented unity was seen regarding this particular issue all over the country. The Indian National Congress issued a direction to all that there would be a general strike all over the country on the day the Commission set foot on the Indian soil. It was also decided that whenever and whichever city it would visit, there would be general strike and protest movements. Accordingly, on the said date, when the Commission landed on the city of Bombay, they were greeted with the protesters with banners carrying slogans like 'Go Back Simon'. The strike was most spontaneous and successful in Bengal owing to the untiring effort of Bose who delivered speeches after speeches in protest against the dubious motives of the Commission throughout Bengal. As a matter of fact, before the Commission arrived, the provincial Congress adopted a programme of boycott of foreign goods, strikes, meetings and processions to express popular resentment. Bose reiterated in all his speeches that the people of India had the same rights and privileges as the others in any part of the world. The people of a vast country like India were being ruled by just a handful of English bureaucrats only because there was a myth — the myth of the English being racially superior to the Indians who were inferior to them in every respect and hence worthless. "We have to get over this misconception. We must make them realize that the Indians do not want to live in subjugation, they want Independence."[7]

An IB report on the political situation in Bengal during the Second half of January 1928, states:

"Interest is centered on the proposed hartal on the 3rd February, which the Swarajists are sparing no effort to make a great success. The Calcutta Corporation has decided by a majority to close its offices, schools, workshops and stores on February the 3rd, and Mr. Subhas Chandra Bose has issued a manifesto calling on all sections of the community to cease work on that day and processions are going round with the same object. He is endeavouring also to put a stop to train, tram and bus traffic. The results of his efforts are not yet known. Undoubtedly there is great difference of opinion regarding the hartal, and in the Mufassal, generally speaking, the Mohammedans are against the proposal. One interesting feature of the agitation is that Mr. Subhas Chandra Bose has issued a letter to the head masters and principals of the various schools and colleges of Calcutta, asking them to close their institutions on the 3rd in sympathy with the agitation against the Simon Commission."[8]

There were some positive implications of the anti-Simon Commission agitation resulting from the far-sightedness of Bose. He tried to motivate people against the use of English clothes and salt, as he believed that this boycott would strengthen the struggle for freedom. He appealed to the Bengali women in particular not to fall a prey to the temptation of 'foreign clothes'. If the women stayed firm on it, then their male counterparts would not dare buy those commodities. He requested them to wear indigenous clothes instead of the fineries that symbolized nothing but slavery. Bose wanted to revive the patriotic spirit generated earlier in the minds of the people during the

"The Dare-All Bengal Patriot" (1928-1933)   37

movement against the partition of Bengal. He got his first book published in 1929, namely, *Boycott of British Goods* having made an extensive study on the subject. Early in 1928, the Bengal revolutionary leaders summoned a workers' conference in the city of Calcutta over which Bose presided. He was released from the Mandalay jail just a few months earlier. It is interesting to note that a Medical Board examined him before his release, as he was seriously ill at that time. The Government insisted that the Board should give a report recommending a change of climate as essential for Bose preferably in Switzerland or if it had to be in India, somewhere near the Himalayas. It was obvious that the Government was not willing at all to keep him in India, at least not in Bengal since to the British, Bose was 'the most dangerous enemy of the Empire'. Fortunately the members of the Board did not oblige the British Government.

It was, however, decided at the Workers' Conference that Bhupen Dutta's Workers' League should, from then on, be known as the Independence League of Bengal as decided earlier. It was also decided that the revolutionaries, to strengthen the cause of the country's freedom, would try to gain control over the Bengal Provincial Congress Committee.

It may be mentioned here that Kate L. Michelle, an English journalist, commented on the Government report regarding the Commission findings.

"In most Western discussions of the 'Indian problem', the main emphasis is laid on the diversity rather than the unity of the Indian people. India has been repeatedly pictured as a vast welter of races, religions and languages, possessing only the unity imposed upon it by the British rule and ready to fly into hostile and warring fragments if that rule should be weakened or removed..."

"The same thesis is implicit through the 'survey volume' of the Simon Report, which laid the basis for the new Constitution granted in 1935. Issued in 1930 as a scientific and objective presentation of the facts about the Indian problem, this report is filled with references to the 'complication of language', with no less than '222 vernaculars', the rigid complication of innumerable castes', the 'variegated assemblage of races and creeds', and similar expressions which suggest the utter impossibility of unity among the Indian people and the consequent importance of British rule as the only means of preserving internal peace and order, among the diverse elements composing Indian society.

"Yet what would an American think if an English commission visited US and made the following 'impartial' report on conditions in the United States?

"The subcontinent of the United States is characterized by the great diversity of climate and geographical features, while its inhabitants exhibit a similar diversity of race and religion. The customary talk of the United States as a single entity tends to obscure, to the casual British observer, the variegated assemblage of races and creed which make up the whole. In the city of New York alone, there are to be found nearly a hundred different nationalities, some of which are in such great numbers that New York is at once the largest Italian city, the largest Jewish city and the largest Negro city in the world. The contiguity of such diverse elements has been a fruitful cause of the bitterest communal conflicts. In the Southern States specially, this has led to inter-racial riots and murders, which are only prevented from recurring by the presence of an external impartial power able to enforce law and order. The notoriety of the rival gangs of Chicago... has diverted attention from the not less pressing problems presented to the Paramount Power by the separate existence of the Mormons of Utah, the Finns in Minnesota, the Mexican immigrants up the Mississippi and the Japanese on the West Coast; not to speak of the survival in considerable numbers of the aboriginal inhabitants." This was mentioned by *The Englishman* to illustrate Bose's objection to the spirit in which the Simon Commission approached the task of surveying conditions in India, and to the Report's one-sided emphasis on factors justifying the continued existence of an 'external impartial power'.[9]

Although Bose was a part of the Congress movement, he never accepted the non-violent non-cooperation method of Gandhi whole-heartedly as did Jawaharlal Nehru, Rajendra Prasad and Ballavbhai Patel. He felt that the all-mighty British could not be ousted from India by means of a weak device of compromise and even if independence was granted by them through a compromise, it would not be without conditions. Most of the Bengalees were also opposed to the idea of a compromise, which was, to them, nothing but sheer cowardice. The path shown by Gandhi, i.e. the patient, prolonged, never-ending process of prayer and petitions did not have any appeal to the Bengali psyche. There were some exceptions no doubt like Satish Dasgupta, Prafulla Ghosh and the like. But to the average Bengalee, revolution was the right device for driving out, once and for all, the alien rulers from India, neither the spinning wheel nor the *Khadi* as suggested by the Gandhians. The non-cooperation movement impressed them initially, because there was some novelty about it, and a hope of achieving Swaraj within a year as promised by Gandhi. The revolutionary activities did not fizzle out in Bengal due to the Gandhian non-violent movement. Sometimes it was overt, sometimes covert, and at times, associated with the Congress movement.

Bose was recognized by everyone as a Congress leader and he also projected himself as such for the British as well as the public but in reality, he never dissociated himself from the revolutionaries with whom he always maintained a clandestine relationship.

Two ardent followers of Bose— Hem Chandra Ghosh and Dinesh Gupta of Dacca – were known for their exceptional organizing ability. As mentioned earlier, Ghosh built up a strong organization in Dacca known as the *'Mukti Sangha'* composed of an army of trained young volunteers comparable to Garibaldi's *'One Thousand'*. Dinesh, had an enthusiastic band of young workers headed by Amar Chatterjee in Midnapore who were ready to sacrifice their lives for the motherland.[10]

When Bose was released from imprisonment after three long years, Deshabandhu Chittaranjan Das was no more. He breathed his last on the 16th of June 1925, in Darjeeling. Bengal was moving through a leadership crisis at that time, as there were two rival groups within the Bengal Congress itself, one following Bose, and the other following Jatindra Mohan Sengupta. Bose tried to persuade Basanti Devi, the widow of C.R.Das, whom he respected and loved as his own mother, to accept the leadership of the Bengal Congress to fill in the void. He found that after the untimely death of Das, Bengal Congress looked like a rudderless ship. But Basanti Devi did not want to get involved in active politics. Bose wrote to her from Shillong, in June 1929:

"He who was at once my friend, philosopher, and guide in my life's mission is no more. Today I am utterly destitute. You are the only refuge of this helpless person. Even if I lose everything else while going through vicissitudes of fortune, conflict and struggle, may I not lose your affection ever."[11]

It may be noted that the Swarajya Party was gaining popularity within Congress while Das was alive. As a matter of fact, with the support of Motilal Nehru, the Congress organization as a whole came to be controlled by the Swarajya Party. After the demise of C.R.Das, the aggrieved Congress leaders got an opportunity to recapture the lost control as a result of which Bose, very much attached to Das, found himself marginalised and opposed on almost every issue. Gandhi, at this juncture, came forward to rescue the Bengal Congress by allowing J.M.Sengupta to hold the three very crucial public positions, the "Triple Crown", the offices of the PCC president, the Mayor of Calcutta and the leader of the Swarajya Party in the Council. Thus, Gandhi showed his overwhelming

"The Dare-All Bengal Patriot" (1928-1933) 41

confidence in J.M.Sengupta, which, instead of solving the problem, rather aggravated groupism within the Bengal Congress.[12] It is still not known whether Gandhi wanted wholeheartedly to restore unity in Bengal Congress or to disrupt it by offering three important offices to the same person to the utter disappointment of the Bose group. Gandhi was the undisputed leader of INC during those days, as a result of which no one in Congress dared to question the decision, no matter how unjust or unconventional it appeared to be.

The revolutionaries of Bengal, were also in a state of dilemma whether to follow Bose or Sengupta. Anushilan Samity preferred to go with J.M.Sengupta and Jugantar Dal decided to follow Subhas Chandra Bose. The Chittagong revolutionary group led by Surya Sen (Master-da) maintained a close relationship with Jugantar Dal and Bose.

When the Calcutta Session of the Congress started, it was found that the young volunteers were clad in full military uniform, all in *Khaddar* though, instead of the traditional *Dhoti Kurta*. On both shoulders, they had the brass insignia 'B. V .' (Bengal Volunteers) and Bose himself appeared as the G.O.C. The disciplined women's wing of the B. V. was highly acclaimed by Vijay Lakshmi Pundit who came to attend the session with her father Motilal Nehru. As she writes:

"The Calcutta Congress is still fresh in my memory. There was always a good deal of pageantry at a Congress session in those days, including the President's procession and many forms of entertainments for the delegates. But Calcutta outdid previous sessions both in the enthusiasm it generated and in the entertainment it provided. Subhas Chandra Bose, the hero of young Bengal, was the captain of the volunteers. In a smart uniform and on a prancing white horse he led the President's procession.

"Calcutta was then a city of wealth and sophistication and to my provincial eyes, it was full of glamour. The whole family, including my new baby Nayantara, had gone to the Congress session. ..

"Father and C.R.Das had been close personal friends but we had not met the members of the Das family. Now we did so and were drawn to one another. Basanti Devi (Mrs. Das) was a lovely woman."[13]

The Calcutta Congress, however, did not at all impress Gandhi. To the utter astonishment and despair of those who worked day and night to make the Congress session a great success, Gandhi said:

"But the demonstrators had gone not to demonstrate strength, they had gone as if to a circus as sight -seers. And strange as it may appear, the Congress pandal was constructed as an adjunct to and in the midst of an enlarged edition of Filis' circus."[14]

Although the Calcutta Congress earned Bose innumerable words of praise from many veteran Congressmen including Motilal Nehru, Gandhi criticized the volunteer corps organized by Bose as he wrote:

"The volunteers dressed in European fashion presented, in my opinion, a sorry spectacle at Calcutta and the expense incurred was out of keeping with the pauperism of the nation."[14-A] No one, however, had the guts, in those days, to ask him whether it would have been proper for the people at that time to dress up like paupers to match with 'the pauperism of the nation'.

Perhaps it was some kind of a stage rehearsal of the Indian National Army, which was formed by Bose fifteen years later in East Asia with the sole purpose of attaining India's independence. The pomp and grandeur with which Motilal Nehru, the president of the Congress was given reception was a feast for the eyes. At the Howrah railway station, on his arrival, Nehru was received with 101 gun salutes. According to an I.B. report, this type of reception used to be given only when His Majesty the King Emperor or the Governor-General arrived in the city. The British Government, however, was very much perturbed by this grand show, which they felt, was their monopoly. They made some caustic comments even regarding the posting of sentries in front of Motilal Nehru's temporary residence in the city.

The Bengal Volunteer Corps came into existence at the time of the Calcutta Congress. At this Congress, Bose made elaborate arrangements to put up a great show with the help of the well-trained volunteers drawn from the different revolutionary groups, young men as well as women. For the Congress and the national exhibition connected with it, a large body of volunteers was required and Bose was entrusted by the Congress authorities with the task of organizing and training the Corps. Though the Corps was a peaceful and unarmed body, military discipline and training in military drill was imparted to the volunteers and they were also given a semi-military uniform. There were mounted volunteers, motorcycle riders, marchers and ambulances, coming in processions.

A few days before the Congress session, Bose made an appeal to people through newspapers for the procurement of horses.

"This is to inform those who wanted to be cavalier volunteers, that after the 14th, no more members will be taken in the Volunteer Corps.

"Quite a few volunteers have joined the cavalier corps, and passed the test. But unfortunately many of them do not have any horse. I hereby appeal to those who possess horses to lend me 50 horses for our cavaliers. From the 11 instant, the cavalier training will start. They will take part in the procession, which will come out on the day the President arrives. Besides, they will have the responsibilities of maintenance of order and security, controlling the movement of people and vehicles from the 20th onwards. The horses may be sent everyday to Park Circus. After the day's work, they will be either sent back to their own stables or kept in the stables of Park Circus Maidan. They will be taken special care of. I hope those who own horses, will help us in this matter."[15]

The historic Bengal Volunteers stirred up the nation as never before. Bose wanted to convey a message to the colonial masters that if necessary, the Indians would not hesitate to launch an armed attack on them by organizing themselves into a disciplined army.

A complete Indianization of the Royal Indian Army was not only his dream, it was also his political objective. The British Government was, naturally, very much opposed to this idea. Indians were never recruited in the higher echelons of the Military services in those days and Bose was the first person to draw people's attention to this deprivation.[15A] The contemporary newspapers however, reported vividly the kind of excitement Bose and his volunteers roused amongst people.

"Well-trained volunteer corps will remain as the main achievement of this year's Congress Reception Committee.

"Nearly two thousand young men have got themselves admitted in the volunteer corps so far in response to the call of Sreejukta Subhas Chandra Bose, the supremo of the corps. They have been trained in the different parks in mornings and evenings under the tutelage of the ex-army men of the military services."[16]

The two groups of the volunteer corps - one from the Shraddhananda Park and the other from the Hazra Park came out to have a route march through the main roads of the city with bands. People in large numbers, enjoyed the wonderful sight standing on both sides of the roads. Park Circus Maidan, named Deshabandhu Nagar on that occasion, had a new look altogether. No one, no matter how famous he was, could enter without showing his identity card and without permission — even Mr. J.M.Sengupta, and Dr. B. C. Roy, were challenged and denied entry as they did not have, with them, the entry card. The discipline of the Volunteers was remarkable and praiseworthy in every way. Subhas Chandra Bose inspired them in the service of the nation by his continuous presence, a spirit of militancy was generated in the minds of the people all around. Women volunteers were parading playing bugles and drums. Their march practice reminded one of the *Shaktikas* of the Vedic Age. The Calcuttans received the President of the 43rd Indian National Congress in style. How much love and respect the leader had infused in the minds of the people for him and for the country can be assessed from this celebration. Even old and elderly ladies took part in this celebration withstanding all the difficulties.

Motilal Nehru delivered his Presidential address at Deshabandhu Nagar in which he said that the city reminded him of the departed leader C.R.Das and his burning patriotism. He had a feeling as if the people became really independent, as if India had become an abode of wealth and happiness. He said that the people of Bengal had proved that they were really the deserving heir of Deshabandhu Das— by means of that inheritance, people would surely be able to fetch Swaraj.[17]

The Calcutta Congress of 1928 was historic in every way. This was the occasion when the Gandhi-Subhas difference on some principles came to the forefront with its inevitable repercussions on national politics. Earlier, when Bose campaigned for boycott of British clothes, Gandhi inquired why the BPCC president was not campaigning for foreign clothes in general, why only British clothes. In July 1928, Gandhi stood by Satish Dasgupta (the staunch Gandhian and *Khadi* campaigner) who was very much critical about the exhibition the Bengal Congress was preparing for the Calcutta Congress. In *Young India* of 26 July 1928, Gandhi wrote that his preference for the post of the Congress President in Calcutta was Jawaharlal Nehru, although Bengal wanted Motilal Nehru. Even "the dare-all Bengal patriot" (that was how Gandhi referred to Bose) wanted Motilal Nehru as the President.

Gandhi was well aware of the fact that Bengal as a whole wanted Motilal Nehru because the latter was a close associate of C.R.Das in the Swarajya Party that changed the course of Congress policy upheld by Gandhi's followers like Rajagopalachari, Vallavbhai Patel and Rajendra Prasad.[18]. C.R.Das was known not just as a politician, but as a renowned barrister famous for his magnanimity and so popular in Bengal that whoever was with him had been accepted by Bengal with open arms.

Gandhi was very much annoyed with Bose because of all this and he could not conceal his displeasure when, on the 14th August 1928, he went to the extent of threatening to take the All-India Spinners' Association out of the Calcutta Congress exhibition if Bose did not follow the guidelines as to the things to be displayed there.[19]

Gandhi's aversion to Bose was revealed also in the letters he wrote during this period. One such letter written to Satish Dasgupta went like this:

"Subhas Babu will never pardon the loin cloth. We must bear with him. He cannot help himself. He believes in himself and in his mission. He must work it out, as we must ours."[20] In what context he wrote it, is still unknown as the letter sent to him by Dasgupta, to which he gave this reply could not be traced.

It was rather unfortunate that a leader of Gandhi's stature could pass such a comment on a very young leader who was about thirty years junior to him and released from jail just a few months earlier after a long exile in Burma and was working in Bengal just for a short while. Gandhi's comments appear to be harsh considering the fact that Bose always held Gandhi in high esteem all through his life and on many occasions expressed his admiration for Gandhi's extraordinary leadership quality that India could boast of.

The Bengal revolutionaries considered the volunteer

"The Dare-All Bengal Patriot" (1928-1933) 47

corps their fighting force when the uprising would be brought about. According to an IB report of 1930, due to the persuasion of the revolutionaries, Bose moved an amendment proposal for complete independence against the official Dominion Status resolution of the Congress. This action on his part was, by itself, a revolutionary stand in view of the fact that no other Congress leader of that era had the guts to present an opinion contrary to Gandhi's. Bose's speech on this occasion was very significant as he reminded everyone of the probability of a second world war on the basis of a prudent analysis of international politics. He said that under the present circumstances, India had to generate a new spirit all around in order to stay alert, an ethos that would demand nothing short of complete independence.

Jawaharlal Nehru, however, was in favour of complete independence but when it came to voting, he changed his mind and opted for Dominion Status as proposed by Gandhi. The amendment proposal of Bose and the revolutionaries were defeated by 1350-973 votes. As Bose writes: "...the vote could hardly be called a free one as the followers of the Mahatma made it a question of confidence and gave out that if the Mahatma was defeated, he would retire from the Congress. Many people therefore voted for his resolution not out of conviction, but because they did not want to be a party to forcing the Mahatma out of Congress." [21]

The British, however, was certain about their idea that Bengal Congress had a clandestine relationship with the militant nationalists whom they called 'terrorists'. A brief note on the "alliance of Congress with terrorism in Bengal" stated :

"At the Calcutta Congress in 1928, Subhas Chandra Bose moved an amendment to Mr. Gandhi's resolution. His amendment was to the effect that there could be no freedom as long as the British connection remained and that the goal of the Congress should be complete Independence. His amendment was lost however, by 1350 votes to 973. Two thirds of the Bengal revolutionaries had strived (sic) hard to get this resolution carried.

"They were successful at the Lahore Congress of 1929, however, for Mahatma Gandhi himself moved the Independence resolution which was then adopted. It was at the Lahore Congress that the Congress proved themselves to be largely 'terrorist' in sympathy by the voting on Mr. Gandhi's resolution deploring the attempt to wreck the Viceroy's train and congratulating Lord Irwin and Lady Irwin on their escape from death. This resolution was passed, it is true, but only by a majority of 148, no fewer than 794 votes being recorded against it.[21A] As a matter of fact, the Congress, at that time, consisted of quite a few followers of Bose who were associated with the Jugantar group of revolutionaries and a few others. It was mostly for them that the resolution, mentioned above, was opposed by 794 members.

Satya Ranjan Bakshi, the editor of *Forward* wrote an article under the title *'Muddled'*, on the 2nd January 1929:

"It will be a grievous blunder on the part of the older leaders of the Congress if they run away with the idea that the numerical voting strength in favour of Gandhiji's resolution is any index of his popularity... He who runs must take note of the determined and articulate rebellion against authority; he who runs must take note of rebellion against popery, political or otherwise. No one is content today to take things as accepted, or trim one's convictions to the conveniences of fancies of men however reputed.

"...It is no doubt true that persons and personalities do count, and the older order does not change in a day. A course of action that has to secure the approval of the ballot box by marshalling on its sides all sorts of distinguished names of the country – revered Pundits and Maulanas, and above all, the mysterious spell of Sabarmati, does not seem to show intrinsic strength. It is a losing cause, and principles do not take long to defeat personalities.

"There is nothing so dissipating and so demoralizing as the confusion of thought and ideas...A programme of 'muddling on' does not encourage or inspire...It was hoped that the mental weaknesses or the intellectual hypocrisies involved in impossible compromises would be got over. ..The older leaders have again sought refuge in reservations and subterfuges.

"Sj. Subhas Chandra Bose's amendment made the issue both clear and straight... That is the beginning of the struggle. The next few months will show whether subterfuges and mental reservations win, or a bold idea, boldly conceived, grips the heart, the intellect and the imagination of the country."

With indomitable spirit, Bose said at the Calcutta Congress:

"India's youth is no longer prepared to hand over all responsibilities to the old leaders and follow them like a dumb flock of sheep. They have realized that an independent and strong India will be built only by the youth and they have accepted that responsibility. The ideas of Sabarmati is trying to generate a notion that modernity is an evil, ...it is better to go back to the days of the bullock carts and instead of building a good physique or having military training, one should aim at spiritual development alone.

"In India today, we want the philosophy of *Karmayoga* (cult of action). We have to live by adjusting ourselves with the present world. We cannot afford to live in isolation.

"When India will be free, she will have to fight against the modern enemies with the help of the latest methods of warfare — in the economic as well as political spheres.

"Gone are the days of bullock carts, they are gone for ever. Independent India will have to keep ready all the time with armaments — waiting until the day when the noble ideal of non-violence would be put into practice by the whole world."[22]

Just a year earlier, at the Madras Congress (1927), complete independence was declared as the goal of the political movements launched by Congress, but the Nehru Committee Report[23] considered Dominion Status as the mission to be accomplished. This decision was certainly a political compromise suggestive of retrogression and Bose opposed it though he had to sign the Report later to avoid a direct confrontation with the Gandhians. He said that had he protested against it, then several protests would have come on various issues, which would create problems for the committee members to formulate a report collectively. The result might have been disastrous. It shows that Bose was, willy-nilly, ready to cooperate with the Congress leaders for the sake of unity. But he was not to deviate from the main purpose for which he joined the Congress movement, i.e. complete independence of India. Evidently, his differences with the Congress leaders came on the surface regarding vital issues before the 1930's.

Bose, as has already been pointed out, never moved away from his original standpoint, i.e. achievement of complete independence, which he reasserted time and again in all his interactions with people. When he went to Barisal in 1929 for attending the District Congress Conference there, he reminded his audience that their goal should be *"Purna Swaraj"* (complete independence) and not Dominion Status. Bose in his Presidential address reminded the audience how the Barisal Conference was dissolved by the Police in 1906. He was of the opinion that the country should be independent not only politically but also economically and reiterated that their political aim should not be Dominion Status but complete independence. He insisted on the awakening of women, youths, the depressed classes, cultivators and labourers to the need for freedom.[24] It may also be pointed out here that the newly developed concern for the marginalized people in independent India owes its origin in the 1920s in the minds of Gandhi, Das and Bose.

Because of Bose's charismatic leadership, all the leading revolutionary groups not only from Bengal but also from outside came forward and joined the bandwagon with unprecedented enthusiasm, in the Calcutta Congress. It was a remarkable achievement of Bose that he could assemble all the leading revolutionary groups of the country in Calcutta to discuss and decide on the ways and means of a militant movement without which it would never be possible, he believed, to drive away the Imperialists from India. *Anushilan*, *Jugantar*, the *Madaripur* group of Purna Das, *Mukti Sangha* of Hem Ghosh, the Chittagong group of Surya Sen and the different militant organizations of North Bengal, all rallied round Bose. They wanted to give a new direction, a new motivation to the freedom movement through this session of Congress. These revolutionary organizations wanted to fight against the British Raj from the Congress platform under the leadership of Bose. As regards the strategy, the official policy of Congress was that of non-violence as a creed to which the revolutionaries were all opposed. But they realized that since Congress was an All-India organization, it would be easier for them to mobilize the teeming millions of the country for a nationwide uprising from this platform rather than from some unknown secret societies. Hence they decided to come under the banner of the Congress to achieve the common goal i.e. *Purna Swaraj*.

This strategy of the revolutionaries did not fall flat as it was found at this Session (1928) of the Congress that the revolutionaries, who did not have any faith in its professed ideology of non-violence, were on the forefront. Gandhi watched the developments with a lot of anxiety, as he was aware of the fact that no popular movement in India could succeed unless the Bengalees got emotionally involved with it. The impact of the Bengal *Renaissance* of the previous century was so overwhelming that the leading personalities of India including Gandhi realized the importance of the Bengali psyche in any national movement whatsoever. He needed the support of the Bengalee youth who demanded complete independence, which he himself had to support, ironically, one year later in Lahore.

Hem Chandra Ghosh, the celebrated revolutionary of Dacca, was ready with his cadres of *'Mukti Sangha'*, publicly presented as the 'Bengal Volunteers' in 1928. Satya Gupta, a leading member of *Mukti Sangha* and a close associate of Bose, was there with his martially trained personnel, which added gorgeous colour to the session. There were proper military-styled ranks for the officers of the Bengal Volunteers. In this corps, there were four Companies, named, A, B, C and D. Major Satya Gupta was in charge of the B Company. The sophistication, smartness, discipline and above all, their military outfit, impressed everybody around. It is interesting to note that quite a few eyebrows were raised amongst the Gandhian hardliners to whom the whole thing appeared to be ridiculous and resembled a circus.

Representatives from different revolutionary organizations outside Bengal also came to attend the Calcutta session of Congress (1928) as Bengal, they believed, was the pathfinder of militant nationalism under the able leadership of Bose. The most memorable of them were Bhagat Singh and Jatin Das, both of whom subsequently, died a martyr's death and left their names inscribed in golden letters in the history of Indian freedom struggle. Bhagat Singh gave his life at the gallows two and a half years later as a convict in the Lahore Conspiracy Case and Jatin Das sacrificed his life in the Lahore Jail through hunger-strike unto death in protest against the sub-human treatment meted out to the fellow freedom fighters.

It is known from *Anushilan* leader Jogesh Chatterjee's account that the Dacca *Anushilan* group had some serious internal problems with the veteran leader of the group named Pulin Das. The leaders disowned Das and allowed Pratul Ganguli and Narendra Mohan Sen to assume the group's leadership. The group's network expanded across the borders of Bengal to North India. Since *Anushilan* was not a familiar name in North India, the formation of another party as an offshoot of the *Anushilan* took place in Tripura. In the presence of Pratul Ganguli, Narendra Mohan Sen and Sachin Sanyal, the Hindustan Republican Association was formed in 1923/1924 which, later, spawned the Hindustan Socialist Republican Army. Bhagat Singh, Batukeshwar Dutta and Ajoy Ghosh were among Jogesh Chatterjee's young acolytes in U.P.[24A]

Jatin Das, the young dedicated social worker, was not unknown to Bose as he was always on the look out for sincere and hardworking youth who would be ready to sacrifice their career for the sake of the country. He organised an association called *Dakshin Kolikata Sevak Samity* which consisted of a library, and centres for training in weaving and spinning. He also made arrangements for procuring yarn spun through the spinning wheels from households against fair price.

Bose was aware of the fact that human resource was an extremely valuable resource that needed to be developed and in keeping with this awareness, he established an orphanage in a rented house for the poor and the destitute. The children there got the opportunity for education, physical exercise and training in handicrafts.

In 1924, however, Jatin Das was elected the Assistant Secretary to the South Calcutta Congress Committee. Around this time, there was a devastating flood in North Bengal. Pabna, Bagura, Rajshahi and Rangpur were devastated by flood caused by overflowing rivers due to torrential rain. In Calcutta, Acharya Prafulla Chandra Ray, the well-known scientist formed a flood-relief committee and help started pouring in form different parts of the country on appeal. It seemed as if the people who due to various reasons, could not participate in the Civil Disobedience Movement came forward to compensate for their non-participation in the said movement and extended their helping hand to the noble cause of flood-relief. Foodstaff, clothes, medicine and money, thus collected, needed to be properly distributed. Satish Dasgupta, the then director of Bengal Chemicals, took the responsibility of keeping the relief commodities in safe custody but who would venture to go to the flood-stricken areas as the leader of the team of volunteers? Prafulla Chandra was a good friend of Janakinath Bose, the father of Subhas Chandra and he knew that having been released from jail, Subhas devoted all his time and energy to social work. Social service was considered by Subhas nothing but a service to the nation. Prafulla Chandra, therefore, considered him as the ideal person to be sent to the flood-stricken North Bengal for proper distribution of relief. Bose convened an all-India youth convention with Meghnad Saha, the internationally acclaimed scientist as the chairperson.

Meghnath Saha was a member of the Anushilan Samity. Earlier, some Indian freedom fighters in Germany sent a message to Bagha Jatin that the German King Kaiser Wilhelm II was sympathetic towards the Indian revolutionaries, particularly towards the Anushilan Samity and was sending weapons to India by a ship for the Anushilan Samity fighters at the Sundarbans. Saha was assigned for picking up the weapons from there which did not happen as the ship did not reach the Sundarbans. (Archive of the Saha Institute of Nuclear Physics, Salt Lake, Kolkata).

The youth was very much inspired by the speeches delivered by Bose and Saha and expressed their willingness to come forward and take part in all kinds of social service work. For the flood victims, Bose organized a team of dedicated volunteers to take part in the relief work under his leadership. He took them along to Santahar, the station that was lying between Bagura and Rajshahi. Enormous tents were fixed on the huge stretches of empty lands adjacent to the station to house the office of the relief centre. Within a few weeks, Santahar became the hub of relief work under the able leadership of Bose. Jatin Das was one of the members of Bose's team working amongst the poor villagers for several days,

"The Dare-All Bengal Patriot" (1928-1933)   55

during which he came into close contact with Bose who was staying there at that time working relentlessly day in and day out for the flood victims.

Bose had an inherent capacity to pick and choose sincere workers from amongst the youth for the cause of the nation and Jatin Das was one such person. His mind was permeated with the spirit of revolution, which led him, in his early life, to join the Hindusthan Republican Association organized mainly by Sachin Sanyal, once a close ally of the well-known *Anushilan* revolutionary Rash Behari Basu. He took the leadership in organizing revolutionary activities throughout Uttar Pradesh and tried to unify the various revolutionary groups under the banner of one single all-India organization. To put his plans into practice, Sanyal came to Calcutta and contacted the leaders of the *Anushilan Samity*. His plans, however, did not materialize due to various reasons which included the ego hassles of some of the leading members of these groups.

Bose wrote in his *Indian Struggle*:

"At the time of the Calcutta Congress in 1928 and after, he (Das) had taken a leading part in organizing and training volunteers and in the Bengal Volunteers Corps, of which the writer was the Chief Officer or G.O.C., he held the rank of Major... Though the Corps was a peaceful and unarmed body, military discipline and training in military drill was imparted to the volunteers.. .After the Congress was over, the Volunteer Corps was maintained and branches were opened all over the province. In this arduous work, Jatin had played an important role."[25]

In Lahore Jail, it may be pointed out here, that the prisoners of the Lahore Conspiracy Case headed by Bhagat Singh made a demand for better treatment than the criminals on the ground that they were political prisoners and under trial, who should be considered innocent until they were actually convicted. These prisoners resorted to hunger-strike when they found that no remedy was forthcoming through usual legal methods.

"Among the prisoners was a young man from Calcutta, Mr. Jatindra Nath Das, who was at first rather averse to hunger-strike because he regarded it as a dangerous game to play. The enthusiasm of the rest forced him to join the strike but before doing so, he warned them that come what may, he would not turn back until their demands were fully conceded. ...As the days rolled by, one by one the hunger- strikers dropped off but young Jatin was invincible....He marched straight on towards death and freedom. Every heart in the country melted but the heart of the bureaucracy did not. ...After his death the whole country gave him an ovation which few men in the recent history of India have received."[26] A message of condolence came from the family of Terence McSwiney, the Lord Mayor of Cork, who had died a martyr's death under similar circumstances, in Ireland. The message runs like this: "Family of Terence McSwiney have heard with grief and pride of the death of Jatin Das. Freedom will come." Bose sent telegrams after telegrams to Gandhi requesting him to send a message on the occasion of Jatin Das's death. The latter labeled this self-sacrifice as a 'diabolical suicide' although later he spoke of the death of Bhagat Singh as a great martyrdom.[27]

The presence of Jatin Das and Bhagat Singh, however, at the Calcutta Congress, are suggestive of Bose's contacts with the sprawling world of armed revolutionaries in various parts of India. People, who were not in the know of things, thought that it was all an extravaganza, signifying nothing. They could not even dream that those young men and women were ready to sacrifice not only their career but also their life in an armed struggle and that the springing 'Bengal Tiger' had his 'gory claws' as much as the British Lion.

However, Bose, who was the General-Officer-Commanding of the Bengal Volunteers, had four Companies, in this corps as mentioned earlier, directed by four Majors Major Jatin Das ('A' Company), Major Satya Gupta ('B' Company), Major Binod Chakraborty ('C' Company), and Major Pratul Bhattacharya ('D' Company).

Bose was severely criticized by the Anglo-American Press in India for having dared to don military uniform himself and to give his volunteers military training. Motilal Nehru, however, praised him for the remarkable way in which the Corps maintained order and discipline both inside and outside the Congress pandal.

It is interesting to note that Pablo Neruda, the well-known Nobel laureate poet of Chile, attended the Calcutta session of Congress at Park Circus. He writes in his autobiography:

"This is a glorious day. We are present at the Congress of the Indian National Congress Party. A nation in the thick of its fight for liberation. Thousands of delegates packed the galleries. I met Gandhi. And Pundit Motilal Nehru, another patriarch of the movement. And his son, the elegant young Jawaharlal, recently back from England. Nehru is all for Independence, while Gandhi favours simple autonomy as a necessary first step. Gandhi: the sharp profile of a very cunning fox; a practical man; a politician along the lines of our early Creole leaders; a mastermind at committees; a shrewd tactician, indefatigable. As the multitude passes by in an endless stream, touching the hem of his white tunic worshipfully and crying 'Gandhiji! Gandhiji!' he gives them a perfunctory salute and smiles without taking off his glasses. He receives messages and reads them; he answers telegrams; all this without effort; he is a saint who never wears himself out. Nehru: the intelligent promulgator of their revolution.

"One of the great figures at the Congress was Subhas Chandra Bose, impetuous demagogue, violent anti-imperialist, fascinating political figure of his country.. .Many years later, here in India, one of his friends tells me how the fortress of Singapore fell.

'Our weapons were trained on the Japanese besiegers. Suddenly we began asking ourselves why. We had our soldiers do an about-face and we pointed our guns at the English troops. It was quite simple. The Japanese invaders were just passing through. The English seemed to be here for all eternity'.[28]"

The Calcutta session of Congress was in every way, a star-studded affair. Surya Sen of Chittagong attended the session with almost all his comrades released from jail and at the end of the session, went back to his home town, charged up like never before. The militant nationalists of Chittagong always considered Bose their role model as the latter stood for an uncompromising struggle for freedom. They organized within a month a well-trained volunteer force constituted by the young and enthusiastic boys and girls in the city. On 26th January 1929, Independence Day celebrations were supposed to take place all over India. Having been released from jail, the revolutionaries observed the Independence Day with a lot of fanfare in Chittagong. The Volunteers assembled in all-white dresses, a band played military tunes, twenty-one indigenous crackers were fired instead of cannons, the flag of the Indian National Congress was hoisted in the midst of loud chanting of *'Bande Mataram'* and *'Inqilab Zindabad'*. Ganesh Ghosh managed the Volunteer Corps in a skilful way. This was the first time that Chittagong celebrated the Independence Day with unprecedented enthusiasm. This kind of an expression of a revolutionary zeal through a celebration caused, obviously, headache to the rulers.

The revolutionaries eventually decided to launch an armed attack on the oppressive rulers, which would be an eye-opener for the ever-compromising, timid leadership of the National Congress. It was essential in those days to awaken the youth on a massive scale with proper leadership and to show the imperialists that the Indian people could afford to disregard them and have a liberation army of their own. The heroic performance of the Bengal Volunteers at the Calcutta Congress under the leadership of Bose inspired the Chittagong revolutionaries to such an extent that they started immediately the preparations for mobilizing the youth of East Bengal to organize a well-trained body of freedom fighters. The Chittagong Armoury Raid that took place on the 18th April, 1930, under the able leadership of Surya Sen, is a remarkable event in the history of Indian freedom movement.

Not surprisingly, the weekly report of the Director, Intelligence Bureau of the Home Department, Government of India, dated 22nd November 1928, New Delhi, expressed concern over the formation of the Bengal Volunteers. The report said:

"Subhas Chandra Bose has issued an appeal for 2000 volunteers for work in connection with the forthcoming session of the Indian National Congress. According to the *Forward*, Subhas will be 'Commander -in- Chief' and will be assisted by three generals, 'all able men and good colleagues'. Half of this force will be in full military uniform and the rest will be in mufti, but both wings will be trained and drilled under expert instructions, who have seen active service in the last world war."[28A]

It is evident from the above report that the Government was watching every move of Bose, collecting informations from various sources regarding his activities. A telegram P. No. 340-C., dated 7th December 1928 from the 'Viceroy's Camp' was sent to the Home Department, New Delhi in which the Viceroy wished to know whether the volunteer corps could be dealt with as an illegal association. [28B] To this, the Home Department, New Delhi replied by saying that they had no information so far that the Congress Volunteers could be brought within the terms of Criminal Law Amendment Act and it might be necessary to have recourse to the Act if situation developed in a menacing way. The reply further stated that if the Government took recourse to the Act, then it might lead to extremely embarrassing results both practically in dealing with masses of volunteers who would defy law and court arrest and also politically in involving probable arrest of principal Congress leaders and in its effect on moderate opinion which would be very slow to believe that such a step was justified.[28C]

There cannot be any doubt about the fact that the 'principal Congress leaders' included Bose in the main whose arrest would lead to political trouble for the Government as he was the undisputed leader of the volunteers belonging to various revolutionary groups spread all over Bengal and outside, and most importantly, the people of Bengal, the rulers knew, were very much sympathetic towards Bose.

Prior to the Chittagong Armoury Raid of 18th April 1930 under the leadership of Surya Sen who was also present at the Calcutta Congress of 1928, the revolutionaries there invited Bose to preside over the District Congress Conference to be held in Chittagong, as he was the president of the Bengal Congress at that time. They had a prolonged, secret meeting with him on 12th May 1929 in a cubicle of the Mahalakshmi Bank in Chittagong. Ganesh Ghosh, Ananta Singha, and Tripura Sen (who died a martyr's death at the Jalalabad combat later) were there, to inform Bose about their organizational strength, their plans for the revolutionary upsurge and the capability of their volunteers for carrying out such a massive attack. Bose wanted to know the details regarding their plans concerning the ensuing Raid.

Way back in 1915, Rash Behari Basu, Lala Hardayal, Jatin Mukherjee (commonly known as Bagha Jatin) and the Ghadar Party attempted to have an armed uprising throughout the country but their attempts failed because of the treachery of Kripal Singh and a few others. The difficulties, therefore, of having a mass upheaval in Bengal or in India as a whole, with the presence of the secret agents of the Police amongst the various revolutionary organizations in different parts of the country, were discussed at length by the Chittagong revolutionaries with Bose. They had enormous faith in him as a result of which they did not hesitate to confide in him as a trusted lieutenant and a dependable guide. They felt that the failure of the earlier attempts had already disheartened the young militants; it was therefore, necessary to have some action to boost their sunken spirit.[29]

The Bengal Volunteers, were backed by ex-revolutionaries like the members of *Mukti Sangha* with Hem Chandra Ghosh as its leader. It is to be noted that neither Hem Chandra Ghosh nor the other members of *Mukti Sangha* were to be considered ex-revolutionaries, as suggested by writers like Sitanshu Das. They were very much active at that time organizing the youth in different parts of East Bengal, giving them physical training, acclimatizing them with the teachings of *Shrimad Bhagavat Geeta* and over and above, instilling in them a spirit of militant nationalism. After the Rodda Arms Raid of 26th August 1914, in which Sreesh Mitra nee Habu Mitra of the *Atmannati Samity*, and Sreesh Pal, Haridas Dutta, Khagen Das of the *Mukti Sangha* took part, Hem Ghosh was arrested by the police and interned in his village home. Till that time the police was suspicious but not very sure about Ghosh and his secret organization. As soon as the police became convinced, they imprisoned him under Regulation III of 1818 first in Midnapore Central Jail, and then in the Hazaribagh Central Jail. He was brought to Alipore Central Jail in 1917 from where he was sent to Dacca Central Jail. In 1918, he was transferred from Dacca to Meherpore village in the district of Nadia where he was interned till 1919. Ghosh was ultimately released in the year 1920 after which he resumed his work in a new environment in a new way. The rulers, during those days, had a tendency of making the arrested rebels move from one place to another, in various jails and this was one of the various forms of harassment the authorities took recourse to at regular intervals.

The prolonged imprisonment of Hem Chandra Ghosh

did not go in vain as he got an opportunity in the jails to do a lot of reading and ponder over his future plans. Initially, after the release, he tried to present a different image of himself before the police and the Government by posing as a law-abiding innocent citizen. Along with his associates, he spread the story of his disillusionment regarding revolution and its concomitants. His original place of work was in Dacca but now he came to Calcutta and proceeded with his plans surreptitiously so much so that the police started considering him a former revolutionary who had given up his rebellious exploits and concentrated on a peaceful, domesticated life. Their names were, thus, deleted from the black list of the police.[30]

It is true that the various militant groups in Bengal welcomed the Bengal Volunteers Movement when it started, with open arms, as a dependable weapon of revolution, but *Mukti Sangha* was so deeply involved in the movement that they accepted it not just as a weapon, but also as the life force of militant nationalism. Even the I.B. reports started referring to them as "B.V". All this was possible because of Major Satya Gupta's skilful captaincy. At that time Hem Ghosh was the secretary of BPCC, this exterior he had to maintain to conceal his extremist interior.

When Swami Vivekananda came to Dacca in 1901, Ghosh was just a boy of seventeen. He was so overwhelmed by Swamiji's personality that he managed to meet him twice on the 3rd and the 4th of April, 1901. Swamiji told him that a subject nation had no religion per se. He said:

"Your only duty is to acquire human power, be brave and drive away the usurper from this country."[30A] Young Ghosh was mentally baptized that very day and chose to follow the path of revolution since then. He was already a disciple of Pareshnath of Dacca, a well-known body- builder who used to say: "Brahma is true, bullet is also true." Ghosh at that tender age accepted these words as a very meaningful gospel. His

Mukti Sangha workers formed a few social welfare organizations in Dacca during the years 1922-23, namely, Social Welfare League and later *Shri Sangha, Shanti Sangha*, and *Dhruva Sangha*. Through these organizations, young boys used to learn boxing, wrestling, swimming and various other games for body building. Secretly, through these associations, capable candidates were selected and trained for revolutionary purposes. Ghosh insisted on quality, not on quantity that was required for a successful uprising.

He assigned leadership of *Mukti Sangha* on Anil Chandra Ray in Dacca when the latter was the secretary of *Shri Sangha*. Under Anil Ray's leadership, *Mukti Sangha* became a strong and well-organized party. Satya Bhushan Gupta, Bhupendra Kishore Rakshit Ray, Bhabesh Nandi, Manindra Kishore Ray, Rasamay Shur and Prafulla Dutta were the leading comrades of Ray during those days. The party continued with its onward march with their collective effort.[31]

From the official records, one gets to know how merciless the Bengal Government was towards the revolutionaries in those days. It did not hesitate to reduce the family allowance granted to the State prisoners in case of any death in their family. One such instance was the case of Satya Bhushan Gupta of the Bengal Volunteers who was a close associate of Bose and eventually a State prisoner during the 1930s. When his mother died, his allowance was reduced by the Bengal Government from Rs. 50/- to Rs. 25/- although he had a number of dependents like an unemployed brother, an unmarried sister and a brother who was a student. Although the Home (Poll) Department of the Government of India considered this reduction to be drastic, the Governor-in-Council in Bengal went ahead to implement its own recommendation with effect from 29th August 1932, i.e. the very day Gupta's mother expired. [31A] It shows that humanitarianism had no meaning to the authorities in those days, for the people in the colonies fighting for freedom. The British upheld the principles of democracy, glorified the doctrines of human rights, but were these all for themselves, for the white-skinned people of the world? Did not the colonized people of the world have the right to liberate themselves and have self-governance? Did not the people of India have the right to possess sovereignty for their own country and promote the interests of their own nation?

However, Lila Nag, the leader of Dacca's *Dipali Sangha*, came into contact with Anil Ray and Hem Ghosh in connection with her social service work. Her joining a revolutionary group was, in every way, remarkable as the women in those days did not have any independence or drive to do something unconventional. Judging from the point of view of women of those days, it was really a very courageous move on her part to come forward from behind the four walls of home and join the firebrands. She published a monthly magazine called *Jayasree*, which comes out even today. It was the *Dipali Sangha* that spread the idea of women's education widely in Dacca and many other parts of Bengal, and also roused a rebellious spirit in the minds of women all around against British Imperialism.[32] Rebati Burman of *Mukti Sangha* introduced Lalit Burman, the revolutionary leader of Comilla, to Hem Ghosh and from then on, the two leaders started working together.

Satya Ranjan Bakshi, the nephew of Hem Ghosh, having completed his Masters from the Calcutta University, joined the daily newspaper called 'Forward' established by Deshabandhu C.R.Das to speak for the Swarajya Party. He did not go back to Dacca, his home town, as he became a very trustworthy comrade of Deshabandhu and subsequently a very good friend of Bose with whom he developed a close relationship that lasted till the end of his life. Deshabandhu inducted Bakshi in his Swarajya party. When Bose came to know that journalist Bakshi was also associated with *Mukti Sangha*, his friendship and faith in Bakshi grew stronger.

The death of Deshabandhu on the 16th of June, 1925 was a big blow to the people of Bengal. Although he had an opposition that could never see eye to eye with him but in front of his towering personality, they appeared to be rather insignificant. The Bengalees, in general, were very much impressed by the growing popularity of his Swarajya Party, the extension of the freedom struggle up to the Council and the capture of the Calcutta Corporation. Long ago Deshabandhu C.R.Das could foresee the possibility of a communal conflict between the Hindus and the Muslims to take place in future that might disturb the unity and integrity of the country. His choice of Sohrawardi as the Deputy Mayor of the Calcutta Corporation was an example of his farsightedness. Sohrawardi was a young barrister at that time without any experience in public administration but his selection by Das for that office was a proof of the latter's political sagacity. In the later years Sohrawardi's communal politics was not acceptable to many but he proved himself to be a competent administrator and an able organizer. Had Deshabandhu not died so early, people like Sohrawardi would not, probably, have moved away from the mainstream of nationalist politics and their continued presence in the Congress leadership would not have led to the partition of the country.

When J. M. Sengupta was honoured by Gandhi with the 'Triple Crown', i.e. the leadership of the Swarajya Party in the Bengal Council, the Presidentship of the BPCC and the Mayoralty of Calcutta, a Congress dissident caucus was created comprising five important leaders namely, Sarat Bose, Tulsi Gosain, Nirmal Chandra, Bidhan Ray and Nalini Sarkar, commonly known as the 'Big Five'. They were from the upper strata of society without much interactions with the people at the grassroots level. The 'Big Five', it may be pointed out here, did not have to struggle for acquiring leadership of the Party unlike Bose.

As there occurred changes at the upper level of the provincial politics, there were significant changes taking place in the districts too. This was the time when the Congress offices at the district level came within the hold of the revolutionaries. They did not have to fight for it because induction of new members was the common forte of the Congress. As a result, the number of their workers never decreased, instead, due to the abrupt suspension of the non-cooperation movement by Gandhi, it increased considerably. Most of the workers were, at that time, young students who, in the late 1920s, came of age. With the exception of one or two districts of the Bardwan Division, by and large, the district Congress Committees came to be controlled by the revolutionaries. It was C.R.Das who had brought small towns and villages into the mainstream movement for Swaraj and Bose wanted to continue with Das's policy of taking the movement deep into the villages with the help of the revolutionaries who were known for their dedication and sincerity. They injected in Congress politics a fighting spirit and a non-compromising attitude. These revolutionaries never accepted the creed of non-violence wholeheartedly and that is why they wanted to use the Congress Party as a national platform to mobilize people in cities as well as in villages for the purpose of an armed resistance nationwide.

Hem Chandra Ghosh was the secretary of the BPCC for quite some time. When Revati Burman introduced a monthly called *Benu* as a literary magazine for the youngsters, Hem Ghosh decided to make it the mouthpiece of the revolutionaries, in the guise of literature. *Benu* was blessed with the affection of Rabindra Nath Tagore and Sarat Chandra Chattopadhyay. *Bipradas*, the famous novel of Sarat Chandra, was published serially in *Benu* for which the author did not charge any honorarium. As a matter of fact, Sarat Chandra and Hem Chandra were so close that the latter used to address him as 'Sarat-da' (elder brother). The famous litterateur and critic Professor Subodh Chandra Sengupta heard of the name of Hem Chandra Ghosh for the first time from Sarat Chandra only. In an interview in the latter's village home, Sarat Chandra told Sengupta that his well-known novel *Pather Dabi* (proscribed by the British Government) was, to a great extent, inspired by Hem Ghosh. As Sengupta writes: "He (Sarat Chandra) repeated more than once that the materials and inspiration for the novel were supplied by Hem, the rest was his own fancy and the work its own apology."[33]

However, in the formation of the volunteer corps, in the Calcutta Congress, Major Satya Gupta was assisted mainly by Jyotish Joardar, Tejomoy Ghosh, Binay Bose, Dinesh Gupta and Haran Dutta. They had organized volunteers in different parts of Dacca, Narayangunge, Comilla, Bikrampur, Mymensingh, Calcutta and Midnapore as a preparation for the ensuing Congress session. Simultaneously a few secret societies also came up about which the police was ignorant.

As has already been pointed out, Bose was a symbol of revolutionary struggle for national liberation to the youth of not only Bengal, also other provinces. On August 4th, 1929, a procession of about 100 Bengalee volunteers and 25 Punjabis was taken out in Calcutta carrying placards bearing such inscriptions as "Down with Imperialism", "Long Live Revolution" and "Death is at our door". Placards were seized by Police and the Commissioner of Police who was informed that another procession would be taken out on the 11th when efforts would be made to bring in large number of strikers for joint celebration of "Political Sufferers' Day", issued order forbidding procession or open-air assembly except with permission. As a telegram dated 30th August 1929 from the Viceroy (Home Dept) to the Secretary of State for India, London states:

"Being subsequently assured, however, that strikers would not be allowed to join procession, he agreed to "Political Sufferers' Day procession while hinting that objectionable placard would not be allowed. Procession organized by South Calcutta Youth Association and Punjab Nau Jawan Bharat Sabha consisting of about 100 Congress Volunteers in uniform and 300 young men in ordinary dress carrying objectionable placards in spite of warning, was taken out on 11th afternoon under the leadership of Subhas Chandra Bose and others prominent in Congress party." It is evident that Bose was very much known to the British Government as a militant nationalist within the Indian National Congress and he was always under the watchful eyes of the Government. It is also clear from above that the Government viewed the other prominent Congressmen as just "others", Bose was their focus of attention. The telegram further stated:

"Local Government who instituted prosecution against certain persons in connection with procession on 4th August wired on 26th August that they proposed to file complaint on 28th August under Section 124-A and 120-B, Indian Penal Code against Subhas Bose, three other members of the Bengal Legislative Council and nine others for participating in procession of 11th in which placards were displayed inciting to armed revolution and advocating establishment of Republic and revolutionary cries were uttered."[33A] When the police seized the placards, however, Bose protested against the seizure. The Bengal Government considered "prosecution necessary to show that the Government would not tolerate advocacy of violence or revolution and that failure to prosecute leaders after instituting proceedings against smaller men for previous week's occurrence will be bad."[33B] It is evident from above that Bose was trying to mobilize the youth and spread the message of revolution all around to win public support in favour of a republic. Evidently he was successful in getting popular support for his endeavour and the rulers were well aware of it.

Around this time, a storybook called *Chalar Pathe* written by Bhupendra Kishore Rakshit Ray with an introduction by Sarat Chandra Chattopadhyay was published. Through the stories, an appeal was made to the womenfolk of Bengal to come forward and join the revolutionary movement. Later it was proved that the appeal did not fall flat as the women of Bengal like Pritilata Waddedar who later became a martyr,

Shanti Ghosh, Suniti Chowdhury, Bina Das, Ujjwala Majumdar and many others joined the rebellious campaigns with courage and fortitude. About this time, Hem Chandra's *Mukti Sangha* had a split giving rise to two different groups, namely, *Mukti Sangha* and *Sree Sangha* of which a mention has already been made. It may be noted in this connection that the police arrested Anil Das of the latter group because he was involved in a train robbery at Nilkhet level crossing in Dacca to collect funds for revolutionary purposes. On the 17th of June 1932, Anil Das died in police custody as he succumbed to the merciless physical and mental torture inflicted upon him by the British Government.[34]

Actions organized by the revolutionaries were going on in different parts of Bengal and the youth of Bengal came forward leaving behind their career prospects only for the liberation of the motherland. Binay Bose, a very bright fourth year student of Mitford Medical College in Dacca, coming from a well-to-do family and a member of the B.V, killed Lowman, the Inspector General of Police on the 29th of August 1930. After the action, Binay came to Calcutta in disguise with Supati Ray of the B. V. Subhas Chandra Bose wanted Binay to go abroad and stay there as an absconder as India would not have been a very safe place for him. Bose's elder brother Sarat Bose, Acharya P .C.Ray and Lady Abala Basu, the wife of Acharya Jagadish Chandra Basu, the great scientist, were of the same opinion but Binay himself was unwilling to leave India because he was determined to take part in the next action. The youth during those days, were so very charged up for a rebellion that they were ready to give up their life and career, no matter how bright it was going to be, for the sake of motherland and Binay's case was one such incident.

Dinesh Gupta, another young activist, was the founder of the Midnapore branch of the B.V. He came from Dacca as a student but his main purpose was to organize the youth in Midnapore, to train and motivate them for revolutionary outrages. The policy of the B.V was 'white life forfeiture' which the volunteers of Midnapore tried to implement wholeheartedly without any care for their own lives.

The alien rulers left no stone unturned to nip all rebellious possibilities in the bud. Accordingly the Government in Midnapore, blacklisted many educational institutions that appeared to lend themselves to the propagation of seditious and revolutionary ideas in the province. The Government blacklisted Midnapore College, Town School, Collegiate School and Hindu School. As a result, punishments like disaffiliation, minimization of grants, close down of the institution for a certain period of time, and giving warnings to the teachers as well as the parents, became a regular feature.[35] According to many, Midnapore was the hub of revolutionary activities in those days in West Bengal and the rulers felt that the educational institutions were nothing but the breeding grounds for 'terrorism'.

The decade of 1930's saw plenty of actions planned by the revolutionary leaders and implemented by the young activists. Simpson, the Inspector General of Police was killed at the Writers' Buildings, Calcutta on the 8th of December 1930 by three young revolutionaries, namely Binay Bose (who killed Lowman in Dacca), Badal Gupta and Dinesh Gupta, a student of Midnapore College and an activist; all of whom belonged to the Bengal Volunteers. During the action, Badal killed himself on the spot, Binay died a few days later in hospital due to severe injury, Dinesh recovered in the Medical College Hospital and was then sent to the condemned cell of Alipore Jail to be hanged. The alien rulers during those days preferred to hang revolutionaries with a fit body, not with injuries and that is why they kept these boys in hospital first for their treatment and recovery and then sent them to the condemned cell.

Bose was there in the Alipore jail in 1931 along with Hem Ghosh, Bipin Ganguli, Purna Das and many other prisoners serving sentence of imprisonment for civil disobedience. Bose

"The Dare-All Bengal Patriot" (1928-1933)

wanted to perform the Saraswati Puja inside the jail. Jailor Mr. Swan was an Irishman who respected Bose for his leadership quality and an uncompromising attitude. Bose requested him for permission for *"Pushpanjali"* (the ritual of offering floral tribute to God) in which he wanted all the prisoners including the inmates of the condemned cell, to participate. It was rather difficult for Swan to allow the condemned cell inmates to come out and take part in the ritual, but Bose was adamant. Swan gave in ultimately and watched them worship the Goddess in a pandal where they hoisted the Indian flag. While accompanying Dinesh on his way to the pandal, Bose pushed him hard to give him a forced entry into Ward no.1 where Sunil Sengupta of BV was present waiting for his comrade. Bose wanted to give a chance to Dinesh to convey a message, if there was any, to his people through Sengupta. Dinesh could not even dream of coming out of the condemned cell ever, on top of it, meeting a comrade and communicating with him was beyond his imagination. He asked Sengupta to tell Hem Ghosh that he was fine, and he would stand by his ideal till the last day of his life. He spent the last few days of his life inside the condemned cell taking refuge in the *Gita*. The revolutionaries in those days used to take oath at their initiation ceremony by chanting hymns from the *Gita*, the most impressive lines for them were:

"Paritranaya Sadhunam Vinashaya Cha Dushkritam Dharmasangsthapanaya Sambhabami Yuge Yuge", which means "to protect the innocent and annihilate the evil, I [God] shall appear ages after ages."

Dinesh Gupta was hanged in the Alipore Jail on the 6th of July 1931. His letters written to his family members were of immense literary value. They were published in the monthly magazine called *Benu*. Having read the letters, Subhas Chandra Bose commented:

"these are not just letters, they carry an invaluable philosophy of life." In one of his letters Dinesh wrote:

"we are scared of death, that is why death conquers us. If we can overpower the fear, death will appear to be trivial. ..we know that we do not perish, our mortal remains perish. The soul is immortal. This soul is Me and this soul is the Divine Spirit. When one realizes this, one can say 'I am Him, fire cannot immolate me, water cannot moisten me, wind cannot dehydrate me'. The *Gita* describes the soul in the following way:

'arms cannot pierce it, fire cannot ignite it, water cannot moisten it, wind cannot dehydrate it, the soul is indestructible, all-pervasive and perennial.'

"You might say, if I know all this then why my mind is still restless. The only way of having mental peace is to surrender oneself to God...Do we really love God wholeheartedly? The one who loves Him wholeheartedly is not scared of death like Nemai of Bengal, Jesus Christ, and all those men of our country who welcomed death with a smiling face."[36]

While Bose was in jail, the meeting of Gandhi with Lord Irwin started on February 17, 1931 in the Viceroy's new palace, now called the Rashtrapati Bhavan.

"It is a historical fact that in the course of his talks, Gandhiji told Lord Irwin that Subhas Babu was his 'opponent' who would 'denounce' him for favouring the British."[37] The meeting, however, led to the signing of the Gandhi-Irwin Pact which was published in the Gazette of India Extraordinary on the 3rd of March,1931. The Delhi Pact disillusioned many people about Gandhi's leadership. Bose was extremely unhappy because of Gandhi's refusal "to espouse the cause of the Garhwali soldiers, the state-prisoners, the Meerut Conspiracy prisoners, and the revolutionary prisoners, which deprived the Indian National Congress of the claim to be the central organ of the anti-imperialist struggle in India."[38]

According to a confidential I.B. report on the political situation in Bengal during the 1st half of March, 1931 "...there were processions. ...the members of which gave vent to revolutionary cries and extolled the perpetrators of murder such as Bhagat Singh, Dinesh Gupta and the rest, while a particularly objectionable speech in favour of violence and bloodshed was delivered by one speaker and received with approbation. There are signs that there may be a break away on the part of the younger elements from Mr. Gandhi and his teaching."[39] The report indicates clearly that the youngsters of those days were very much perturbed by Gandhi's stand on the nationalist prisoners who were fighting fearlessly against the imperialists and while fighting for freedom, they were also sacrificing their young lives which they thought, was not being appreciated by Gandhi.

During those stormy days, Bose left no stone unturned to save the lives of Bhagat Singh, Rajguru and Sukhdev who received death sentence due to the Lahore Conspiracy Case. As he writes :

"Before my release from prison on March 8th, I ascertained that the political prisoners, as a rule, were hostile to the Pact and I naturally shared their feelings. But after coming out, I realized that the Pact was a settled fact and there was no possibility of preventing its ratification at the Karachi Congress. The only question that we had to decide was whether we should put up an insignificant opposition at Karachi or whether we should refrain from dividing the House while disapproving of the Pact. Before coming to a decision, I considered it advisable to meet the Mahatma personally. I therefore undertook a journey to Bombay, which also enabled me to gauge public feeling in the provinces through which I passed. At Bombay I had long conversations with the Mahatma. After criticizing the Pact, the point that I urged was that we would be prepared to support him as long as he stood for independence — but the moment he gave up that stand, we would consider it our duty to fight him. At the end, the Mahatma gave the following assurances:

"* * * 3. He would use all his influence and strain every nerve to secure amnesty for those who had been left out in the Pact. From Bombay the Mahatma left for Delhi and I travelled in the same train with him. This gave me a further opportunity not only of supplementing our talks at Bombay but also of observing how the public were reacting to the Pact.. .At Delhi, no sooner did we arrive than we received a bombshell in the shape of news, to the effect that the Government had decided to execute Sardar Bhagat Singh and two of his comrades in the Lahore Conspiracy case. Pressure was brought to bear upon the Mahatma to try to save the lives of these young men and it must be admitted that he did try his very best. On this occasion I ventured the suggestion that he should, if necessary, break with the Viceroy on the question, because the execution was against the spirit, if not the letter of the Delhi Pact. I was reminded of a similar incident during the armistice between the Sinn Fein Party and the British Government, when the strong attitude adopted by the former, had secured the release of an Irish political prisoner sentenced to the gallows. But the Mahatma who did not want to identify himself with the revolutionary prisoners, would not go so far and it naturally made a great difference when the Viceroy realized that the Mahatma would not break on that question. However, at that time, Lord Irwin told the Mahatma that he had received a largely signed petition asking for the commutation of the death sentence passed on the three Lahore prisoners. He would postpone their execution for the time being and give serious consideration to the matter, but beyond that he did not want to be pressed at the moment. The conclusion, which the Mahatma and everybody else drew from this attitude of the Viceroy, was that the execution would be finally cancelled and there was a jubilation all over the country and especially in Bengal, where some revolutionary prisoners were also going to be executed.

"About ten days after this incident the Congress was to

meet at Karachi. The general expectation being that the execution would be cancelled, it was a most painful and unexpected surprise when on March 24th, while we were on our way to Karachi from Calcutta, the news was received that Sardar Bhagat Singh and his comrades had been hanged the night before. Gruesome reports were also afloat in the Punjab about the manner in which their dead bodies had been disposed of. It is impossible to understand at this distant date the poignant grief, which stirred the country from one end to the other. Somehow or other, Bhagat Singh had become the symbol of the new awakening among the youths. ...he was the father of the Nau Jawan Bharat Sabha (the Youth Movement) in the Punjab — that one of his comrades, Jatin Das, had died the death of a martyr and that he and his comrades had maintained a fearless attitude while they were in the dock."[40]

It was, by all means, a triumph of the British policy of Divide and Rule, " have compromises with Congress and crush the revolutionaries ruthlessly."[41]

Gandhi never concealed his negative mental disposition towards the revolutionaries. In his own words: "Bhagat Singh worship has done and is doing incalculable harm to the country ...The result is goondaism and degradation whenever this mad worship being performed. It was the peremptory duty of the A.I.C.C. to condemn at the forthcoming meeting, the treacherous outrage and reiterate its policy of non-violence in unequivocal terms".[42]

There was a nationwide uproar from Kashmir to Kanyakumarika against the execution of Bhagat Singh and his compatriots. As soon as Gandhi reached Karachi, a huge crowd gathered under the leadership of Nau Jawan Bharat Sabha, shouting slogans, holding him responsible for the hanging of Bhagat Singh and the others. The Congress leaders were under the apprehension that there would possibly be a deadlock regarding the question of approving the Delhi Pact in the wake of the execution of Singh and the others. Only Bose possessed the strength and the leadership quality required to mobilize support for an open resistance. But in the Karachi Congress, which was presided over by Ballav Bhai Patel, Bose came up with a mature sagacity and farsightedness to avoid a possible split in Congress. He expressed the opinion of the Leftists criticizing the Pact, but did not want to create a serious obstacle to the acceptance of the main proposal of the Congress, for the sake of national unity.

Bhagat Singh's execution was followed by the assassination of the District Magistrate of Midnapore by the young revolutionaries of Bengal. The instruction of taking revenge came from the Buxa detention camp secretly sent by Bhupendra Kishore Rakshit Ray of the Bengal Volunteers to its Calcutta members. According to a confidential report for the 1st half of April, 1931,

"the event which has overshadowed all others during the fortnight is the murder on 7th April of Mr. J. Peddie, D.M. of Midnapore. It should be recorded that Mr. J.M.Sengupta has issued a statement condemning the crime.. .on the other hand, at least one so-called responsible leader, viz. Subhas Bose, with his call for 'thousands of Bhagat Singhs' must be held guilty of inciting impressionable youths to this very type of outrage. His journal *Liberty* has uttered no real word of condemnation and the only comment on the crime is contained in a leaderette, which combines half-hearted regret with a reference to Gandhi's warning to the youth of the country against copying the example of Bhagat Singh. This warning was preceded by the payment of 'all the tributes that could be paid to the memory of Bhagat Singh and his comrades.' Comment is superfluous.. .The murder was committed in furtherance of the accepted policy of the terrorists who consider that the Irwin-Gandhi Pact leads them nowhere, and that they can only get what they want by continued violence. It is perhaps significant that the latter part of March was characterized by numerous speeches apropos of the execution of Bhagat Singh which were incitements to bloodshed, pure and simple, and by a flood of revolutionary leaflets which, experience has proved always to be a prelude to outrage of some sort."[43]

Bose was very close to a Barisal revolutionary named Satin Sen who subsequently died a martyr's death in a jail in the then East Pakistan (now Bangladesh) after India's independence. The same IB Report goes on to say:

"It is evident that at least one notorious agitator, released under the amnesty, viz. Satin Sen of Barisal is going to show no response to this act of clemency. He made a most objectionable speech on Bhagat Singh's Sradh Day in Calcutta and evidently intends to give as much trouble as possible."[44]

The impact of Bhagat Singh's execution was far-reaching, particularly upon the young revolutionaries of Bengal. "Outwardly there is little change to note in the general situation. The 'lull' continues, but the Congress people continue steadily, as they have done ever since the announcement of the Delhi settlement, their efforts to consolidate their own position and undermine that of Government. The 'youth' element becomes more and more conspicuous. At a meeting in Calcutta on 3rd May, 1931, Subhas Bose warned his audience that the truce must not be regarded as a permanent peace treaty but that they must be prepared for a fresh fight keeping their powder dry. This atmosphere of preparation is specially noticeable in Midnapore. The Commissioner, Burdwan Division, reports as follows: 'the reports received from District Officers and the information one picks up at interviews and on tour, all confirm the growing apprehension that the Delhi Settlement is merely a drop-curtain between the acts of a tragedy and that the stage is being set behind for further and more serious trouble. ...The consumers and vendors of excisable articles and foreign goods generally are being interfered with by methods which are far from 'peaceful'. Meetings and conferences are being held all over the country at which people are exhorted to boycott foreign goods and stop the consumption of liquor, to hoist the

National Flag and keep it flying and to prepare earnestly for the coming struggle by collecting funds and joining Congress organizations. Loyal persons are being threatened with serious consequences once provincial autonomy is established, complainants and witnesses are being brow-beaten into denying what they have already said or concealing what they undoubtedly know and offenders are being held before the self-constituted tribunals and fined for the benefit of Congress funds".[45]

Bose was always under the watchful eyes of the British Intelligence as he never concealed his feelings towards the revolutionaries who were to him, a symbol of unadulterated patriotism.

Like Bose, the revolutionaries were very much disappointed with the outcome of the Gandhi-Irwin pact and they were convinced that their colonial masters would never grant them complete independence they aspire for, because of the compromising attitude of Gandhi and his followers. Bose continued his feat of preaching the ideal of complete independence, come what may. The Karachi Congress approved of the Gandhi-Irwin Pact (29th March, 1931) and leaders like Sardar Patel sang praises of the Dominion Status forgetting about the proposal adopted in Lahore Congress for complete independence. At this point of time, the Government was carefully watching the happenings in the arena of Bengal politics as it always did, but this time with an extra zeal, for there was some difference of opinion between J.M.Sengupta and Subhas Bose within the Bengal Congress itself. The Government was eagerly awaiting a showdown between these two leaders and their respective followers, which might escalate into a split in the Congress Party itself. Even over the Gandhi-Irwin pact, the two leaders had differences which were a source of amusement for the rulers. The report on the political situation in Bengal during the second half of March 1931, states:

"The present center of political unrest is, of course,

Karachi and there the Bengal leaders with their staffs are now assembled. J.M.Sengupta is supporting the Gandhi-Irwin Pact while his rival Subhas Bose is biding his time until he is strong enough to wreck it. His open connection with the Nau Jawan Bharat Association is sufficient evidence of his views. ..the situation is tolerably good in the majority of districts, with, however, exceptions. These exceptions relate to those districts on which civil disobedience obtained its strongest hold, in particular, Midnapore and Bakarganj......

"The execution of the Lahore murderers was the signal for a good many processions and meetings, and speeches eulogizing their deeds were delivered... The Corporation as was to be expected, adjourned its meeting of the 25th instant. 'as a mark of protest against the unwise, ill-considered action of the Government in executing Bhagat Singh, Sukhdev and Rajguru in utter disregard of strong and united public opinion throughout the country'.

"In Calcutta, there has been a revival of picketing in the last few days. The Congress people repudiate it and the Commissioner of Police reports that it is the work of the Jubak Satyagraha Samiti and there is reason to believe that Subhas Bose and his relatives are not unconnected with it."[46]

By the term 'his relatives' the authorities probably meant Sarat Bose, the well-known barrister and elder brother of Bose who was with the latter almost always as a source of his strength.

According to some observers, there were some apparent contradictions in Bose so far as his outlook on the policies and activities of the revolutionaries were concerned. This one can ascertain, they argue, from his speeches and programmes during the period of 1929-1932. He expressed his lack of faith in terrorism more than once in his public speeches and statements. In this context, his speech delivered on the 28th of September, 1929, in the Howrah District Political Conference, may be cited. In the very beginning, Bose paid his homage to

Jatin Das by saying that he ignited the fire of independence on his own bones. But in the very same speech he mentioned that he did not know whether there were people who still believed that India could attain freedom by means of two and a half pieces of bombs and one and a half pistols. It was not so easy for India to attain freedom, he said. It might be possible to indulge in terrorism with the help of two and a half bombs and one and a half pistols, but revolution was a different thing altogether. One could have terrorist outrages with the help of just a handful of men but a revolution would take place only when the entire nation woke up. He insisted on mass-based organizations spread all over the country to mobilize people for an uprising without which India would never be able to attain complete independence. He felt the necessity of having a huge supply of arms and ammunitions for a successful uprising and that is why he used to talk about the futility of sporadic actions with the help of a few bombs and pistols. It was the lack of arms and ammunitions required to fight against a powerful enemy which was lamented upon by Bose, certainly not the idea of militancy.

With the purpose of mobilizing people, Bose toured the whole country, delivered speeches to inspire people for joining the mass movements, reminding them of the torture inflicted by the rulers upon the freedom fighters.

His whereabouts were meticulously monitored by the British Intelligence, ample evidence of which is found in the IB records kept in the State Archives of Calcutta. One such report states that the Commissioner of the Burdwan Division, referring to Midnapore in particular, pointed out that when anti-Government propaganda had been so widely spread and had penetrated so deeply, "it takes a long time for respect for law and order to reassert itself. Subhas Chandra Bose has been paying visits to a number of places in the 24 Parganas, but his speeches appear to have been moderate in tone, and none of them aroused much excitement."[47]

From 1930 onwards, the vindictive British Government started throwing the revolutionaries into the prisons of Buxa, Deoli, Hijli, Berhampore and quite a few of them were imprisoned without trial. These political prisoners used to be tortured and humiliated by the authorities mercilessly as a result of which there was an undercurrent of hatred permeating the minds of the hapless inmates. On 16th September 1931, all on a sudden, in the dead of night, the unarmed prisoners in Hijli were attacked by the jail guards, bullets showering on them killing on the spot, Bengal's young revolutionary Santosh Mitra, a close ally of Bose and Tarakeshwar Sengupta. More than a hundred prisoners were badly injured by this brutal assault.

Earlier, Bose held the British jail authorities responsible for the pathetic death of Jatin Das in Lahore Central Jail, but this Hijli incident appeared before him as a dastardly act. It was to him, not just a stray incident taking place in a particular region or area, rather something of a greater magnitude. He roused public opinion throughout the country to protest against the British atrocities and requested the All-India Congress leadership to consider the matter seriously, as an event of national importance. At the same time he expressed deep anguish at the way the Congress leaders were showing their indifference towards Bengal. Besides, he summoned the Bengal leaders to act in unison putting an end to narrow group-politics. Soon after, he started moulding public opinion in favour of a widespread programme for prison reforms and a proper policy regarding the treatment of detenues in the detention camps. He was shocked by the lack of concern shown by Gandhi who was in England at that time, and by the Congress leaders as well which led him to write a letter to the Congress President Sardar Patel on 25th October, 1931 expressing his concern regarding the whole matter.

The British Government was so very scared of Bose that books carrying his name in the title used to be proscribed, e.g. the book entitled *Babu Subhas Chandra Bose* written by

T.S.Chokkalingam, was proscribed under Section 19 of the Indian Press Emergency Powers Act, 1931, although the book contained nothing seditious. [48] The Government was all the more fearful about books written by Bose himself. His *"Indian Struggle, 1920-1934"*, published abroad, was prevented from entry into India under Section 19 of the Sea Customs Act.[49]

It is true that Bose was planning to launch an armed attack against the British Raj with the help of a well-trained and well-equipped army of volunteers composed of the revolutionaries with help from abroad, but suggestions regarding the implementation of his plans came from different quarters, in different ways. The Subject Committee of the Howrah Session of the Bengal Provincial Conference, 1927 at Maju proposed that a permanent body of Bengal volunteers, constituted by five thousand dedicated, healthy, and strongly built boys should be formed. For them, training in physical exercise, military drill, ambulance etc. should be arranged under the supervision of the various District Congress Committees. The name of the proposer was Narandas Dey.[50]

The Subject Committee wanted to organize a well trained volunteer force which would eventually spread over the country as a whole and take the form of a national army in course of time. This idea tallied with that of Bose and to motivate people in favour of an armed resistance, he travelled extensively all over Bengal attending meetings and delivering speeches as many as possible. The government, as usual, kept on monitoring all his whereabouts with the help of secret agents.

After the Calcutta Congress, however, on the 13th of July, 1929, he went to attend the District Congress Conference held in Barisal.

"The local agitators wanted to welcome Subhas Chandra Bose at the Nalchiti Steamer Ghat on his way to Barisal but the sub-agent did not allow anyone to go on board the steamer....Subhas Chandra Bose, the President-elect for the District Conference with Kiran Shankar Roy, Dr. Subodh Kumar

Bose, Mrs. Latika Bose and Jalaluddin Hashmi and several others reached Barisal by the Khulna Express steamer on 13-7-29. They were received at the station with shouts of *Bande Mataram* by about 150 volunteers in Khaki Khaddar uniform and about 200 students of the Braja Mohan and the Banipith schools and the prominent agitators of the town viz. Niranjan Sen, Aswini Ganguli and others. ...In all about 500 men attended the Ghat. The volunteers carried short bamboo lathis. After a procession through the town, the guests were conducted to the house of Saral Kumar Dutta. Subhas Bose was accommodated in the house of Amiya Kumar Raychowdhury. .."

"On 13-7-1929, the Conference started at about 5-30 PM. About 1200 persons attended including about 300 ladies. Amongst those present, were Purna Chandra Das, Kiran Shankar Ray, Pratul Ganguli ex-detenue, Aswini Ganguli ex-detenue, Jalaluddin Hashmi and most of the local agitators. The proceedings commenced with the song *'Bande Mataram'* ...The Chairman of the Reception Committee, Rajani Kanta Chatterjee.. .mentioned about the cruelty of the Bureaucracy in arresting Satindra Nath Sen and some Congress workers.

"... The Conference was resumed on 14-7-1929. Subhas Chandra Bose announced that Satindra Nath Sen and his co-workers had broken their fast at his request on condition that he would try his best to redress their grievances in the jail. Lalit Mohan Das of Goila moved the following resolutions which was supported by Narendra Nath Das and Jalaluddin Hashmi and unanimously carried –

a) Enlistment of 6500 volunteers by 31st August
b) Boycott of foreign goods
c) Removal of untouchability
d) Physical culture in villages
e) Propaganda of non-cooperation in the interior

"Narendra Nath Das said that for the sake of freedom,

the measures adopted by Shivaji, Guru Govinda, Lenin and others were not condemned in any independent country. He further said 'India would never have become dependent had she had swords.' ...Ashutosh Mahalanbis moved a resolution of respect for Satya Ranjan Bakshi...He said that the object of sending Satya Ranjan to jail was to crush the *'Forward'* ...the resolution was unanimously carried.

"...Dr. Subodh Chandra Bose said that Section 110 Cr. P.C. is applicable to thieves, robbers, dacoits only and not to Satin Sen and Subhas Bose.

"The following resolutions were read by the President and carried unanimously –

(1) Protest against the confiscation of the book' *Desher Parichaya'* written by Arun Chandra Guha
(2) Sympathy for the people of the flood-affected areas
(3) Unity amongst all castes for attainment of Swaraj
(4) Necessity for retention of and exercise with weapons
(5) Removal of water hyacinth from Khals and rivers
(6) Protest against the lending of the Town Hall at Barisal to the Cinema Company.

"Subhas Chandra Bose concluded with a speech in which he said that the strength of the country has increased since 1921. He said 'England's weakness is our opportunity. A worldwide war is very near. All nations are discontented. We will tell the English that we will take this opportunity. A decision for India is wanted before this worldwide war. If you satisfy our claim to the full, there will be a compromise. Do what lies in your power, we will do what we think our duty.' The Conference ended. ..with shouts of *Bande Mataram* and Subhas Babuki Jay."[51]

The kind of enthusiasm generated by Bose all over Bengal in favour of a mass upheaval was unprecedented. All over the city of Calcutta, training camps were being set up by the revolutionaries with a view to organizing the youth for an armed resistance. "Active preparation for training camps for male and female volunteers in public parks in Calcutta, presumably with the tacit consent of the Corporation, led to the declaration of the Bangiya Seva Dal as an unlawful association under Para II of the Indian Criminal Law Amendment Act, 1908, and it may be necessary to take similar action against other such bodies. Mr. Subhas Bose, before leaving for Bombay, made speeches in Nadia and Khulna districts urging an intensive boycott of British goods."[52]

When Bose paid a visit to the District of Mymensingh in December 1931, "the District Magistrate draws attention to the fact that Mr. Bose made a point of going to those places which have the most active revolutionary gangs."[53]

Besides appearing at the Berhampore Conference, he also paid a visit to Burdwan District "where in addition to his usual speeches about the shooting in the Hijli Camp, and the incidents which followed the murder of Inspector Ahsanulla at Chittagong and the attempted murder of Mr. Durno at Dacca, he spoke of the Governor-designate of Bengal as a 'repression-specialist' and warned his hearers that difficult times were coming for which they must prepare."[54]

It is true that Bose did not have much of a faith in the sporadic actions perpetrated by the revolutionaries in different parts of the country, but at the same time he never really condemned these acts of violence as an unproductive exercise. Rather he wanted the rulers to delve deep into the matter and find out why these youngsters embarked on the method of violence. After the killing of Simpson I.G. (Prison) by three young revolutionaries on the 8th December 1930, one IB record shows :

"The outrage of Dec. 8th is outwardly condemned, but like Subhas Bose's speech, at the Corporation meeting, this condemnation is coupled with the strongest implication that the outrage was really only the inevitable outcome of Government's policy. In fact, it is difficult to comment in terms of moderation on the attitude of the Press to this abominable deed. The sympathies of the Press would appear to be with the murderers and not the murdered. Thus Liberty devotes much space and large headlines to the sufferings of Binay Bose, while Advance on December 11th, while throwing a single sentence of sympathy to the murdered man's survivors, devotes the rest of a long leading article to proving that such outrages are an inevitable (and — the tone of the whole article implies-a quite commendable) result of 'repression'."[55]

Bose, with a dauntless spirit, formed committees consisting of revolutionary leaders with large followings amongst the youth. "Apart from the committees of Mr.Subhas Bose, political activity of the ordinary kind outside Calcutta, has not been marked during the first half of November (1931). ..In East Bengal, where the Congress organizations are dominated by the violent sections, interest is centered in terrorism and crimes of violence. This is illustrated by the activities of Mr. Subhas Bose, who, after attending a meeting of the Bengal Jute Workers' Conference at Kankinara on the Labour Day, the 31st October, made a tour in Bakarganj district and then went to Dacca with the Committee which appointed itself to inquire into the 'alleged indiscriminate arrests and assaults and oppression. ..by the Police' that followed the attempt to murder Mr. Durno (the Collector of Dacca). The Commissioner of Dacca points out that Mr. Subhas Bose chose to visit those places in Bakarganj district, which are the principal centers of revolutionary activity. He made speeches on the Hijli and Chittagong incidents and urged his audience to prepare themselves for the next war. Mr. Subhas Bose was stopped at Narayanganj by an order under Section 144, Criminal Procedure Code, forbidding him to enter the Dacca district, but was arrested later when after a brief visit to Comilla, he disobeyed the order. The Commissioner reports that he asked the District Magistrate to take this action because after the

"The Dare-All Bengal Patriot" (1928-1933)

attempted murder of Mr. Durno, there was wild rumours in Dacca of impending communal disturbances; the people had been reassured with some difficulty by the efforts of the Commissioner and the Nawab and the Commissioner was assured by several Hindu leaders that the visit of Mr. Subhas Bose was most undesirable."[56]

It may be pointed out here that two young revolutionaries named Saroj Guha and Ramen Bhowmik who were absconding, attacked Durno, on the 28th of October 1931. As a result, the police, not being able to get hold of the culprits, indulged in unprecedented atrocities causing innocent people to suffer. As soon as Bose came to know about it, he rushed towards Dacca but was arrested at Narayanganj on the 7th of November. J.C.Gupta and the other members of the Enquiry Committee accompanying Bose were allowed to go to Dacca, whereas Bose was sent to Chandpore by a steamer so that he found no option but to go back to Calcutta. But indomitable as he was, Bose took another route to Dacca, through Comilla, Akhaura and Bhairab and reached his destination on the 11th November. Unfortunately he was arrested again at the Tejgaon Station, four miles away from Dacca. The sub-divisional magistrate asked him to go back but he refused to oblige as a result of which he was offered a conditional release on bail and asked to come back on the day of the hearing. Bose did not agree to this proposal and was, consequently, sent to the Dacca Central Jail.[57]

Even in jail, Bose was restricted in his interviews with people. Narendra Narayan Chakrabarty, Abinash Bhattacharya, Suren Sengupta and the two lawyers, Rajani Das and Jogen Guhathakurta appealed to the District authorities for permission to meet him in Dacca jail. They were permitted to meet him standing in front of the iron rods and nets behind which Bose would be present. This arrangement was evidently quite humiliating for him, so he told the jail authorities that he did not want to meet anyone in this way.[58]

Bose was, however, released on the 14th of November on personal bail of Rs. 500 after which he visited almost all the houses raided by the Police on the 28th of October 1931. He came to Dacca only to find out to what extent the bureaucracy had gone to take revenge on the local people for the attack on Durno. He listened to everyone affected and inspected the damaged properties, sympathized with the people tortured by the Police and told them that the whole country would be on their side.[59] From Dacca, he went over to Mymensingh, from there to Netrakona, and visited subsequently places like Kishorganj, Jamalpore, Sirajganj and several other towns and villages in East Bengal. When he was planning to go to Midnapore, the Government was scared as the said district was well known for its revolutionary campaigns. A C.I.D. report informed the Government that Bose was planning to go to Tamluk within a day or two in order to revive the Salt Campaign there, and volunteers from outside the district were already coming in. The District authorities were scared and started thinking in terms of issuing an injunction order against the entry of Bose.[59A]

Bose, according to previous IB Reports, supported the revolutionaries in more ways than one. He used to assist them financially so that a strong and powerful militant organization could be built up which would pave the way for a countrywide uprising.

"In September, a reliable agent reported that the Bengal Provincial Congress Committee was giving Rs. 300/- a month to the Bengal Provincial Students' Association for organizing a students' movement in the Mufassal for carrying on with the Civil Disobedience movement and that the terrorists of the future would be drawn from among the members of this association. According to the same agent, Subhas Bose, who was released from jail on the 23rd September 1930, intended to build up a new students' and young men's organization with the double object of maintaining his own power in politics and starting a fresh fight with the Government. In October, another agent reported that Subhas Bose hoped to raise a fund of Rs.3 lakhs, which was required by the revolutionaries of Bengal, for purchasing bombs and revolvers. The agent said that although Subhas Bose had said nothing in public to support the impression that he believed in terrorism, nevertheless his long association with the terrorists who have always turned to him for help and advice, compelled him to support them.

"In December, information was received that Subhas Bose had urged a member of the Jugantar Party to commit some act of terrorism and had told a member of Binayendra Ray Chowdhury's Bhabanipore group that he was trying to amalgamate all parties. In his opinion, sporadic crime was of no use, but if the parties combined and kept on committing terrorist crimes, the result would be good. Continued acts of terrorism even by one party would be effective, he is reported to have said."[60]

Informers were very much active in those days working for the Government as agents within almost all the revolutionary organizations. The Government depended on these spies heavily as they often supplied useful information on the basis of which it became possible for the Government to arrest revolutionary leaders or activists from their secret dens. The revolutionaries were nothing but terrorists to the British as they were posing a serious threat to the Raj. The Raj was justified in considering the revolutionaries as terrorists from their point of view because the latter were trying to wreck the rule of the Raj in India but sadly enough, some of the Indian people including a few national leaders, the Gandhians in particular, also looked upon them, with contemptuous eyes, as terrorists, not freedom fighters.

No one can deny the fact that India was by all means, the jewel on the British Crown, which the Colonists did not want to part with for obvious reasons. On this particular issue, the hardliners in Congress were of the same view that these revolutionaries were not patriots; they were terrorists disturbing the law and order situation of the country. The well-known Bengalee novelist Sarat Chandra Chattopadhyay had sympathy for the militants, as he never believed that freedom would ever come through prayer and petitions and through the spinning wheel. Gandhi once asked him openly: "But why don't you believe that the attainment of Swaraj will be helped by spinning?" To this Sarat Chandra's reply was:

"I think attainment of Swaraj can only be helped by soldiers, not by spiders." Then he asked Gandhi,

"You think non-violence is the only weapon to fight the British?"

"I have no doubt about that. Those who believed in armed resistance, are wrong, and those who are terrorists, are the enemy of the country.", Gandhi retorted. Sarat Chandra replied:

"What does the word 'enemy' imply? If difference of opinion is enmity, then you might also be considered an enemy by many people. I respect these terrorists because they love their motherland as much as you do. That is why they are ready to sacrifice the most prized possession, their own life for the sake of the motherland. This spirit of self-sacrifice, this dedication may appear to be wrong to you, but how come you consider them enemy of the country?"[61]

Inspite of this stigma attached to them, the freedom fighters of Bengal did not give up their revolutionary campaign to please the Gandhians. According to a confidential report from R.E.A.Ray,

"the Jugantar Party has proved itself to be the most dangerous party in Bengal...In most districts during 1931, the Jugantar groups have been speaking of organizing district risings. Such risings, however, require months of quiet preparation and a well-organized body of local terrorists. A period of intense police activity at a time when most of the experienced district leaders and many of the rank and file have already been arrested, is not, therefore conducive to the success of such schemes. The result is that the groups have to be satisfied with stray murders and the commission of dacoity with the object of securing money for the purchase of arms and reorganization, but the idea of an eventual rising is always in the background."[62]

Bose was trying, by all means, to bring together the *Jugantar* Party, the Dacca *Anushilan Samity*, *Mukti Sangha*, Chittagong groups and all the other like- minded revolutionary organizations in 1928 and this attempt led to the emergence of the Bengal Volunteers (B.V.) with whom he maintained contact till the end of the Second World War. It will not be an exaggeration to describe the B.V. as a para-military force, which inspired the militant nationalists also in the other parts of India to come up and organize themselves for a nationwide uprising. According to a confidential police report,

"this amalgamation was short-lived on account of the mutual jealousy of the leaders of the parties but there is no doubt that when the present terrorist campaign is scotched and the leaders are released, there will be a further attempt to bring all terrorist groups in Bengal under central control. The terrorist campaign, which began in 1930, surpasses even the long-drawn out first campaign (1907-1918) in respect of achievement. The leaders of both parties must realize that, had the Dacca Anushilan Samity combined with the Jugantar Party in the initial stages, even more striking results might have been achieved. The realization of this may make the leaders of all parties forget their quarrels and work together for their common object, the expulsion of the British from India by terrorism.

"Whether the rival parties bury the hatchet and work together or keep separate, the next campaign, if allowed to germinate, will be fiercer than the present one. Terrorist organizations, which are on a permanent basis, cannot be dealt with satisfactorily by temporary legislation. Now is the time, therefore, to make a permanent statute of such powers as are deemed necessary at present to deal with these very dangerous organizations."[63]

The Government, accordingly, enacted a series of statutes and ordinances like the Bengal Suppression of Terrorist Outrages Act, 1932 (Bengal Act XII of 1932), Bengal Emergency Powers Ordinance, 1932 and a series of amendments of the existing laws to make them more repressive.

After his release from jail, Bose became the rightful heir to the political heritage of Deshabandhu C.R. Das who was portrayed by the British Intelligence as an ally of the terrorists.[64] He preferred to follow the course that he felt to be beneficial to the country even if it was not acceptable to Gandhi and his followers. During the early 1930's, Bengal Congress was subjected to a prolonged period of severe repression not experienced by any other region during the same period. Because of the extremist outrages, the central leadership of the Congress Party tried to put Bengal at the back seat, as the central leadership consisted of the staunch adherents of the doctrine of non-violence. This gradual marginalization of Bengal Congress was reflected in the ordeal Bose had to go through during this period, as he was the most popular Congress leader of the time, in spite of his young age.[65]

An important incident occurred around this time that revealed the anguish in the minds of the people due to the execution of Bhagat Singh and his comrades on 23rd March 1931. Angry young demonstrators protested at railway stations as Gandhi was going by train to Karachi where the plenary Congress session had been due with Sardar Patel as the President. Gandhi scornfully described these protesters as "Subhas youths".

REFERENCES
1. Samanta, A.K., *Terrorism in Bengal*, A Compilation of Documents, Vol. 1, Government of West Bengal, 1995, pp. 632-633.

2. Ghosh, Kalicharan, *Biplabir Bhumikaye Subhas Chandra*, (article in Bengali), published in Netaji Subhas Chandra Bose Birth Anniversary Number, 1999, Jayasree Patrika Trust, Calcutta, p.118.
3. A.K.Samanta, op.cit. p.633
3A. Ibid. p.633
4. Ibid. p.634
5. Ibid. p. 634
6. Majumdar, Ramesh Chandra, *Bangla Desher Itihaas* (in Bengali), Volume 4, General Printers and Publishers Pvt. Ltd. Calcutta 1982, p.319.
7. Basu, Nimai Sadhan, *Desh Nayak Subhas Chandra*, (in Bengali), Ananda Publishers Pvt. Ltd., Calcutta, 1997, p. 108.
8. Confidential File No. 90/1928, IB, The State Archives of West Bengal
9. Chattopadhyaya, Sabitri Prasanna, *Subhas Chandra O Netaji Subhas Chandra*, (in Bengali), Jayasree Prakashan, Calcutta 1986, pp. 85-87.
10. Interview taken by the author with Amar Chatterjee, a veteran revolutionary, on the 31st of January, 1998 in Calcutta.
11. Bose, Subhas Chandra, *Correspondences 1924-1932*, Netaji Research Bureau Calcutta, Oxford Book and Stationary Company 1967.
12. Das, Sitanshu, *Subhas: A Political Biography*, Rupa and Company, New Delhi, 2001, pp. 157-158.
13. Pundit, Vijaylakshmi, *The Scope of Happiness*, Vikas Publishing House, New Delhi, pp.91-92.
14. *Young India*, dated 10th January, 1929; *Collected Works' of Mahatma Gandhi*, Vol. XXXVIII, pp. 325-328, Publications Division of the Government of India, © Navajivan Trust, Ahmedabad 1970.
14A. Ibid.
15. *Anandabazar Patrika*, 12/12/1928, (Bengali Daily published from Calcutta).
16. Ibid. 13th December 1928
17. Ibid. 22nd Dec. 1928
18. *CWMG* Vol. XXXVIII, op.cit., pp. 91-92
19. Das, Sitanshu, op.cit., p. 259
20. *CWMG*, Vol. XLI, op.cit. p. 319
21. Bose, Subhas Chandra, *Indian Struggle*, 1920-1942, Oxford University Press, pp.174-175, © Netaji Research Bureau, 1997
21B. File No. 26/32, Part 1, Introductory, State Archives, West Bengal.
22. *Anandabazar Patrika*, op.cit. 26th December, 1928

23. Markandeya, Subodh, *Netaji Subhas Chandra Bose,* Arnold Associates, New Delhi, 1990, p.68.
24. Confidential File No. 80V /28, IB, State Archives, Calcutta
25. *Indian Struggle* op.cit. p. 180
26. Ibid. pp. 178-179.
27. Chattopadhyaya, Sabitri Prasanna, op.cit. p.92; Basu, Nimai Sadhan, op.cit. p.127
28. Neruda, Pablo, *Memoirs,* translated from Spanish by Hardie St. Martin, A Condor Book, Souvenir Press Ltd, London, 1977, pp. 81-82.
28A. File No. 233/28, Home Poll, National Archives, ND
28B. Ibid.
28C. Ibid.
29. Singha, Ananta, *Subhas Chandra 0 Banglar Biplabira* (article in Bengali), published by Girish Maity in *Netaji Prashasti Smarak Grantha,* 1967, Calcutta; Singha, Ananta, *Agni Juger Ekti Adhyaya* (article in Bengali), published in *Saptahik Basumati* 14th July 1966.
30. Ghosh, Amalendu, *Biplabider Smarane 0 Sanniddhye* (in Bengali), Purna Prakashan, Calcutta 1999, p. 25.
30A. Ibid. p.21.
31. Ibid. pp. 26-27
31A. File No. 31/53, Home Poll, National Archives
32. Author's Interview with Mrs. Helena Dutta, a veteran revolutionary of Dacca Sri Sangha, on 1st March 2000 in Calcutta
33. Sengupta, Subodh, *India Wrests Freedom,* Shishu Sahitya Samsad Pvt. Ltd. Calcutta, 1982, p. 4
33A. File No. 223/1929, Home Poll, State Archives, West Bengal.
33B. Ibid.
34. Ghosh, Amalendu, op.cit. p. 30.
35. File No. 562/32, Sl.No. 55, West Bengal State Archives, Calcutta
36. Letter of Dinesh Gupta, dated 30/3/1931 from Alipore Central Jail, Calcutta.
37. Markandeya, Subodh, *Netaji Subhas Chandra Bose,* op.cit. p. 83
38. Ibid. p. 84
39. Confidential File No. 90/28, IB, West Bengal State Archives
40. *Indian Struggle,* op.cit. pp.225-227.
41. Singha, Ananta, *Agnijuger Ekti Adhyaya,* (article in Bengali), in *Saptahik Basumati,* 18th April 1968, Calcutta.

42. CWMG op.cit.
43. File No. 90/1928, IB, State Archives, On the political situation in Bengal during the first half of April 1931.
44. Ibid.
45. Ibid. On the political situation in Bengal during the first half of May, 1931.
46. Intelligence Report on the political situation in Bengal during the second half of March 1931.
47. File No. 90/28, IB, West Bengal State Archives.
48. File No. 37/1934, Home Poll. National Archives, New Delhi.
49. 35/8 of 1934, Home Poll, National Archives.
50. File No. 80 C/27, Part I, p. 27, West Bengal state Archives.
51. File No. 80 V -28, IB, State Archives.
52. File No. 90/1928, IB, West Bengal State Archives
53. Ibid.
54. Ibid
55. Ibid.
56. Ibid.
57. *Anandabazar Patrika*, 12/11/1931
58. Ibid. dated 13/11/1931
59. Ibid. dated 16/11/1931
59A.. File No. 850/1930, State Archives, West Bengal.
60. Samanta, Amiya, *Terrorism in Bengal*, op..cit.
61. Ghosh Ray, Dilip, *'Gandhibad Ki Sachal?'* (article in Bengali), in *Saptahik Basumati*, 15/8/1968, Calcutta.
62. Samanta, Amiya, *Terrorism in Bengal*, op.cit.
63. Ibid.
64. File No. 840/32, Home Poll., West Bengal State Archives
65. Das, Sitanshu, op. cit. p.265.

4
THE YEARS OF EXILE (1933-1938)

The Indian revolutionaries had an emotional involvement with the Irish freedom fighters ever since the Easter Rebellion had taken place in 1916 on the Easter Monday (24th April). It was a remarkable event in the history of Irish freedom movement. 1500 rebels took over the Dublin Post Office and other key buildings in the city. They raised the Irish Flag and read a Proclamation of Independence and formation of the Republic of Ireland.

The mode of operation of the Irish revolutionaries, their dedication and patriotic spirit attracted Bose since his student life. That is why in *The Indian Struggle,* he referred to the strategy of the Irish revolutionaries more than once in connection with the Indian freedom struggle. At the same time, in this book he gave an indication of his attempt at the establishment and widening of an Indian-Irish Independence League.

According to Dilip Roy, his close friend, Bose was in favour of forming powerful revolutionary organizations by Indian freedom fighters to combat the Raj. He even claimed that the Bengal revolutionaries in the post-Swadeshi period did not fail at all and he cited an Irish parallel:

"You might just as well say that the Sinn Fein movement is a failure also since it has not delivered the goods yet. When

De Valera was sentenced the other day to death, whoever thought that he would be released and then re-imprisoned again in 1918 only to escape from Lincoln Jail and visit America where he would raise six million dollars for the Irish Republican movement? A revolutionary movement for national liberation is not like a chance detonation, which makes the age-long prison walls topple once and for all. It is a slow laborious work of building up brick by brick, a citadel of strength without which you cannot possibly challenge the power that be. The Bengal revolutionary movement at the dawn of this century was the first real movement, real in the sense that it gave our supine prostrate people the first hint about the reality of their own unaided strength. It was the first movement that created a nucleus of national consciousness."[1]

On the 31st of October 1929, Viceroy Lord Irwin declared that the British cabinet would ultimately grant Dominion Status to India and on this occasion the plan to call a round table conference was also indicated. Welcoming this announcement, in November, the conference of different political parties in Delhi greeted the proposal of the Viceroy. As Bose was against Dominion Status, he issued a separate manifesto along with Dr. S. Kitchlew and Abdul Bari opposing the acceptance of Dominion Status and also the idea of participating in the so-called Round Table Conference.

The manifesto pointed out that in a meaningful Round Table Conference, only the belligerent parties should be represented and the Indian representatives should be selected not by the British Government, but by the Indian people themselves. It also warned the Indian people that the Viceroy's pronouncement was a trap laid by the British Government. It was reminiscent of a similar move made by the British Government some years ago in the case of Ireland when the Prime Minister Lloyd George suggested that an Irish Convention consisting of all parties should be held for framing a Constitution for Ireland, but the Sinn Fein Party were clever enough to see through the game and boycott the convention.²

During the early 1930's, aggressive attacks like the Chittagong Armoury Raid, killing of three District Magistrates in Midnapore, and storming of the Writers' Buildings in Calcutta strengthened the acts of repression to be administered by the British. As Bose observed in Indian Struggle,

"A golden opportunity of putting an end to the regrettable state of affairs arose in March 1931, when the Delhi Pact was concluded. But instead of turning over a new leaf, the authorities decided to copy the Black and Tan methods that had been employed in Ireland."³

Bose criticized vehemently the British policy of 'Divide and Rule' as in case of India, this policy, he believed, would inevitably lead to a partition of the country causing a permanent damage to the political and the territorial integrity of the country.

"If the Indian people cannot be divided, then the country — India — has to be divided geographically and politically. This is the plan, called Pakistan, which emanated from the fertile brain of a Britisher and which has precedents in other parts of the British Empire.. .Immediately after the last war, Ireland which was always a unified state, was divided into Ulster and the Irish Free State."³ᴬ

In his presidential address to the Haripura Congress in 1938, Bose said:

"In accordance with this policy, before power was handed over to the Irish people, Ulster was separated from the rest of Ireland." He could foresee a similar fate for his own country as he observed:

"An internal partition is necessary to neutralize the transfer of power...I have no doubt that British ingenuity will seek some other constitutional device for partitioning India and thereby neutralizing the transference of power to the Indian people." This premonition of his was an outcome of a thorough

The Years of Exile (1933-1938)

study of history of the other countries of the world, particularly the ones under the direct or indirect control of the British. That his forewarning was not baseless had been proved in 1947 when the British left India after partitioning the country creating thereby not two sovereign nations but several dominions like the two pieces of Pakistan, East and West, more than 500 princely states and the rest of British India as India.

Bose was perhaps the only national leader of that time who predicted partition of India by the British resulting from a compromise, the very idea to which he was opposed throughout his public life. The Partition could have been avoided had the power- loving leaders of India paid heed to what Bose told them repeatedly through radio broadcast from abroad. It seems as if the leaders were in a hurry to grab power, come what may and the price paid for this 'transfer of power', not hard-earned Independence so to say, was unprecedented suffering for a large number of people in Punjab and Bengal, the magnitude of which beggars description. In Bengal, these uprooted people, uprooted for no fault of theirs, are still considered to be 'refugees' by many and frequently looked down upon even today.

However, one may consider now the Ireland question over which Bose and Jawaharlal Nehru had difference in their respective outlook. Having been released from prison, Nehru went to Europe in autumn of 1935 to visit his ailing wife Kamala and stayed with her till March 1936. Most of the time he resided in Badenwiler in Germany with his wife, but occasionally he went to London and Paris but never to Ireland probably because of the anti-British atmosphere pervading the country. He himself once said:

"I had imbibed most of the prejudices of Harrow and Cambridge and am perhaps more an Englishman than an Indian. I looked upon the world almost from an Englishman's standpoint."[4] Herein lies the difference between Bose and Nehru, the two important political personalities of India. Both of them came from the upper strata of society, both studied in the Cambridge University but they had different mindsets altogether. The two leaders came from different cultural backgrounds. When Bose went to Cambridge, he was already grown up with the cultural heritage of India ingrained in him. Nehru, while studying abroad, was very much influenced by Western culture. Their family backgrounds were also dissimilar. Bose belonged to an aristocratic family with faith in the Indian value-system. The Nehru family was different in this regard. Bose was well-versed in Indian as well as Western Philosophies, whereas Nehru was trying to trace the discovery of India.[4A] To Bose, India was the divine motherland, the one and only reality in existence, in front of which everything else was superficial.

Bose visited quite a few European countries during the 1933-1936 period, with the purpose of acquiring knowledge regarding the existing state of affairs prevalent in those countries. Towards the end of his sojourn, Bose arrived in Ireland, the country revered by him the most. He paid visits to President de Valera and other members of his ministry. He also met the leaders of the Irish Republican movement.

The freedom struggle of Ireland against British imperialism, which was prolonged and bloody, was undoubtedly the source of inspiration for the Bengal revolutionaries.

Since September 1931, revolutionaries were trying to establish direct contact with Ireland. Mrs. F. M. Woods, the General Secretary of the Indo-Irish League, invited Gandhi to come to Dublin in that year. Madame Maud Gonne McBride was the President of this League and Robert Briscoe, who became the Lord Mayor of Dublin twice, was one of its leading members. Madame Charlotte Despard, a well-known leader of the Irish Republican Party and a sympathizer of Indian national movement, went to Dublin from Belfast in 1936 to interview Bose who was, to the Irish militants, the epitome of Indian freedom movement.

It may be recalled that in June 1932, Madame Charlotte Despard met V. J. Patel, the well-known nationalist leader of India, belonging to the Swarajya Group, in London and was overwhelmed by his determination and uncompromising attitude regarding Indian freedom struggle. Patel expressed his willingness to go to Ireland and set up an association called 'The Friends of India Society' over there. He wanted to win the support of the Irish people in favour of India's right of self-determination. With this aim in view, Patel went to Dublin in July 1932 and organized an association consisting of the like-minded people, leading to the formation of 'Indo-Irish Independence League'. It was V. J. Patel who, later, entrusted Bose with the responsibility of furthering the cause of India's freedom movement with the help of this League. While in Dublin, Patel sent an activist called I.K. Yajnik to Mrs. Woods for the work of the League; he wrote to her in a letter dated 8th September 1932 that for the smooth functioning of the League, he depended heavily on her active cooperation.

It is to be noted that Bose used to speak to the Indian youth while in India about the Irish freedom movement, during 1928-29 and Ireland also was very much sympathetic towards India's struggle for freedom. For almost two decades, Ireland exerted a tremendous impact upon Bengali nationalists such as Subhas Chandra Bose and members of revolutionary groups.

The impact of Irish nationalism in Bengal suggests a model for decolonization in the non-Western world and a source of the tactics needed to achieve it. Irish actions seemed to create a new paradigm for guerilla warfare to which Bengali revolutionaries, already committed to the goal of forcing the British from India by force of arms, enthusiastically responded.[4B]

Bose wrote to Mrs. Woods on the 7th of December 1933:[5]

"It was good of you to send the sympathetic message of Irish friends to the Indian Press. I am sure it will be greatly appreciated. I remember that in September 1929, the family of Terence Macswiney sent a short but magnificent message on the occasion of the death from hunger strike of Jatin Das in Lahore prison. The message was received with grateful appreciation.

"Thank you very much for the invitation to come to Ireland. I have been longing to visit Ireland for years and I hope to do so before I return to India. In my part of the country (Bengal), recent Irish history is studied closely by freedom-loving men and women and several Irish characters are literally worshipped in many a home. At present I am not allowed to visit the United Kingdom—nevertheless I shall be permitted by the Irish Free State Government to visit Ireland (Free State). But I want to keep this fact a strict secret. Some friends of mine in London are trying to secure permission for me to visit England. But if the British Government comes to know that I am planning to visit Ireland, it will put their back up and they will never issue a passport for my visit to England. Until the question of my visiting England is finally decided, one way or the other, I desire to keep quiet regarding my intention to visit Ireland.

"For Madame Gonne McBride I have a message from my brother (Sarat Bose) whom I met in prison just before I sailed for Europe. My brother met Madame in 1914 in Paris and ever since then, has been one of her admirers. I daresay Madame does not remember my brother. He has been in internment since February 1932. My brother went with Mukherji, an Indian friend of his, to visit Madame.

"I duly received a copy of your bulletin and I liked it. Do you get any of the Indian papers (in English) regularly? If you get them, would it be possible for you to pick out the interesting news – or would it be necessary to supply you with the news in a ready form? How often do you publish the bulletin? I am anxious to supply you with information about India.

"Kindly let me know which papers in Ireland are likely to publish interesting news, exposing the true character of British Imperialism. Irish Press of Dublin is Dev's paper – 1 think, which is the organ of the I.R.A.? We shall try to send some news from time to time, if you could supply me with a list of the friendly Irish papers and journals.

"I hope letters are not secretly censored in Ireland now-a-days, as they are in India. It is necessary for me to know that."[5A]

It is worth mentioning here that Terence Macswiney died a martyr's death like Jatin Das by fasting unto death for his countrymen. Through this letter in which Bose mentioned the words of condolence from Macswiney's family as a 'magnificent message', he strengthened the bond of fellow feeling between India and Ireland. Even his elder brother Sarat Bose was impressed by the achievements of the Irish revolutionaries and was very much interested in the activities of the Indo-Irish League in promoting the cause of Indian freedom movement.

V.J.Patel, however, had enormous faith in Bose, hence he assigned on the young leader the responsibility of mobilizing support for India's freedom movement through the Indo-Irish League. Bose himself was nonetheless hopeful about the prospects of the League in furthering the cause of India's independence. The mainstream Congress leaders, with their avowed ideal of non-violence, did not support him at all in this regard but Bose was bent on following the path of the Irish revolutionaries who were a role model, so to say, for him and the other like-minded freedom fighters of Bengal.

The British bureaucracy was also aware of the influence of the Irish freedom fighters on the revolutionaries of Bengal. Wilkinson, the District Magistrate of Chittagong, wrote in 1930, to Tufnell Barret, the Second Additional Deputy Secretary to the Government of Bengal (Pol. Dept.) that he wanted the book called *My Fight for Irish Freedom* by Dan Breen, published by the Talbot Press Ltd., Dublin 1924, to be proscribed by the

Government and its import into India prohibited under the Sea Customs Act. In the letter, Wilkinson said that he had read the book which might aptly be described as 'the revolutionaries manual'. He wrote further that Dan Breen appeared to have been one of the originators of the Irish volunteers and later a leader of the Irish Republican Army.

"He definitely belonged of the Violence Party of Sinn Fein.... The book throughout extols armed rebellion against constituted authority and is written in such a way as to win the sympathies of young emotional minds for the spirit of revolt..... Apart for the injurious influence which such a book must have upon the impressionable minds, it is bad from another point of view also. There can be no doubt that the revolutionaries here obtained several of their ideas from the book and applied them in the outbreak of April 18th as the following quotation will show : 'our new plan for more active operations against the British was in short to attack them in their strongholds – the police barracks throughout the country' (p.162)." The outbreak mentioned in Wilkinson's letter was the Chittagong Armoury Raid of 1930.

V. J. Patel wanted India to revert to the programme of the Swarajya Party and advocated the methods of President De Valera.[6] Patel was for adopting the tactics of De Valera and firmly believed in capturing all offices and key centres of power in the country so long as the members of the Swarajya Party commanded a majority in the Congress. If they had no majority, Patel opined, they should merely remain in the position of the Opposition. He spoke vehemently against the policy of the existing leadership of the Congress.

In an interview, V.J.Patel, when questioned whether it would not be better if the Swarajya Party captured the Congress, he replied that at present the Congress organization was saturated with Gandhism, that it would be very difficult for it to capture the Congress.

Having returned from Dublin in September 1932, Patel's

health started deteriorating. In spite of ill health, he enquired about the activities of the League through letters written to Mrs. Woods from the sanatorium of Germany. But after May 1933, the replies to the letters of Mrs. Woods were found to be written by Bose.

Hence, it may well be presumed that Patel, at that time, was not able to write due to ill health. In a letter dated 12th of October, 1933, from Switzerland, Bose writes to Mrs. Woods:

"Your letter dated the 4th instant, to Mr. V .J .Patel is to hand. He is very glad to receive your kind message and desires me to convey his warmest thanks for the same. I am sorry he is not well enough to write. Doctors are still unable to say if he will survive his present illness."[7]

As has been pointed out, Bose was an ardent admirer of the Irish freedom fighters as their patriotism was in every way more militaristic than India's freedom movement. Relatively few Irish people collaborated with the British against their own people, whereas in India, the situation was different. Here, the number of Indians who actively and wholeheartedly served the British Empire was much greater than that of those who struggled for the country's complete independence. This put the Raj in India in a better position than it had in Ireland.

Sir John Anderson tried with all his might, to execute the ill- famed repressive policy of the British called *'Black and Tans'* (mention has already been made) during the Irish War of Independence. He did not really succeed there because local informers on the Irish Guerillas of Michael Collins, the nationalist leader, were scanty. Collins was the leader of the Irish Republican Army, previously known as the Irish Volunteer Force (IVF). The combination of black police uniforms and tan army outfits gave rise to the term Black and Tans for the ex-First World War soldiers used by the British to crush the revolutionaries.[8] Anderson found himself handicapped in Ireland while implementing his repressive policy to give the insurgents a lesson. The British Intelligence agencies in India, on the other hand, were in a better position, as they never suffered from lack of information on the freedom struggle and its active participants here, particularly Bengal. Unfortunately local informers here, were very much active in supplying information to the Intelligence agencies regarding the revolutionaries. It was mainly due to the lure of pecuniary rewards that the localites in Bengal served the British by supplying information regarding the revolutionaries.

As described by Sir Oswald Mosley, in his autobiography *My Life* :

"The Irish as fighting men had become very good indeed. They were making monkeys not only of the Black and Tans but also of the whole administration. It may not be true that Michael Collins, dressed as a charwoman, was able to read the papers on the desk of Sir John Anderson, then Under-Secretary to the Lord-Lieutenant in Dublin Castle, but he was certainly better informed than his antagonist. This favourite son of the Home Office, later described by his admirers as the Tiger of Bengal, found the Irish air not nearly so congenial as his later experience of the gentle clime of India, where eventually he was able to play the strong man with more success. Baffled and looking foolish...the 'Black and Tans' faced a situation in which firmer characters and stronger discipline have been known to break down. ..Confronted with triumphant guerilla tactics by a weaker force supported by a civilian population, the dominant force is often tempted to employ two instruments: torture and terror...The Black and Tans were the first of many to succumb to that vile temptation, but in the Irish, they met a people of particular fortitude."[9]

Anderson was notorious as the key person responsible for the severe regime of repression against the Irish people. The British Home Office preferred him as the Governor of Bengal in place of Sir Stanley Jackson who ordered Bose's release in 1927. Sir John Anderson came to Bengal in 1931 as the new Governor who, it was expected by the British, would be able to bring the rebellious Bengal under control, as the revolutionaries here, were a perennial source of trouble for the Raj. Against Michael Collins's Irish Guerillas, Sir John Anderson could not achieve success in Dublin in spite of his ill-famed policy of Black and Tans, but here in Bengal, the Government felt that Anderson would surely have success in crushing the Bengali militants with the help of the local informers.

In India, particularly in Bengal, Anderson's Bengal version of the Black and Tans did not have to face any resolute armed resistance because the mainstream of the nationalist movement preferred the path of non-violence and it was this lofty ideal of non-violence that created 'the gentle clime' in India as spoken of by Sir Oswald Mosley. The nationalist leaders virtually brought down their aspirations to a desire for constitutional advancement, not an early grant of Dominion Status. It is an irony of fate that when Anderson commenced his regime of repression in Bengal, in the early 1930's, several nationalist leaders were regularly meeting him to work out a justification on the basis of which the Congress would find it easier to accept the new Constitution to be gifted by the British to the Indians. The Bengal revolutionaries, on the other hand, were suffering due to the repression of Anderson who employed two of his ill-famed instruments, of torture and terror indiscriminately. The mainstream nationalist leaders did not really bother about their sufferings; instead, they wanted to prove to their colonial masters that they had only some modest aspirations, like constitutional reforms or Dominion Status, nothing else.

In 1934, when most of the radical leaders of Bengal were behind the prison bar, Jatish Guha, Sukumar Ghosh and Madhu Banerjee of the Bengal Volunteers were absconding. The Bengal police could not get hold of them in spite of conducting a severe manhunt. Jatish Guha and his compatriots decided to give Anderson a fitting reply as the latter's repression was going beyond the limits of tolerance. Guha was in charge of the BV at that time and under his leadership Burge, the third District Magistrate of Midnapore was assassinated on 2nd September 1933. As per instructions from the leaders of Bengal Volunteers, Ujjala Majumdar, Manoranjan Banerjee, Bhabani Bhattacharya and Rabi Banerjee, all from Dacca, rushed to Darjeeling to kill Anderson on the race course of Lebong on the 8th of May, 1934, where the latter came to give away the prizes personally to the winners. It was a golden opportunity for the revolutionaries to take revenge for all their sufferings. Bhabani and Rabi belonged to a place called Jaidevpore in Dacca where BV had a small unit under the leadership of Sukumar Ghosh. Ghosh planned the whole operation and selected these two young boys for launching an attack on the Governor on the said date.

Unfortunately a tragedy occurred during the preparatory period. In Narayangunge, BV had a small branch inside a village called Deobhog. For the purpose of dacoity, Sukumar Ghosh with Madhu Banerjee and Mati Mallik, two of his trusted lieutenants, assembled in the latter's house. The revolutionaries, in those days, used to collect funds through the method of dacoity which more often than not, involved a great risk, but the fear of risk never deterred them from embarking on actions. On 10th April 1934, as they were moving towards Narayangunge at the dead of night, a few vigilance guards, specially trained under the authority of Anderson, suddenly pounced on them from a hidden place and a scuffle followed. Madhu managed to take out his revolver and fired at them as a result of which one guard died and he could run away with Ghosh. Unarmed Mati got caught as he fell down into a ditch and subsequently served with a death sentence. Inspite of unbearable torture in prison, Mati did not utter the name of Madhu or Sukumar nor did he disclose their whereabouts; had he done so, he would have been spared by Anderson. The revolutionaries in those days, had to take oath at the initiation that come what may, they would never divulge anything before the authorities, even if it was at the cost of their own life. Mati was hanged after a judicial farce, on the 15th of December, 1934 in the Dacca jail. Sadly enough, Mati Mallik's self-sacrifice is still not known to many Indians for whose Independence he, like many others gave away his life at the altar of the nation.

As per Jatish Guha's instructions, Sukumar Ghosh and Madhu Banerjee went ahead with the plot of killing Anderson. Accordingly the team with the assigned duty reached Darjeeling in due time. Rabi and Bhabani put up in Darjeeling's Luis Jubilee Sanatorium, Manoranjan Banerjee, the younger brother of Madhu, from Dacca took shelter in the Snow View Hotel along with Ujjala Majumdar who carried a harmonium with firearms and bullets inside.

On the scheduled date, Manoranjan and Ujjala dropped the two boys, clad in European outfit, at the race course for action and left Darjeeling for Calcutta. The two boys managed to hide themselves carefully amongst the audience and at an opportune moment, shot at Anderson, their target, but as he was surrounded by policemen, IB people and a whole lot of bodyguards, the bullets missed him. Both the boys got seriously injured as the guards fired at them immediately afterwards. Having regained his senses in the hospital, the first thing Bhabani asked was "Is Anderson still alive?" In the court room, in answer to a question put forward by the chairman of the tribunal, J. Yuny, Bhabani said," I came to assassinate the Governor. My object was to finish him. I have nothing more to say. None but myself and Rabi took part in the action connected in this conspiracy." (*Amrita Bazar Patrika.* 26.8.1934.).

Both Bhabani and Rabi were served with a death sentence along with Manoranjan Banerjee. Ujjala Majumdar was served with a deportation order for twenty years, and fourteen years' rigorous imprisonment, Sukumar Ghosh and Madhu Banerjee got fourteen years' deportation. As Rabi was a brilliant student of the Baptist Mission School of Dacca, the missionaries protested against his death sentence. Ultimately the Court changed its verdict and ordered for his exile outside India never to return to his motherland without Government permission.

In a letter written from the condemned cell to his younger brother, Bhabani said that a coward feels scared in the crematorium at the dead of night but in the same place and at the same hour of the night, a saint achieves *nirvana*. Bhabani achieved his *nirvana* on the 3rd of February 1935 in the Rajshahi jail (now in Bangladesh) where he was hanged till death.

In this Governor-shooting case, Sukumar Ghosh was declared by the court to be the ring leader and served with a life sentence with rigorous imprisonment. Except Ujjala Majumdar, all the others were sent to the Andaman cellular jail far away from India. In 1937, Sukumar Ghosh actively participated in the historic movement covering 37 days of fasting for bringing the political prisoners back to mainland India and the very next year participated again in the movement spanning over 35 days of fasting in the Alipore Central Jail for the release of the political prisoners. Bose met them in the jail and worked for their release. Sukumar Ghosh was released ultimately in 1946, joined Bose's Forward Bloc and started organizing party units in different parts of East Bengal as a leading member of the party although Bose was not physically present in the country at that time.

However, the British Government firmly believed, on the basis of information gathered through their Intelligence network that behind all these operations, the mastermind was Bose who, instead of condemning these actions, paid homage to the revolutionaries as martyrs, praised their courage and self-sacrifice and summoned the youth of the country, particularly Bengal, to emulate their uncompromising spirit of patriotism.

G.D.Birla, the well-known industrialist and a close friend

of Gandhi's, told Anderson on 10th April 1932, that Gandhi had been rushed into "things" (that is, continuation of Civil Disobedience Movement after the failure of the Round Table Conference in London) by an unsympathetic Lord Willingdon, the Viceroy. "If Gandhiji was released and satisfactory solution found about the terrorist movement, the situation could be eased and Gandhiji could cooperate."[10]

Obviously the 'cooperation' spoken of by G.D.Birla would have been with the Raj but what he meant by 'satisfactory solution' is still not clear. Anderson, however, did not pay any attention to all this and continued with his policy of repression in an effort to break the backbone of the revolutionaries which ultimately led to the occurrence of the Lebong outrage. On the occasion of Anderson's departure in 1937, Ananda Bazar Patrika wrote that the Bengali people would not soon forget the painful memory of Anderson's regime just as Ireland had not as yet been able to forget the story of the Andersonian era in that country, (Ananda Bazar Patrika, 23rd November, 1937, Kolkata).

The two radical organizations of Bengal, which became a matter of concern for the British, were obviously the Bengal Volunteers and the Jugantar group. As the "Notes on the policy of the Terrorist Parties in Bengal" issued by the then Bengal Government, wrote:

"The Jugantar Party has proved itself to be the most dangerous party in Bengal. Its record of achievement — the Chittagong Raids, almost all the murders and many armed robberies and dacoity —is one which must, in the future, draw to it, adherents, in large numbers from all over Bengal. It also has the advantage over other terrorist parties, of being the fighting force of Subhas Chandra Bose, who is more outspoken than any other Congress leader of Bengal in praise of terrorists and in his demands for Complete Independence, which is the avowed object of the terrorist campaign. This advantage is great, for it opens out avenues of employment for terrorists in all institutions controlled by the Congress Party and vast opportunities of recruitment.

"At the present time, the most dangerous of the Jugantar parties are at Chittagong, where the absconders of the Raid Case are plotting further outrages and at Dacca, Calcutta, Tippera where the groups of the Sri Sangha, the party responsible for so many assassinations and other crimes, are in considerable strength under the guidance of fanatical absconders. The policy of these two groups of the Jugantar Party (the Chittagong group and the Sri Sangha group) is to paralyze the administration by the murder of European officials, selected Indian officials, and selected non-official Europeans. They have given effect to this policy, ever since 1930, when the chances of successful risings on a large scale, in several districts, simultaneously faded into remoteness... They are still dangerous in those districts where they were particularly well-organized.

"In most districts during 1931, the Jugantar groups have been speaking of organizing district risings... The probable failure of the Round Table Conference was often discussed by the terrorists who expected that Gandhi would then declare Civil Disobedience again. In this, they saw increased possibilities of terrorism. In 1930, the Jugantar leaders planned to launch their attack at a time when the country was disturbed by the lawlessness of the non-cooperation movement. The ready response to the recruiting agent and the success of their campaign prove that their selection of the right moment was not at fault. It was suggested that in 1932, if Civil Disobedience were declared, the Jugantar Party should carry on with terrorism at the same time as the Congress waged a 'non-violent' war. Subhas Chandra Bose, however, is said to have stated that the terrorists should give Civil Disobedience a chance and resume terrorism only if Civil Disobedience failed. Subhas Chandra Bose is the last man to object to Europeans being murdered, and his desire to suspend terrorism during the

Civil Disobedience movement was probably merely in order that the Congress, under the garb of non-violence, and the shelter of the Gandhi-Irwin Pact, might stir up the people and thus prepare the ground once more for the terrorists. Subhas Chandra Bose's attitude at the recent Berhampore Congress is instructive. He clearly intended to force Gandhi's hand over the Bengal Ordinances and compel him to start Civil Disobedience. Subhas Chandra Bose got his resolution passed largely through the support of a communist-cum-terrorist group known as the Samyaraj Party. This party, the leaders of which are persons who were at one time, members of some terrorist group, aims at bringing about a mass revolution in which all terrorist groups and the communists will combine. Satindra Nath Sengupta is stated to have said in November, that terrorism should continue in order that the revolutionary spirit might be maintained and that mass action would be possible when Civil Disobedience were declared. Government's attitude towards Civil Disobedience is now clear. Subhas Chandra Bose has not been given the opportunity to work out his schemes..."[11]

However, V.J.Patel, it is to be noted, arrived in Vienna after more than a year of travels in America and the Irish Free State. Arrested in January 1932, after the failure of the Round Table Conference in London, he was released because of serious illness and was allowed to leave the country in March 1932, when he went to Vienna for a complicated surgical operation. Thereafter, in spite of his failing health, he travelled in America to address meetings on India and went to the Irish Free State where he met Eamonn de Valera. As his health deteriorated he returned to Vienna for a medical check up.

This was the first meeting of Bose with a front-ranking nationalist leader of India in sixteen months. Since he left Calcutta at the end of December 1931 for Bombay, where he met Gandhi and attended a meeting of the Congress Working Committee, Bose had not interacted with anyone of V. J. Patel's stature and political experience. To Bose, he represented a phase, now forgotten, of the Swarajya Party initiatives to take the country out of bondage. Most of those hopes disappeared with the death of C.R.Das. Of the great leaders who were on the side of Das at that time, V. J. Patel was among the very few still around. As the aging leader moved towards the end of his life, he turned to young Bose for his leadership qualities about which Patel was more than confident. Swarajya Party never believed in the device of prayer and petitions for the achievement of independence although it was within the Congress Party itself the official creed of which was non-violence. It may be pointed out here that Bose, a born rebel, never criticized the creed of non-violence, rather accepted it as a strategy but in his heart of hearts he knew that the device of non-violence would never be able to fetch independence from the Raj. He also knew that a revolution could not succeed without overwhelming mass support and Gandhi had a tremendous mass appeal as the father figure in the country. Bose had a conviction that some day in future, Gandhi would realize the futility of non-violence and would support the idea of an armed resistance the likes of which people saw a few years later in 1942 all over the country during the Quit India movement. In August 1942, Gandhi's slogan was *'Karenge ya marenge'*, i.e. 'do or die' which turned the freedom-loving agitators all over the country violent leading to the arrest of almost all the top leaders of Congress.

In May 1933, however, Bose got permission to go to Germany. He toured Germany, Czechoslovakia and Poland for about two months. His keen observation on the Czech and Polish legions helped him form Indian Legion in Germany in 1941.

In July 1933, he arrived in Berlin's Friedrichstrasse railway station but declined to accept the hospitality offered to him by the German Foreign Office and preferred to stay in a hotel instead in Charlottenburg on his own expense.

Bose was curious to know about the devices used by the Nazi supremo Hitler and Italy's Mussolini to galvanize their masses into strong units and inspire them with a new vision of 'the nation above everything'. But no less critical of many aspects of this ultra-nationalistic philosophy of Nazism and Fascism, he preferred to be an 'unofficial ambassador' of India in Germany to make an objective assessment of the emergent nation. He wanted to meet Hitler personally to get amended the latter's contemptuous remarks about India and her freedom struggle in his book *Mein Kampf*. But several other urgent commitments barred his meetings with Hitler in Germany during the 1930's. However, the important officials of the German Foreign Office like Pruefer, Diekhoff and Rolke gave him a patient hearing and appreciated his viewpoints.

Bose registered his protests through a letter to the official press organ of the Nazi party, namely, *Volklischer Beobachter* which in its issue of July 1933 wrote that Germany had no interest whatsoever in the internal affairs of India. He observed much to his dismay, how ignorant the German press and the country at large were about India and her freedom struggle. Even Hitler's comments about India were a product of inadequate knowledge gathered from some works of a few English writers translated into German. The attitude of the Germans towards Indians reflected their prejudice towards coloured races even though theoretically Germany accepted its kinship on the foundations of 'a common Aryan stock'. It may be pointed out here that Germany showed sympathy towards Indian freedom movement during the 1st World War when an arms consignment was released from Germany for the Bengal revolutionaries in order to jeopardize the British rule in India. The Treaty of Versailles, following the 1st World War, only sowed the seeds of another war in Europe and Bose hoped that Germany could help the Indian freedom fighters to make the British empire collapse in its largest colony i.e. India.

During his stay in Germany, Bose was assured by a

dissident group within the Nazi party itself that technical help would be provided to the Bengal revolutionaries for the purpose of de-stabilising the British rule in India. But unfortunately the plan did not materialize due to various reasons.

In Berlin, the head-quarters of an organisation called the Indian Students' Association was the meeting point of the like-minded Indians. This organization was set up by Bose as a publicity and propaganda office during his European sojourn of the 1930's; it was supported by the representatives of the German Foreign Office at that time.

Bose observed the situation which the Indians in Germany were found to be in. During the period that followed the 1st World War, the Indians living in Berlin could be placed in three different categories; the first include those political exiles who during the War, worked along with the German Foreign Office to have a successful uprising in India. People like Virendranath Chattopadhyay, a noted Communist and a dedicated worker of the Comintern, whom Jawaharlal Nehru fondly called *Chatto*, belonged to this category.

The second group was linked with the German Socialist Party with a global network.

The third group comprised of the Indian scholars strongly committed to the Communist ideology that included A.C.N.Nambiar who was driven out of Germany when Hitler came to power. The former was related to Chattopadhyay by marriage. Apart from his regular contacts with the Soviet comrades in Leningrad and Moscow, Chattopadhyay had a very cordial relationship with the Soviet representatives of the TASS in Berlin which was one of the main sources supplying information to the USSR about India. It was Chattopadhyay who introduced Nambiar to the then TASS representative Z.H.Menkes in Berlin.

In 1933, when Bose arrived in Berlin, Nambiar helped him to be in regular touch with the TASS representatives there, namely Menkes and V.I.Annankova.

Bose was, during those days, not permitted by the Government to visit England, USA and USSR. Realizing the importance of propaganda for winning sympathy from the other countries of the world, he took initiative to set up friendship societies in various European countries.

The Comintern's India section was observing Bose's endeavour to win international sympathy and to formulate plans with the help of the Indian communists in Germany like Nambiar, Habib-ur Rahman, J.K.Banerjee and Pramode Ranjan Sengupta.

In Berlin, he gave much later, the responsibility of the Azad Hind Radio to Habib-ur Rahman who was in Europe since 1937. J.K.Banerjee was a young journalist in Paris associated with Hindustan Standard, (a well-known news paper in India) who brought the invitation of Bose to Sengupta, (a noted communist in Paris), for coming to Berlin and discuss the possibility of his collaboration with Bose in the freedom movement. It was not easy for Sengupta to accept Bose's invitation as he was an anti-fascist activist and therefore to go to Germany in the midst of the war, would tantamount to a betrayal of his own cause, he thought. But later he realized that the war had created a new situation that generated many opportunities for furthering the cause of Indian independence. Sengupta finally decided to meet Bose in Berlin and subsequently joined his movement.

Bose had to overcome immense difficulties before he could have his way in Germany. Some of the German militarists had plans of conquering India having defeated the British. There was also a powerful section of some racist officials hostile to any colonial struggle for independence who wanted to exploit Bose's passionate nationalism by setting up a special department to deal with the Indian affairs known as *Das Indienreferat*,[11B] under the German Foreign Office. Bose refused to cooperate with the German Government unless India was recognized by Germany as a free nation. He was however, fortunate enough to have support from some of the leading foreign office men like Adam von Trott zu Solz who, a couple of years later, introduced him to Hitler and the Reich foreign minister Ribbentrop.

Sadly enough for Bose, however, V.J. Patel, whom he adored probably the most after the expiry of C.R.Das, died on 22nd October 1933 in a sanatorium in Switzerland at Gland. Gandhi in his tribute of 24th October 1933, acknowledged with warmth the care and attention Bose gave to the dying leader. "I cannot close this tribute without placing on record my deep appreciation of Mr. Subhas Chandra Bose's magnificent and devoted nursing of Vithalbhai at much risk to his own health."[12]

On 27 October 1933, Gandhi wrote to Vallabhbhai, the younger brother of V. J. Patel, who was in the Nasik Jail at that time:

"I was certainly grieved by Vithalbhai's death, though for himself it was a deliverance...He seems to have been looked after very well. Subhas, it seems, was beyond all praise. From all sources 1 hear reports of his wonderful attention to Vithalbhai. 1 have written to him. You also should write."[13]

There is, however, no evidence of any letter Vallabhbhai wrote thanking Bose for what he did for his elder brother especially when Bose himself was recuperating from a serious illness. On 21st November 1933 Vallabhbhai wrote to Mathuradas Trikamdasji expressing his grief over his brother's death when he had no one with him "to whom he could say whatever he wished to say freely and frankly."[14] V .J .Patel' s personal relations with Bose were either not known to Vallabhbhai or he did not like it. The two brothers had differences over political issues, particularly over the younger brother's unflinching loyalty to Gandhi.

Towards the end of his life, Vithalbhai saw in Bose "a

great fighter with an incomparable determination to carry on India's struggle without any kind of compromise... Even at this early age he has all the merits of a great leader, and his statesmanship and diplomacy are something which I have not seen in any other young man in India. ..Where can you find such a man? It is for this reason that all my hopes are centered on him, and I am leaving all my moneys to him to be disposed of for any foreign propaganda that he may decide upon for the uplift of India."[15]

But even before V.J.Patel's dead body could be brought to Bombay, Vallabhbhai wrote to Gandhi complaining of the bequest of money by his elder brother to Bose. His letter to Gandhi is not available but the reply he received from Gandhi mitigated his unhappiness. "...As for the stories we hear regarding Vithalbhai's last wishes, we can say nothing. I, too, have my doubts as you have."[16]

When Gandhi expressed his doubts about reports that V.J.Patel in his will bequeathed a huge amount of money for Bose to carry out work in the interest of Indian independence movement, Vallabhbhai's grievances, naturally, became stronger about the whole episode. As he could not do anything to his brother, Patel played all out to prevent his brother's money from going to Bose who was neither a relative nor a person liked by him politically.

Vallabhbhai was not one who would express his gratitude to Bose for what he had done to nurse V.J.Patel during the terminal stage of his life in Europe. Reports of the bequest infuriated him. According to Govardhanbhai Patel, one of the two people appointed by V.J.Patel, to be the executors of his will, when he went to meet Vallabhbhai with a copy of the will in Nasik Jail, he had to face a searching cross examination, the kind a lawyer would indulge in, to rouse misgivings about the authenticity of Vithalbhai's will.[17]

Vallabhbhai ultimately took the matter to court and

succeeded in getting it nullified in 1939. This was the time when he was also opposing by all means, Bose's re-election as the Congress President. The statements against the will, in this case, were comparable, in their squalor, with any nasty property dispute that some aggrieved relatives might take to court. Here, the disputant was a former Congress President and the pillar of the "Gandhi Wing" of the Congress movement, none other than Sardar Vallabhbhai Patel. It was rather unfortunate that he brought a charge against the incumbent Congress President Subhas Chandra Bose that the latter managed to get, by unfair means, a monetary bequest from a renowned nationalist leader, V.J .Patel, while he was on his deathbed. The British Indian courts readily decided to deprive Bose of the money V.J.Patel had left for the young leader in whom he had enormous faith.

The episode must have brought deep personal humiliation to Bose but as he was an archetypal *bhadralok*, he did not want to get himself involved in this filthy litigation and hence, decided to stay away from it. He really prided himself on his family background which he expressed in a letter to Gandhi on the unresolved Congress crisis precipitated by the resolution passed at the Tripuri plenary session in 1939.[18]

In a letter written to Mrs. Woods, however, on the 21st December, 1935, Bose said:

"You will be surprised to know that owing to the machinations of the official party in the Congress, the executors of the will of Mr. V .J .Patel, are sitting tight over the money. All the other payments provided for in the will have been made with the exception of the money that should come to me for publicity work abroad. The High Court of Bombay granted the probate nearly fourteen months ago but the money is lying idle. The official party seem to be opposed to the idea that I should undertake the work. They were of course opposed to the late Mr. Patel in his life time but I never expected that meanness would go so far."[19]

The mud slinging that took place over the will of V .J

The Years of Exile (1933-1938)

.Patel, in which some Congress stalwarts participated, caused Bose deep hurt. Still, he made no mention of this incident in his subsequent writings, although he left an account of his association with V.J.Patel in Geneva in 1933 in connection with the possibility of help to come from the League of Nations for Indian independence. He mentioned that the League machinery was so completely under the control of Britain and France that "it was impossible to utilize the League for India's liberty, though India was an original member of that body." Bose wholeheartedly wanted to forget about Patel's Will and the bitter experience associated with it.[19A]

In 1933 he went to Rumania where he came into contact with the well-known Maharashtriyan ophthalmologist Dr. Narsingh Mulgand who helped him establish contacts with the highly placed personalities sympathetic to the Indian cause. From Rumania, he went to Poland where the Oriental Society of Warsaw gave him felicitation and there he spoke on the necessity of establishing a Polish-Indian friendship society. In Warsaw he met a few Indologists amongst whom Stainslav F. Mikhailsky was noteworthy.

He attended the convention of the students of Asia that took place in Rome in December 1933. The convention was inaugurated by Mussolini. There is a controversy regarding the first meeting of Bose and Mussolini. According to some, soon after the convention of Asian students, they met each other for the first time in Rome in January 1934. There is yet another belief that when Bose came back to Europe once again as an exile after father's Sradh rituals, he met Mussolini for the first time in January 1935 in Rome. During this period, he also met Maxim Litvinov, the Soviet ambassador in Italy and Prince Amanullah of Afghanistan, then in exile there.

There is yet another account obtained by the author from the Seely G. Mudd Manuscript Library of Princeton University (courtesy : Helen Van Rossum) which states that in 1933, Bose came to Rome and met Mussolini. (See Appendix III) Wherever he went in Europe, he tried to convey the message of India in bondage and win sympathy of the people there in favour of his country's independence.

Bose, as pointed out earlier, had a long-standing interest in and admiration for Ireland, its long and tenacious struggle and the methods its leaders employed not only against savage repression but also to outmaneuver the imperial power of England and, on occasion, at the conference table. Ireland, he felt, had lessons for the Indian revolutionaries as both countries were confronted with the same imperial power and the militants in both, had similar hopes and aspirations. Bose was probably the only national leader who used to study closely the international situation during the inter-war years and ponder over the question how India should conduct her external relations as long as she was a dependency striving, above all else, for national independence.

At that stage, Bose was very much keen on having the Irish revolutionaries and their leaders as sympathizers for India's militant nationalism. He was eager to make the Irish people aware of the situations prevalent back home, as a result of which he, during his European sojourns, maintained regular contacts with the Indo-Irish Independence League. He informed Mrs. Woods about his plan of bringing out, on a monthly basis, a bulletin in three languages— English, French and German. It seems Mrs. Woods was very much sympathetic towards the Indian freedom movement and held Bose in high esteem. In the same letter Bose expressed his willingness to write articles on official repression in India on the points suggested by Mrs. Woods. He requested her to place his articles in the best paper of Ireland, preferably the Irish Press so that the people there could get to know what was going on in India. He wanted to inform as many people abroad as possible about the condition of the colonized Indian nation so that the Indian freedom movement could win sympathizers all over the world.

The Years of Exile (1933-1938)

Bose requested her also to send him a list of the friendly papers in Ireland and said that he would send Indian bulletins to them direct to save time. He was told by Mrs. Woods that they were getting, among the dailies from India, the *Hindusthan Times, Free Press Journal and Amrita Bazar Patrika*.

Bose was very much keen on the continuance of the Indo-Irish Independence League as a collaborator of the Indian freedom fighters. When he received a letter from Madame Maud Gonne McBride, President of the League, stating that owing to want of funds the work of the I. I. League might come to an end, Bose was very much worried and expressed his faith in Mrs. Woods who, he believed, would manage to continue the work of the league, come what may. On his side, he wrote, he was determined to do his best to foster that contact. The Secretary of the India Committee in Geneva at that time was a Danish lady – Madame Horup whom he informed about the Indo-Irish Independence League and about the friends in Ireland. Bose found her genuinely interested in Indian affairs.[20]

That the interest Bose had in the Irish freedom movement was not one sided, but mutual, is amply proved by the various letters and statements of the eminent personalities of Ireland. Ms. Charlotte Despard, the well-known leader of the Irish Republican Army, wrote in a letter sent to an Indian doctor called Dr. Dey that she sent a message of hope and encouragement to the young men and women of India. She mentioned in that letter that ever since she was a young woman she was fascinated by the ancient history of the Indian people, their glorious traditions and through many descriptions which she came across in books, about the beauty and riches of India. Later in her life she became familiar with the history of the East India Company and of the formation of the British Empire in India. She wrote that the educated Indians had more or less forgotten the glorious history of their past, but she noticed that there was an ever-growing recognition amongst the youth of India of both sexes and several different races that the subjugation in which India had been held by the British, checked their development and prevented them from fulfilling their true destiny. She wrote about her two visits to India and her latest findings about the country and her people. She was impressed by the fact that so many women were getting educated, gave up *Purdah*, and were doing splendid work in education, in healing, in science and research. She believed that one could count them by millions, and young men and women all over the country could recognize their present situation and were determined to achieve independence of their country. In her opinion, the subjugation of India was one of the great crimes of history. Much was made by those who desired to throw dust into the people's eyes of the Pax Britannica, which was an illusion following the old imperial policy of "divide and conquer". She was happy to see that the workers of India who were being so disgracefully exploited by their British masters would now follow the examples set to them by the Meerut workers, and create unions for themselves. Finally, she congratulated Dr .Dey on the beginning he and his countrymen made; many people suffered and many would suffer in the future but she firmly believed that if they were true to themselves, this tyranny would come to an end and the people would once more be masters of their own glorious country.[21]

It will not be wrong to say that Bose single-handedly internationalized Indian freedom struggle during the inter-war period and it was not an easy task considering the kind of ordeal he had to undergo for this arduous task both at home and abroad. Foreigners had to be convinced in various ways before their sympathy and patronage could be obtained. It is true that the Indian revolutionaries abroad, tried before him to mobilize support from outside in favour of Indian independence. But there is a basic difference between the efforts made by Bose and those of his predecessors so far as external patronage is concerned. The Indian revolutionaries abroad built up anti-imperialist propaganda-machinery outside India, made arrangements for arms supply secretly to the militant nationalists back home and leaders like Mahendra Pratap even went to the extent of forming a provisional Government in Kabul. In 1915, M.N.Roy left India for Germany for the purpose of procuring arms to fight against the British. In July 1931, as per Bhagat Singh's instructions, Sardar Prithvi Singh went to Moscow with the purpose of obtaining revolutionary training from there. Rash Behari Basu went to Japan to organize an army with Japanese help for India's independence. There he formed the Indian Independence League in 1937. Around the same time Lala Hardayal, who formed the Ghadar Party in California, went to Germany for collecting arms and ammunitions for fighting the Raj. Quite a few revolutionary organizations were formed in different parts of Europe and Asia by the Indians. Different types of periodicals including newspapers with revolutionary messages used to be published in different parts of the world for the purpose of winning popular support for Indian freedom movement all around and amongst these, *Free Hindusthan, Talvar* and *Bande Mataram* were very popular in Europe.

It may be pointed out here that early 20th century saw the noteworthy revolutionary activities of Madame Cama, Shyamaji Krishnavarma, S.R.Rana, Govind Amin, V. Chattopadhyay, Madhav Rao, Lala Hardayal and the revolutionary Guru of Subhas Chandra, Rash Behari Basu abroad. Madame Cama, in spite of being a woman, scared the British by means of her fearless revolutionary activities in Europe. To the Raj, she was "anarchical, revolutionary, anti-British and irreconcilable."(History sheet of Madame Cama, National Archives of India). In August 1907, Cama attended the International Socialist Congress at Stuttgart, Germany in the company of S.R.Rana, a well-known Parsee revolutionary and at the meeting of this body on August 22nd, she said that she was speaking "for the dumb millions of Hindusthan, who are undergoing terrible tyranny under the English capitalists and the British Government. She said that 35 million pounds were taken annually from India to England without return and in consequence people of India died of poverty at the rate of half a million every month. At the close of her speech, she unfolded the Indian National flag designed by her, a tri-colour in green, yellow and red with the words *Bande Mataram* on the middle band with emblems to represent the Hindus, Mohammedans, Buddhists and Parsees. She implored everyone to read Hyndman's paper on the impoverishment of India and waving the flag before them she said she had every hope of seeing the republic of India established in her life time. Cama and Rana attended this Congress as delegates from the Paris- Indian Society.

Cama had contacts with Bipin Chandra Pal, a well-known revolutionary of Bengal who was, initially, opposed to the idea of extremism preached by Aurobindo Ghosh and Tilak. Uptil 1902, he supported the Congress policy of 'prayer and petition' but with the inception of the movement against Partition of Bengal, his political stance underwent a radical change which made him lean towards aggressive nationalism. When the movement started, he appealed to the Congress leaders for adopting the policy of total non-cooperation with the British and preached the utility of the device of passive resistance for achieving independence. During the early 20th century, his writings published mainly in *New India*, an English weekly, roused national sentiment and inspired people all over the country to come forward and fight for independence. His articles were also published regularly in the English daily called *Bande Mataram* of Aurobindo Ghosh. When Pal was arrested and thrown into the prison for his fiery speeches and writings, Madame Cama was terribly upset and felt the necessity of having a central press in Paris 'beyond the reach of the tyrannical English' where the revolutionaries could publish all necessary circulars in different Indian vernaculars. She wrote to the editor of *The Indian Sociologist* in 1907 that if Russian methods were carried on in India rigorously by the oppressors, the so-called British rulers, then people must meet it with "measure for measure." The Russian people were getting everything printed in Switzerland, and thus "they do not risk the freedom of their most valuable hands like Mr. Pal." She further wrote

"I wish I could go to Calcutta and take up the thread where he has left it and keep up giving open-air lectures to the masses while he is absent, but I have already made arrangements for going to America..." To an interviewer in New York, she said

"No one conceives how we are persecuted. I could not return to India, I am sure. Only recently two cultured men were arrested and deported without trial for speaking the truth about our country's condition. Now they are locked up in Burma. Talk about Siberia and its injustices! The most hopeful thing is the enthusiasm that is spreading over our entire people. Starved and uneducated, as many of us are, the past few years have shown an increase of millions of patriots. We shall have liberty, fraternity and equality some day. We hope for freedom within ten years." (History sheet of Madame Cama).

Cama addressed many gatherings and had gone on tour in the USA only for this purpose. In 1908, Lala Lajpatrai, another well-known extremist leader visited Paris and met the militant nationalists there. Cama could not meet him as she was away in the north of France but in the same year, she returned to Paris specially for the purpose of meeting B.C.Pal when the latter was passing through Paris on his way to England. She attended one of a series of lectures on 'Indian Nationalism' by Pal. At a meeting of the London Indian Society held on February 20th, 1909, at Essex Hall, Strand, Cama delivered a speech and before she commenced, took out from her pocket a silk flag on which were inscribed the words

'*Swadeshi*' and '*Bande Mataram*'. She said that she was in the habit of speaking under that flag. In her speech, she mentioned that she liked Muhammadans better than Hindus because they were a stronger and more warlike people, force and violence had become inevitable and without their use liberty would remain a dream and a farce. Cama used to give financial help to the revolutionaries in various ways. In April 1909, she contributed 10 pounds towards the funds of B.C.Pal's *Swaraj* magazine. When a boy named Harnam Singh was expelled for disloyalty to the Crown from Cirencester College, it was given out by the youth himself during the Mutiny celebrations at the India House on the 10th of May that he was not at all worried as Madame Cama promised to adopt him and leave him all her wealth. During this period, Cama was one of the recognized leaders of the revolutionary movement in Paris and was said to be regarded by the Hindus as a reincarnation of some deity, presumably Goddess Kali. (History Sheet of Cama, National Archives). A National Fund was also created in Paris in 1910 of which Cama and Virendranath Chattopadhyay were the treasurers and Cama herself contributed 5000 francs to this fund for the promotion of Indian freedom struggle.

Apart from Europe, freedom movements were going on in North America under the leadership of the Ghadar Party of Lala Hardayal and the United India League established by Taraknath Das in Canada and USA respectively. In Japan, Indo-Japanese Association was formed in 1903 which brought the people of the two countries close to each other and made the Japanese people conscious about the plight of the Indians under the British. The impact of visits in Japan by eminent personalities like Lala Lajpat Rai, Md. Barkatulla, and Bhai Bhagwan Singh was also noteworthy. Mahendra Pratap set up a provisional Government in Kabul with the help of the Indian insurgents abroad which attracted the attention of many leaders all over the world including V.I.Lenin.

When Japanese goods started capturing Indian markets,

The Years of Exile (1933-1938)

the British Government tried its best to keep the Japanese goods away from India. In keeping with her slogan 'Asia for the Asians', Japan helped the Indian revolutionaries in various ways, by giving the absconders asylum, making arrangements for the shipment of arms and ammunitions and so on. Apart from this, some eminent politicians and defence personnel in Japan expressed solidarity openly with India which appeared to be alarming for the British Government in India. (Lecture Series on Japan, Issue No. 4, Japan Foundation, New Delhi, January 1997).

It should be noted, therefore, that the path followed by Bose was the historic path laid down by his predecessors, the militant nationalists of India. He realized that without international sympathy and support, Indian freedom movement could not be strengthened. During his European sojourn, he left no stone unturned to establish contacts with various European nations and personalities and was considered by many of them as the unofficial ambassador of India in Europe.

In November 1934, however, Bose came back to India, as his father was seriously ill back home. The British Government was extremely unwilling to have him again in India, as they feared that had he come back, the revolutionaries, particularly in Bengal, would be recharged and indulge in acts of violence with a renewed vigour. A letter from the Government of Bengal, No. 22773-X, dated 23rd June 1934 stated:

"Mr. Subhas Chandra Bose, formerly a state prisoner under Regulation III of 1818, was released and allowed to go to Europe for reasons of health on the 23rd Feb. 1933. The Government of Bengal, on some information, apprehend that he is coming back to India and consider that if he does return without permission, he should be arrested and detained under Regulation III of 1818. It was our intention to give a warning to Bose vide Secy's note Dt. 29-12-32 that action would be taken against him, should he return to India without permission of the Govt. of India; and the Secy. of State and the Govt. of Bengal were informed accordingly, but the warning was not embodied in the Order issued to him. It is for consideration whether we should ask the Secy. of State to have the warning conveyed to him now. It might have the effect of keeping him from wishing to return. It seems, however, that the warning circular issued by the Secretary of State under which no endorsement on his passport will be given without prior reference to the Secretary Of State or the Govt. of India, will serve the purpose of preventing an endorsement for India from being given, as we shall have to be consulted to this end. Foreign and Political Dept. may perhaps first see as to whether this interpretation of the circular issued by the Passport Office is correct; if so, we could have the warning conveyed to Mr. Bose when he asks for an endorsement to return. In regard to return, the position is that we cannot indefinitely refuse permission to an Indian to return to India, though in special circumstances we can refuse to grant passport facilities owing to existing conditions in India at any particular time." The British Government was unwilling to see Bose again in India as they considered him "the most dangerous enemy of the Empire" and that is why they tried to find some loopholes in his passport so that his re-entry into India might be prevented. They insisted on 'Empire wide Endorsement' to be found stamped on his passport without which they were not to allow him to come back.[22]

Thus it is evident that there was an unprecedented hue and cry at the Government level over the question of Bose's homecoming. Report shows that the Foreign and Political Department, Home Department of both Bengal as well as India, were extremely worried about the possibility of his coming back to India.

Some British officers in the Foreign and Political Department, however, had a different opinion altogether as the following Confidential Report shows:

"The question concerned arose over the possibility of Mr. Subhas Chandra Bose returning to India.

"The literal interpretation of the rules, as insisted on by the Legislative Department, that a man cannot return to his country, in which (and by which) his passport is issued to him, unless that passport is endorsed for return to that country, amounts in practice, to denationalizing him, as pointed out by Mr. Smith. Since D.I.B. however regard the present ruling as advantageous to them, we need not press the point. Mr. Caroe may however be interested to see.

Sd/- D.J.K.Coghill (of the Foreign and Political Department) 23-9-34.

"The working of the passport rules in their bearing on British Indian subjects is, I think, really a matter in which Home Department is most intimately concerned, though I observe that under the Rules of Business 'passports' are dealt with in the F & P Department. The strict legal interpretation of the Passport Act and the Passport Rules as applied to the present question introduces anomalies which I am inclined to think, whatever may be the legal position, would be difficult to defend on wider grounds, if a challenge were made.

Sd/- O.K.Caroe (of the Foreign and Political Dept) 24-9-34.

The Report goes on to say that the Home Dept was worried as to the question of granting Bose permission to re-enter India with the help of a passport with endorsements on it only for certain European countries. Home Dept quoted the note given by G.H.Spencer of the Legislative Dept which said that Bose could not re-enter British India without being in possession of an endorsement for India. It seems the Home Dept was quite happy with the note given by Spencer regarding this matter as it says that it was indeed as it should have been and it was an important result of the existing passport system.

Fortunately enough, there was N. P. A. Smith in the

Home Dept who felt that to exclude a British Indian subject from India came very near to denationalizing him and he found it difficult to resist the feeling that the Passport Act could not have been intended to be an instrument for such an extreme measure. Smith wrote in his note that he wanted his point of utmost difference with the Legislative Dept to be recorded. He said that administratively the Legislative Department's decision was of definite advantage to the Government and it might therefore be unprofitable to pursue the matter further. D.J.K. Coghill also agreed with Smith on the issue of refusal that would amount to nothing but denationalization. Hence it would certainly be impossible to prevent the return of many undesirable Indian agitators and revolutionaries who were, at that time, kept out of India by the refusal of permission to return.

It is true that there was the well recognized principle that each country was responsible for consuming its own smoke, but while recognizing this, the Government of India had obtained the concurrence of the Secretary of State to the policy that permission to particular Indian British subjects to return to India might be refused on the ground that the conditions in India might be such as to make it undesirable to permit return of certain individuals at a particular time. Indefinite exclusion was not contemplated, they argued, but the policy of excluding for special reasons was a well-understood one. A copy of the notes they kept for record with their file about Bose.[23]

Janakinath Bose, Subhas Bose's father, was on his deathbed when his wife, Prabhabati Devi requested the British Government to allow her son Subhas to come back to India to see his father probably for the last time. A telegram from the Government of Bengal dated 27-11-34, stated that the Government of Bengal had received a communication from the mother of Subhas Bose stating that she cabled to him to come to India immediately by air in view of his father's critical condition. She requested that facilities might be given to him to return for a few weeks. His warrant under Regulation III of 1818 was cancelled and he was allowed to go to Europe for reasons of health on the 23rd February 1933. It was intended to warn Mr. Bose that should he return to India without the permission of the Government of India then action would be taken against him. This warning was not, however, embodied in the order issued to him although the Secretary of State issued a warning circular to the effect that no endorsement on his passport should be given without prior reference to the Secretary of State or the Government of India. It is evident that the local Government was strongly opposed to Subhas Bose's return to India at that time and they also felt that his father's illness should not be taken into account as he was unlikely to survive till Subhas could return. The telegram conveyed the opinion of the Bengal Government that permission should be refused and the local Government might be instructed to inform Mrs. Bose accordingly. The Bengal Government's telegram was to be repeated to the Secretary of State to enable him to take the necessary action in regard to the refusal of an endorsement for India.

The Home Department's telegram dated 13th December, 1932, to the Secretary of State stated that it would seem sufficient to inform Mr.Subhas Bose that if he returned without permission he would again render himself liable to detention under Regulation III of 1818. As stated in the office note, this warning was not embodied in the order issued to Bose.

The Government decided to consider later the question of the action to be taken against Bose in the event of his return to India in the absence of passport facilities. In this connection sections 4 and 5 of the Indian Passport Act were cited. Section 4 authorized the arrest without warrant of any person who attempted to enter in British India without a passport and Section 5 authorized the removal of any such person from British India. It was decided that if he returned to India without permission, action against him would be taken under

Regulation III of 1818.[24]

The kind of resistance Bose had to face for coming back to his own country was perhaps unprecedented in the history of India. The then Government left no stone unturned to prevent him from home coming but when, on receiving a telegram from his mother, he rushed to India to pay the last visit to his father, the Government became panicky and arrested him at the airport. Unfortunately, Bose could not see his father as the latter expired one day earlier and he was kept interned at his father's Elgin Road residence for six weeks.

It is evident from various records that the Government of India, Government of Bengal, the highest echelon of the British Government in London and the various Consulates of Britain all over Europe were very much perturbed by the activities of Bose, as he was performing the role of the unofficial ambassador of India in the various countries of Europe spreading messages everywhere about India's plight under British imperialism, and about the false propaganda against Indian people and Indian culture. The Government was in a dilemma, whether to keep Bose in Europe or permit him to come back to India as both the options appeared to be equally dangerous for the Raj.

On the other hand, it was not easy for the Government to keep him in custody, without trial, for an indefinite period of time. Apart from the fear of a nationwide storm of protests, quite a few members of the British Parliament used to embarrass the Government with questions regarding Bose. The members of the Central Legislative Council too showed concern about his health.

The Government, as has been pointed out, considered his presence within the country as dangerous because of his connections with the revolutionaries. It did not even have the guts to allow him to enter into England in case the anti-imperialist feelings already prevalent there, got further

The Years of Exile (1933-1938)

intensified amongst the Indian students due to his presence. Some of the members of the House of Commons wanted to know on what grounds he was not permitted to enter into England. According to an India Office records File of 1935, Ernest Thurtle, a Labour member, wanted to know why Mr. Subhas Chandra Bose was not permitted to pay a visit to England.[25]

In an answer to Mr. Thurtle's question dated 9.12.1935, the Government replied that the honourable member was presumably aware of Mr. Subhas Bose's connection with the Bengal revolutionary movement, which made it necessary to order his detention in India under the Bengal State Prisoners Regulation. The sole reason for his release from this detention in February 1933, was to enable him to visit particular countries on the Continent where specialist medical treatment could be obtained. The answer from the Government side further stated that his presence in the said country would be undesirable, and in view of the circumstances of his release, Govt. was not prepared to authorize passport facilities for a visit to England unless it could be shown that it was essential for medical reasons for which the passport had been originally granted.

Departmental notes on this subject offer an interesting reading. It stated that in October 1935, Bose applied to the Consul in Vienna for a new passport. The Consul was authorized to give him one bearing the same endorsements as that in his passport but did not follow the instruction and gave one valid for all countries in Europe. When it came to notice, the Consul was instructed to take any opportunity that offered to rectify his mistake but at the same time to be careful not to reveal to Bose that the passport in his possession was perfectly good for England. Conscience did not prick the minds of those in power belonging to a country that preached the glorious principles of Rule of Law.

The Foreign Office, however, was unable to obtain from the Consul information as to the exact terms of the correspondence that took place between him and Bose or as to how he might hope to correct his error. In the circumstances it appeared desirable to be careful in replying to this question not to imply that Bose needed permission or an additional endorsement on his passport to enable him to come to England.[26]

Another departmental note stated that it was considered undesirable that Bose should be given facilities for coming to England.

"Our position as we know is weak. Bose himself has not realized this so far; but we cannot and should not try to make the issue if, as is likely, it is raised in Parliament on Monday. We are in fact, coming to the point at which we may have to admit to the public – including Bose – that we cannot stop him from coming here. I think it would be dangerous to gamble, even in a small degree, on the chance that we may not be asked what steps we have taken or can take to prevent his coming to England; and I would therefore make the draft reply scrupulously accurate so that there should be no hedging if we should afterwards have to say that we cannot stop Bose from coming here." The note further said that there were a number of Indian students in England upon whom Bose might exercise an undesirable influence and also his presence there would make it easier for him to improve contacts with the Communist Party of Great Britain. This departmental note to Mr. Morley was signed by R.T. Peel, Secretary, P& J Department, India Office, London on 7.12.1935.[27]

In England some members of the House of Commons were eager to know how Bose was allowed to visit Ireland, the land of militant nationalism. Sir Reginald Henry Craddock, a Conservative M.P .and a member of the Joint Select Committee on Indian Reforms, wanted to know, from the Under Secretary of State for India, under what conditions was Bose, a detenue in Bengal, permitted to leave India and how had he been permitted to visit Ireland. To this the answer from

Mr. Butler the Under Secretary of State for India, was that Bose was permitted to leave India in order to receive particular medical treatment. The territorial validity of his passport was framed accordingly. The question of his admission to the Irish Free State was one for the Free State authorities, not for the British Government.

The colonial government, however, was apprehensive of the fact that Bose might not go back to Europe after the performance of the last rites of his father in December 1934. As a result, they decided to serve him with a warrant under Regulation III of 1818 in case he declined to return to Europe. They even went to the extent of keeping him interned in his own house for six weeks, as has already been pointed out, as a prisoner in anticipation of what he might do if given freedom. It seems as if the values of liberal democracy, like liberty, equality, justice and all those lofty ideals held in high esteem by the British political philosophers were meant for only their own people, not for the others.

A telegram from the Government of Bengal, No.163, dated 4-12-34, stated:

"The local Government suggest that they should take action against Subhas Bose under Section 2 of the Bengal Criminal Law Amendment Act, 1930, in the first instance. After the order has been in force for a week and if Mr. Bose declines to return to Europe after performing the Sradh ceremonies he will be served with a warrant under Regulation III of 1818. The local Government prefers this course as they feel it would make criticism and consequent embarrassment less likely than immediate arrest and confinement as previously contemplated. The local Govt. are in the best position to judge which course would be preferable and the case is submitted for orders. But it would appear prima facie desirable that he should not be given an opportunity to contest his association with terrorists. The use of Regulation III, under which he was detained up to the time he left India, and which has been approved by the

Secretary of State, would appear more appropriate and less open to objection."[28]

The Government was perplexed with the thought of how to handle the Bose affair, particularly regarding the place of his detainment. As the telegram No.2483, dated 12th December 1934, from Home Department, New Delhi, states:

"Please obtain a copy of Bengal's telegram of 11th December 1934 regarding Subhas Bose. Home Department suggests the following reply to Bengal, which, if approved by His Excellency may be issued by you as from Home Department. Please inform me if reply is approved and has issued so that I may repeat telegram to Secretary of State.

"2. Your telegram of 11th December 1934. Subhas. We approve action proposed by you as detailed. ..We are enquiring from Bihar about Hazaribagh, but anticipate no difficulty. You will no doubt consider possible alternative of prosecuting Bose under Bengal Criminal Law Amendment Act if he infringes the conditions of the order in force against him.

"Telegram from the Government of B & O (Bihar and Orissa) No 34 R.C. dated the 14th December, 1934. Submitted. In the circumstances it is for consideration whether B & O should now be asked if they can arrange for Subhas Bose's detention in a private house in Hazaribagh."

The Government was extremely cautious about Bose's contacts with the outside world. They did not want the press to have any sort of communications with him as they were very much apprehensive of the fact that through the media, Bose's sufferings would be known to all which might give rise to problems for the authorities. A letter from the Bengal Secretariat, dated 13th December, 1934, to M.G.Hallet, the Secretary to the Government of India, states:

"In continuation of our Cypher telegram of the 11th instant, I am desired to forward herewith a copy of the representation dated the 7th instant addressed by Subhas

Chandra Bose to the Hon'ble Mr. Reid, referred to therein and to say that, as far as is known, Subhas will not raise any objection to the medical examination proposed by Government. The Board has been asked to submit its report by the 14th instant i.e. tomorrow, but it is understood that there is a possibility that it may ask for further time to enable clinical and X-ray examinations to be made. In that case it will probably be necessary to remove Subhas to the Medical College and there will be a further delay of 4 or 5 days before the final report of the Medical Board is received.

"2. It is impossible under conditions of home detention in Calcutta to prevent communications to the press and actually communications are being issued to the press from Subhas' s house with a view to keep alive public interest in his case.

"3. It is presumed that Behar and Orissa Government are aware that Subhas Bose may have to be sent to the Hazaribagh Jail and that the warrant forwarded with your Express letter No. D. 7765/34/Poll. of the 2nd December, in which the place of detention and the name of the Jail Superintendent have been left blank, could be utilized if and when the occasion for sending him there arises."

It seems as if Bose was the main focus of attention of the British Government, which was frightened by the presence of the former in India and bewildered as to the modus operandi to be used to keep him away and well under control. The same letter goes on to say:

"As regards the point raised....if it is ultimately decided to intern Bose in B & O (Bihar & Orissa), the procedure will be to arrest him in Calcutta under Regn. III and use the blank warrant in question for this purpose. He will then have to be transferred to B & O and detained there on a fresh warrant, which we will issue when the place of detention is known. If necessary, this may be explained to the Bengal Government when we know the result of the discussion between them and the Hon'ble Member. No action would appear to be required at this stage and we may await further developments."

From the Bengal Secretariat, a secret message was sent to M.G.Hallett, the Secretary to the Govt. of India that runs thus:

" ... I am desired to forward a copy of the report of the Medical Board received yesterday. It will be observed that the majority of the Board have recommended an X-ray examination to confirm their opinion. The Governor in Council has, therefore, decided to have Subhas Bose X-rayed at once at the Medical College hospitals and arrangements are accordingly being made to have him taken there on Monday the 17th instant. It is understood that the examination and preparation of plates will take about a week and that the final opinion of the Board as to diagnosis and treatment is not likely to be received till X'mas day. It seems likely, therefore, that the idea of sending Subhas Bose to Hazaribagh before the Sradh will have to be abandoned. A further report will be sent on receipt of the Medical Board's final opinion. ..."[29] This document bears ample evidence to show that the Government was initially planning to send Bose to Hazaribagh jail before the *Sradh* ceremony of his deceased father whom he wanted to see for the last time but could not, due to his late arrival. Because of the paraphernalia and the dilly dally on the part of the Government regarding his home coming, he arrived in Calcutta after his father's demise and the Government was planning to send him to Hazaribagh before the *Sradh* without any concern for his mental state.

The Medical Board recommended a change of climate for Bose preferably in Europe for his quick recovery. Surprisingly, the Board that consisted of two Indian doctors did not recommend any Indian hill station with similar climatic conditions for Bose's recovery. He was seriously ill at that time with fibrosis of the lungs. The abdominal pain he was suffering from, was, in the opinion of the majority of the members of the Board, in all probability, due to Cholecystitis (one member, the dissenting member of the Board considered that there was no room for doubt in this matter). The other members considered that an X-ray examination was desirable to confirm their opinion. The Board considered that, in the first place, medicinal treatment should be fully conducted.

The Board suggested that in view of the past medical history of the patient, treatment of the nature recommended was more likely to be effective when supported by the climatic advantages of Europe. This report was signed by Lt. Col. Anderson, Sir Nilratan Sircar, L.M.Banerjee and Lt. Col. V.Hodge on the 13th of Dec. 1934.

It is an amazing story how Bose horrified the Government of India as well as Britain by his physical presence in his own country even if for a short while. In spite of a close-knit intelligence network exercising constant vigilance on Bose, the bureaucracy used to have sleepless nights during his stay in India.

While in Europe, Bose had his watchful eyes set on the happenings in India . His attitude and reactions used to draw people's attention in and out of India and his presence was always strongly felt by the others even when he was physically not around. Although he possessed a British passport, he was not allowed to enter into England by the Government. Earlier in 1933(11-12th June), he was invited to preside over the Indian Political Conference in London, but he could not attend the Conference, as he was not permitted to enter into the country. He sent his written message to be read by somebody else on his behalf. The theme of his speech was 'Technique of Revolution' which happens to be one of his memorable writings. In it he said that on the road to freedom, there was no question of compromise and the political decisions and attitude of Gandhi was nothing but unconditional surrender to the enemy. He analyzed the causes of the sad demise of the Non-Cooperation and Civil Disobedience movements and did not hesitate to describe the Gandhi-Irwin pact as a disaster for the nation and a boon for the British Government. He compared the British imperialism in India with a well-decorated and well-protected fortress, which could be vanquished by two methods, cut off all supply lines to it forcing the soldiers to surrender or capture it by applying armed force. But unfortunately no attempt had as yet been made to apply armed force to achieve independence, because Congress was tied to the doctrine of non-violence. He further observed that economic embargo had also not been possible due to organizational weaknesses and various other reasons. He suggested that the government should be prevented by all means, from collecting taxes, and during periods of crisis, no cooperation, military or economic, would be assured to them. The Indian soldiers, police and the Indian members of the bureaucracy should be motivated to defy the orders of the foreign masters. The idea of non-payment of taxes to the colonial masters was not new as before the War of Independence, the Americans stopped paying taxes to the British Crown as a pressure tactic which ultimately led to an armed resistance bringing thereby the much coveted Independence.

Bose, however, stated deliberately that an armed resistance was not on his cards, as Congress did not believe in violence. As a matter of fact he could not afford to preach armed resistance openly as he knew that had he done so, it would not have been possible for him to stay outside jail even for a day, the British authorities would have left no stone unturned to finish him off. In his heart of hearts he knew that without a revolution, termination of British imperialism in India would never be possible. For this, all kinds of preparation, mental as well as physical, widespread publicity abroad, and determination to secure help and assistance from the enemies of the British imperialists were necessary. He was pretty sure that a great war was in the offing and India had to utilize the opportunity presented by the situation, and that there was not

The Years of Exile (1933-1938)

a single moment to waste. He had a sense of urgency, which incidentally, became very strong at that stage. He had to use the Congress as the forum for his struggle for independence because the Congress was at that time, not just a political party but a common platform from which it was possible for the nationalist leaders to convey their messages to the people of the nation.

During his five years of exile in Europe, he returned to India twice, and on both occasions, he was immediately arrested, detained in police custody and meticulous arrangements were made to send him back to Europe once again. But he was never perturbed and never accepted any humiliating conditions for his own release. From Home Department at New Delhi, a telegram dated 29th November 1934 was sent to the Govt. of Bengal, which stated:

"There is possibility that Subhas Bose may attempt to return to India either with a valid passport or with no passport or with an invalid one. Newspaper report states that he intended traveling by Dutch Air Mail leaving Rome on November 30th and arriving in Calcutta on December 4th. We are endeavouring to ascertain whether he has actually sailed by this Air Mail.

2. If he had no valid passport, it would be possible for him to be arrested without warrant under Section 4 of Indian Passport Act, but it is doubtful whether a British Indian subject could be removed from British India under the provisions of section 5. It appears necessary, therefore, to deal with Subhas Bose under Regulation III again. A warrant under this section will therefore be sent to you for use against him."[30]

It is evident from above that Regulation III of 1818 was a tyrannical law possessed by the British Government by means of which they could arrest their political opponents any time without giving any justification in the form of a warrant.

Evidence suggests that Sarat Chandra Bose, the elder

brother of Subhas Chandra, was, in more ways than one, the source of inspiration for the latter. In the report of the Political Department of the Government of Bengal sent to the Home Department of the Government of India in August 1932, Sarat Bose was mentioned as a prominent Congress leader, the power behind his brother Subhas Chandra Bose and financier of the Civil Disobedience Movement of 1930 in Calcutta. It is true that even after the advent of Gandhi on the Indian political scene and the acceptance by the Congress of his doctrine of non-violence, there were many in the Indian National Congress like Bose who believed in the method of armed resistance against foreign rule and remarkably enough, the political ethos of the nation as a whole was in keeping with their ideas. Although the official ideology of the Indian National Congress was non-violence and Bose never proclaimed that the principle of non-violence had no value at all, he knew that it had a highly moral value but as has been pointed out, he had a strong feeling that the mighty British imperialists would never leave India unless they were forced to do so. He was pragmatic enough to gauge the futility of the principle of non-violence to be used as a weapon against the usurpers who were themselves a worshipper of force.

Sarat Bose, who was a barrister by profession, financed the defence expenses of the Bengal revolutionaries when they were prosecuted on charges of militant activities. John Anderson decided to punish him because he had, apart from helping Bose, tried to organize the legal defence of those who were arrested for the Chittagong Armoury Raid. So great was the fear of police harassment that at the outset, no legal practitioner would agree to accept the Chittagong prisoners' brief. As a result, on the 5th of February 1932, Sarat Bose was arrested under Regulation III of 1818, which was his first imprisonment. At that time, Subhas was already arrested and detained in the Seoni Jail of the Central Provinces again under Regulation III of 1818.

While in Vienna, Bose wrote the 1st part of his well-known book *The Indian Struggle 1920-1934*, the publishers of which were Wishart and Company, 9 John Street, Adelphi, London W.C. 2. Having received his mother's telegram, when he rushed to India by flight to see his ailing father, the typed copy of the book was with him. On the 3rd of December 1934, as soon as he landed on the Karachi airport in the evening, he received the news of his father's demise. The British police, in spite of his personal bereavement, did not hesitate to ransack his luggage and forfeited the typed copy of his *Indian Struggle*.

Next day, the moment he arrived at Dumdum (Kolkata) airport, now named Netaji Subhas Chandra Bose International Airport, he was confronted with a host of restrictions including an order for house arrest and for leaving India immediately after performing the *Sradh*, the ritual for the departed soul according to Hindu customs. Eminent personalities all over the world including George Bernard Shaw, H.G. Wells and Rabindra Nath Tagore protested against this inhuman act on the part of the British Government.[31]

The famous Bengali periodical *Prabasee* of the Bengali month *Magh* 1341 B.S. wrote:

"When Subhas Chandra landed on Karachi, the typed copy of a political treatise about Indian freedom struggle which is going to be published soon has been seized by the Government. It has come out in newspapers that litterateurs of Britain like H.G. Wells, Aldus Huxley and Earl Russell as well as Rabindra Nath Tagore of India protested vehemently against the seizure of the typed copy of Subhas Babu's book..."[32]

However the book was published on the 17th of January 1935 as the original manuscript was with the publishers. Not surprisingly though, the British Government proscribed the book in India on the 23rd of January (which happened to be his birthday) while the author was in Europe. After his father's last rites, he had to leave India on the 10th of January 1935.

However, a telegram dated 14. I. 1935, signed by M.G.Hallett, the Secretary to the Government of India, Home Department, stated that Bose's return to Europe had not yet been reported to the Secretary of State and this should be done. It was clearly desirable that they should be consulted before any facilities were granted to Bose to return to India. It also seemed advisable to warn him that he would be liable to arrest under Regulation III if he should return without previous permission. They might accordingly forward a copy of the Bengal Government's letter to the India Office and ask them to take steps to give effect to the local Govt.'s requests. So far they were under the impression that Bose's recent visit to India was made on an invalid passport as the U.P .Govt. definitely informed them in their telegram, dated the 17th July, 1934, that his passport did not bear an endorsement for British India which even a British Indian subject was expected to possess before he could return to India. The Bengal Govt.'s letter however, confirmed the statement in the Secretary of State's telegram of the 29th November last and showed that the U.P .Govt. misinformed them.

The telegram further stated that "it also indicated that there was no ground for a complaint to the Secretary of State in regard to the non-observance of the instructions regarding Bose contained in the foreign Office Circular No.2 dated the 21st July 1933. It was no doubt the case that those orders definitely specified that Bose should not be granted any further endorsement without prior reference to them or the Foreign Office, but since his passport was already valid for return to India, it could not legitimately be held that the action of the British Consulate in Vienna in granting him a transit visa merely to enable him to travel by air was ultra vires of those orders."[33]

It is evident from above that the British Government was extremely cautious about Bose's whereabouts and always on an alert regarding his activities as he was "the enemy number one" to the British imperialists. The IB people could not sit at

The Years of Exile (1933-1938)

rest because of his activities in and out of India. Even when out of India, Bose was probably an unbearable pain in the neck for the British. As he was spreading the message of India all around trying to counteract all the anti-Indian propagation outside India, the foreign rulers made it a point to do anything and everything within their might, to prevent him from entering into different countries. As a confidential record shows that since Palestine and Iraq were, in those days, British-mandated States and did not possess Consular representatives in all countries, British Consular and Passport Control officers in such countries were empowered to issue passports, etc. on behalf of those States. That is why the British Consulate at Vienna granted a transit visa for Palestine and Iraq to Bose who, being a foreigner from the Iraqian and Palestinian point of view, was required to possess such a visa to enable him to land when the Air Mail plane by which he travelled broke journey at airports in Iraq and Palestine.

The report also mentioned that the period of validity of British and British Indian visas of the type mentioned was restricted to one year from the date of issue, but the life of the transit visa that was granted to Bose on behalf of the Iraq and Palestine Governments was not known, nor could it be ascertained whether this visa entitled Bose to make any more journeys on it as was the case with a British Indian transit visa. To be on the safe side therefore they decided to ask the India Office to take steps to cancel any endorsement for India on Bose's passport as well as his transit visa for Iraq and Palestine if the latter could be used again. He would then be unable to return to India until he got specific permission to do so. The report made a reference to the telegram sent by the Bengal Government to the Secretary of State No. 1612-S, dated the 2nd August 1927 and the India Office letter No. 1306-27, dated 7th September 1927 regarding the return to India of British Indian subjects. Such persons, the report stated, could be refused entry into India only in very exceptional circumstances.

The Secretary of State agreed that the grant of facilities to the British Indian subjects to return to India could be delayed for special reasons arising out of special conditions in India and the transit visa should not have been granted by the British Consulate in Vienna without prior reference to the Foreign Office or to the Government of India.[34]

The Secretary, however, was very much perturbed with the way things were moving, so he wanted to know whether the action of the British Consulate at Vienna in giving a transit visa across Palestine and Iraq to Subhas Bose was correct and whether this transit visa would enable Bose to return to India by air, and if so, within what period. It appears that the Government was apprehensive of the fact that with foreign help Bose, along with the Bengal revolutionaries might launch a massive attack on the Raj in near future and that is why they did not want him to come back to India.

Earlier the Foreign Office circular of the 21st July 1933 stated that no further endorsements should be granted to Subhas Bose without prior reference to the Foreign Office or to the Government of India. It was said that a visa was an endorsement on a passport and in view of the circular referred to above, the transit visa should not have been granted by the British Consulate without prior reference to the Foreign Office or to the Government of India. On the other hand, as Subhas Bose's passport was valid for return to India, the Consulate probably thought that the grant of a transit visa was a mere formality, the office note said.[35]

Not surprisingly, the British bureaucracy kept on exchanging notes amongst themselves over the issue of Bose's probable return to India. A letter signed by C.M.Trivedi on 19.1.1935 stated that if the transit visa given by the British Consulate at Vienna was of the same kind as a British Indian transit visa, Bose would be able to return to India by air across Iraq and Palestine during the period of the validity of the visa i.e. a period of one year. He further stated that they had no

The Years of Exile (1933-1938)

information either as to the period of the validity of the transit visa or as to whether Bose could on that visa return to India by air within the period of the validity of the visa. If the enquiries by the India Office showed that the transit visa was good for a future journey to India by air within the period of its validity, and if intimation was received of Bose's intention to return to India by air during the period of the validity of the visa, a warning similar to that in the case of receipt of intimation of his intention to return to India by sea should be conveyed to him. In the meanwhile, the telegram to the India Office intimating Bose's sailing for Europe might be issued.[36]

Another record shows how ruthless the British authorities were in handling Bose in exile, how innovative they had been to prevent him from coming back to his own motherland. M.G.Hallett writes to India Office on the 23.1.1935:

"When in Calcutta I discussed with Mr. Reid whether Subhas Bose should be given a warning that he would be dealt with under Regulation III if he attempted to return. I explained the position to H.M. and we thought that on the whole this was not desirable, as it might have the effect of making him refuse to go, and this would have been rather embarrassing. As he has been given a return ticket, which was purchased through the police, it makes the position a little more difficult, but this cannot be helped. All we can do is to ask the India Office to let us know promptly if he shows any signs of returning, in which case we shall have to warn him of the action that would be taken against him on arrival. I therefore put up a letter below to the India Office for approval. It is not in my opinion possible to ask the Secretary of State with any chance of success to have the passport or the visa cancelled."[37]

The said letter addressed to R. T .Peel of India Office stated that Bose, according to Press reports, intended to return to India as soon as possible after his operation and that the local Govt. desired that steps might be taken to prevent the grant of facilities to him to return to India by Air without prior sanction and that if any intimation was received of his intention to return by sea, he would be liable to arrest under Regulation III in the event of his returning to India without previous permission to do so.

Hallett went on to write,

"Bose's passport which I saw myself when in Calcutta, is available for five years from the date of issue and as the Govt. of Bengal observe, is valid for return journey to India. They also draw attention to the fact that he was given a transit visa by the British Consulate at Vienna on November 27th, though this appears contrary to the instructions given in the Foreign Office order of July 21st, 1933. It was as a result of this that he was able to return to India by Air, which was somewhat embarrassing to the Govt. of India and the Govt. of Bengal. It further appears that this visa for transit by Palestine, Iraq etc., is still valid for at least a year and there is thus nothing to prevent his returning to India by either air or sea.

"If Bose shows any signs of attempting to return to India, immediate information may be given to us. We will then consider whether a warning should be given to him that he would be arrested under Regulation III on arrival. Under present conditions we consider that such action will certainly be necessary."[38]

The British Government was extremely fearful, rather panicky about Bose and his activities, that is why they tried to prevent him from returning by hook or crook. The above documents prove that since it was legally not possible under the circumstances to prevent him from coming back to India, the British authorities were planning to serve him with a warning that he would be arrested, immediately on arrival, under the infamous Regulation III of 1818 which did not require any warrant as such. It seems as if Regulation III of 1818 was the most dependable instrument in the hands of the rulers in those days to deal with their 'most dangerous enemy.'

The Years of Exile (1933-1938)

The British bureaucracy however, was rather bewildered about their own decision regarding Bose, whether to keep him out of India or have him back home imprisoned. It is evident from above that there was difference of opinion within the bureaucracy itself. They were apprehensive of the fact that Bose, who was spreading the message of India and her freedom struggle all over Europe, might be able to mobilize support for Indian independence from the other countries of the world. They were also aware of the fact that he had connections with the Indian revolutionaries abroad. A confidential report says:

"Even if Bose arrives in India without warning, the Government of India will be able to lock him up safely before he can start a revolution...1n many ways, Bose in India is a smaller man than Bose in Europe. Here he can be locked up at a moment's notice; in Europe he is at liberty to advertise himself and to give all who wish to hear a harrowing account of this country and of the inequities of its rulers."[38A].

After Deshabandhu's death, however, Bose's political beliefs went through a process of radicalization, which was stimulated by the ideological tumult in the inter-war years and the ruthless repression to which the British Government subjected him. The British employed against him a ruthless policy of suppression. It was not only vindictive in character but also bordered on being a vendetta. As it is, Bengal was the most fertile breeding ground for the revolutionaries during the 1930's and on top of it, Bose, the 'enemy number one' to the British, had a charismatic, flamboyant appeal to the people in general. No other province suffered as much as Bengal did during this period and Bose's personal sufferings went into the making of his assessment of the British Indian Government. To the revolutionaries of Bengal, it was in every way, a ruthless regime that should be terminated without delay. The suppositions made in the early 1920's about the prospects of a peaceful mass movement being able to secure phased advances to self-government were no longer tenable in the

1930's.³⁸ᴮ

Bose was, evidently, considered to be a "terrorist" by the British who alleged in the Bengal Government's secret dossier that he was the indisputable leader of the *Jugantar* group of revolutionaries. These charges, which were never brought before an open court, were the grounds on the basis of which all subsequent punitive measures had been adopted against him. In 1928, he was a signatory to the All-Party Committee's constitutional recommendations, which proposed a dominion government in India in the British Commonwealth. Within a short span of time he moved, under pressure from the revolutionaries, an amendment seeking complete independence as the goal of the Congress in December 1928 at the Calcutta session of the Congress party, as mentioned earliar.

It may be pointed out here that before the Congress split of 1907 at Surat, Lokmanya Tilak and Aurobindo Ghosh gave leadership in the Congress party to those who wanted Swaraj as the ultimate objective of the party, as distinct from the gradual realization of responsible government, which was the goal of the moderate Congress men. The Congress 'Moderates' tried to uphold the existing Congress objective whereas the more progressive section i.e. the Left Wing in the movement wanted to proclaim *Swaraj* as its ultimate goal. Twenty years after that split, after the Congress had adopted *Swaraj* (to mean dominion status) as its political objective, the new Left Wing, according to Bose, consisted of those who stood for *Purna Swaraj* (complete independence) to be achieved by uncompromising struggle.

Even after years spent in detention under the "lawless laws" and in forced exile in Europe, Bose described the revolutionary violence in Bengal as an "expression of despair" induced in the minds of the young men and women by their conviction, generated by their experience in Bengal that it was impossible to win political rights without resort to violence. The regime, under which Bengal lived at that time, was far from a

The Years of Exile (1933-1938)

liberal one. Had it been so, had it not viewed an entire generation of youngsters of Bengal as terrorists, subjecting them and their families to incessant repression and heckling, even when they were out of prison, had they been permitted to work for *Swaraj* on constructive lines, revolutionary violence in Bengal would not have been so rampant (Indian Struggle).

Bose never encouraged the youngsters to indulge in individual assassinations, bomb throwing or similar acts of unorganized violence. But as Leonard Gordon commented in an interview with the author, Bose was so respectful to the unadulterated patriotism of the revolutionaries that he never hesitated to pay homage to them openly when they became martyrs.[39]

No exposition on the revolutionary movement of Bengal could be complete without a reference to the Irish struggle for independence. After the de-colonization of Ireland in 1921, Irish freedom struggle had a special appeal to the Bengal revolutionaries as the first example of a successful rebellion against the British Empire. In February 1936, Bose visited Ireland as he had great admiration for the Irish freedom fighters and the leadership of De Valera in their struggle for freedom. He met him and was received by him with warmth and cordiality. Before his visit, J.P. Walshe, Secretary, Department of External Affairs of the Irish Government, wrote a letter to Mrs. Woods. He said that he had been asked by the President of the Republic to inform her that he would be glad to meet Bose when he arrived in Dublin. Walshe requested Mrs. Woods to get in touch with him before the arrival of Bose so that the Government could arrange his first call with the President.[40]

The visit of Bose, as also his discussions with De Valera was reported extensively in the Irish Press describing it as an important exchange of ideas and experiences between the two revolutionaries, the old Irish and the young Indian.[41]

His meticulous study of various revolutionary movements in Europe against colonial exploitation convinced Bose that the ideological colour imparted to various struggles for liberation was really not important. As a result, he concentrated more on the strategies or techniques employed by the various revolutionary movements regardless of their ideology. His objective study of Lenin and Stalin in Russia, De Valera in Ireland and Kamal Ataturk in Turkey taught him that these leaders were able to awaken the masses in slumber, got them involved in the struggle and used well-thought-out strategies for fulfilling their aims and objectives.

However. *The Sunday Independent*, in Dublin, dated 2/2/1936 wrote :

"Mr.Subhas Chandra Bose, President of the Bengal Congress, former President of the Indian Trade Union Congress, the former Mayor of Calcutta, arrived in Dublin from Cork yesterday evening. He travelled from Havre to Cork having been refused a permit to travel to England."[42]

The report further said,

"Mr.Bose had a great admiration for President De Valera and the Irish people. The Irish struggle for liberty had been followed with profound sympathy by millions of Indians who were also struggling for national freedom at the same time and the success of Ireland had given new heart to India."[43]

A well-known newspaper called *Irish Independent* dated 4/2/1936, quoted Bose while covering his Dublin reception:

"There will be no settlement of the Indian Question except on the basis of complete independence....the people of India keenly followed Ireland's fight for freedom. Many books dealing with the subject had been banned, but those that had passed the Customs authorities were eagerly read and passed from one person to another".

Bose said that he was delighted with the warmth of the welcome accorded him, the interest shown in Indian affairs, and the desire to help Indians in their struggle. The same newspaper covered his visit to the President thus:

"He had had a very interesting talk with President de Valera and was hoping the President would be good enough to accord him another talk. He would have liked to have visited England. He had been at school there and he did not suppose his presence would have greatly disturbed the public peace."[44]

Regarding his talk with de Valera, a correspondent wrote on 3/2/1936, from Dublin for an Indian newspaper called *Patrika* :

"Mr. de Valera has honoured the Indian leader by inviting him to see him yesterday. That was Mr. Bose's first interview in this country. The two leaders discussed many problems and the Irish President asked his Indian friend to make a survey of Irish industries. He will be accorded all facilities... Subhas Bose is particularly anxious to establish, if possible, trade relations between India and the Irish Free State. Though it was a long talk, the President has asked Mr. Bose to see him once again. He has also given him a hint that he might like to see him everyday during his stay in Dublin. ..Tonight there is a big reception arranged in honour of the Indian leader under the auspices of the Indian-Irish Independence League. Though Fianna Fail Party members do not agree with many of the activities of the Republican Party, they have joined hands in making tonight's function, a great success, worthy of the Irish tradition in welcoming a foreign visitor. ..

"Mr. Bose has received letters and telegrams from various organizations in England welcoming him to London. 'We want you to visit London' says one of the communications 'as we are anxious that the working class of this country should be told the truth and the whole truth about the condition of Indian working class and peasantry under the domination of British Imperialist Rulers' .One of the invitations is that from the Rogers Sinn Fein Club, London."[45]

Even when he was leaving Dublin, it was given wide coverage by the Press. A correspondent writes:

"This afternoon Mr. Bose saw Mr. De Valera for the third time during the week......he leaves Dublin for Cork on Tuesday next as he has received a special invitation from Miss MacSweeney, the sister of the late Terence MacSweeney of sacred memory. Another invitation from Cork has also come from Mr. Sean French, who is a Republican Lord Mayor of Cork. According to his present arrangement, Mr. Bose leaves Irish soil on the 12th instant. He sails from Cork for Havre for Paris where he is to attend an international anti-imperialist Conference." The correspondent further said that Bose might meet Ben Bradley of the 'League against Imperialism' there and Harry Pollitt of the Communist Party of Great Britain was likely to make a journey to Paris to meet Bose. When the correspondent wanted to verify this information from a fellow journalist in London, the latter said "if Mountain does not go to Mahomet, Mahomet must come to Mountain."[46]

It is evident from the above records that because of his progressive and genuinely leftist thinking, Bose was considered a like-minded person, a true communist by the CPGB leaders like Harry Pollitt and Ben Bradley. In all probability, this was a sore point for the Indian communists which persisted even after Independence.

It is also evident from above that he was considered by various organizations in England the ideal spokesperson for the Indian workers and peasants, who was capable of presenting the ground realities regarding the plight of the people belonging to those classes under British imperialists.

Amongst all the European countries, Ireland was perhaps, most keenly interested in India's independence. De Valera led the Irish Revolution successfully whereby the British were forced to concede independence to Ireland by creating the Irish Free State. The Irish revolutionaries set up several underground organizations during the 1st World War with German assistance. The Sinn Fein Movement was historically a successful model for the Bengal revolutionaries mainly because it faced the same

The Years of Exile (1933-1938)

enemy, i.e. Great Britain, the country that colonized them for years. The Irish Nationalist Party resembled, in many ways, the Gandhians who wanted constitutional reforms, their aim being the achievement of only "Home Rule". The United Irishmen group, which originated from the Sinn Fein Movement, resembled the Indian radicals of whom Bose was the foremost. United Irishmen wanted a completely independent Ireland. The aid extended by the German Government to the Irish as well as the Indian revolutionaries during the first World War made Bose hopeful of getting similar help from Germany once again for Indian independence.

De Valera was very much eager to extend Irish help and support to the cause of Indian independence and was willing to appeal to the conscience of the world in favour of Indian revolution.

Eamon de Valera stressed on the idea of common cause among nationalists in Ireland, Egypt and India while raising funds for Sinn Fein in the USA in 1920. At a meeting of the Friends of Freedom for India in New York, he emphasized the need for armed rebellion to throw off the yoke of the British Empire. He said,

"We of Ireland and you of India must each of us endeavour both as separate peoples and in combination, to rid ourselves of the vampire that is fattening on our blood and we must never allow ourselves to forget what weapon it was by which Washington rid his country of this same vampire. Our cause is a common cause." (Eamon de Valera, India and Ireland, New York, 1920, pp. 23-24).

The secretary of State for India, Lord Zetland, it may be noted here, used to attend the meetings of the cabinet's Irish Situation Committee out of concern for the effects of Irish agitation on the Indian situation. He commented that revolutionary elements in India took Ireland as their model.[46A]

During his stay in Ireland, Bose wrote a number of letters

to the Irish newspapers and provided them with news and articles on the repressive measures adopted by the British Imperialists for dealing with the Indian revolutionaries particularly in Bengal. He made arrangements for the publication of a monthly bulletin in Ireland on India in English, French and German languages.

There is no doubt about the fact that Bose was the first Indian leader who was exposed to the world outside Great Britain over a considerably long period of time. He felt, even during those days when the term 'global village' was unheard of, that in the fast- shrinking modern world, no country could live in isolation if it had to survive. He, therefore, devoted himself, during the European sojourn, to the work of informing the Europeans about the nitty gritty of Indian freedom struggle. He made efforts particularly to

(a) counteract the false British propaganda about his motherland,

(b) enlighten the world about the real plight of his countrymen under their colonial masters,

(c) inform the world about the remarkable achievements of the Indian people in different spheres of human activity.

Bose was the only Congress leader in those days who realized the importance of international relations in the life of a subject country struggling for national liberation. Unfortunately he did not find too many like-minded people within the Congress rank and file to share and support his strategy which was considered to be right later by many of his political opponents.

In April 1936, Bose decided to come back to India for the purpose of attending the Lucknow session of the Congress, which was to be presided over by Jawaharlal Nehru. When the British Intelligence came to know about it, the Government warned him through the British Consul of Vienna that he would be arrested as soon as he landed in India. The letter dated 12th March 1936 goes like this:

"I have today received instructions from the Secretary of State for Foreign Affairs, to communicate to you a warning, that the Government of India have seen in the press, statements, that you propose to return to India this month, and the Government of India desire to make it clear to you that should you do so, you cannot expect to remain at liberty.

Sd/- J.D. Taylor (His Majesty's Consul)."[47]

Bose wrote to Nehru asking for his opinion regarding his intention of coming back to India. Jawaharlal Nehru wrote in his reply that although this type of prohibition could not be accepted for an indefinite period of time, still under the existing circumstances, he was unable to support the decision Bose had taken to come back to India.[48] Nehru, not very surprisingly, did not want to antagonize the British authorities by supporting the decision of Bose regarding the latter's coming back to India. Instead of fighting together to uproot the imperialists from the Indian soil, these leaders were busy calculating their own future prospects by keeping themselves safe in the good books of the British.

A disheartened Bose, however, wrote to Romand Rolland in a letter dated 8th April 1936 that although there was a possibility of spending the best years of his life in prison, he was not at all scared of the warning given to him by the British Government. This he wrote to Romand Rolland in reply to a letter from the great French literateur requesting him to postpone his home-coming.[48A]

On the 8th of April 1936, Bose was arrested once again as soon as he landed on the Bombay Port. People throughout the country burst into protest, and in demand of his unconditional release, celebrated Subhas Day on the 10th of May 1936.

In the House of Commons, questions were asked by some opposition members regarding the justifiability of the decision of the Government to arrest Bose on his return. Mr.

Thurtle, a Labour Party member of the House of Commons,[49] asked the Under Secretary of State for India whether he was aware that the British Consul at Vienna had notified Bose that if he returned to India he would not retain his liberty. He further asked "whether this Gentleman is not to be allowed to return to his native country without being arrested and, seeing that he was first arrested four years ago, do the Government intend to keep him under control indefinitely without trying him for any given offence?" To this, Mr. Butler said that notification had been served to him that he could not expect to remain at liberty if he returned to India. To the second part of the question he said, since it went beyond the original question, he required a notice of it.

James Maxton, another MP from the Independent Labour Party who earned a folk hero status in the socialist circles,[50] wanted to know whether there would be any limit to the continued persecution of such an eminent citizen of India as Bose. To this Mr. Butler said," 1 have already said that that is wider than the original question and had better be put on the Paper."[51]

Ellen Cicely Wilkinson, another MP from the Labour Party asked whether the Hon'ble Gentleman would tell the House what objections the Government had to Mr. Bose and what was the charge against him. She wanted to know whether the charge had already been formulated or not. Mr. Butler replied by saying that:

"I think Mr. Bose is aware of the reasons which led to his incarceration in India in the first instance. He was allowed to go away for medical reasons." Again, Miss Wilkinson asked:

"Is it not a fact that no charge has been preferred against him? Why do you not try him and sentence him if he has done anything?" [52]

Since there was no definite legitimate charge against Bose and he was constantly subjected to imprisonment or

The Years of Exile (1933-1938)

unnecessary harassment, sensible Parliamentarians in England itself kept on questioning the competence of the Government to do so with a citizen of a subject country. Thurtle asked the Under Secretary of State for India, on the 6th of April, 1936, if, in view of the Government's declared intention to deprive Bose of his liberty in the event of his return to India, he should state whether or not it was the intention of the Government to formulate a definite charge against Bose and bring him to trial on that charge.

Butler, in his reply, said that Bose was previously detained under Regulation III of 1818, a procedure that did not involve trial upon definite charges. When Maxton wanted to know whether 'the Hon'ble Gentleman' would not use his influence to stop the persecution of this gentleman who had a distinguished record of public service in India, the latter replied: "The same reasons that led to Mr. Bose's detention in 1932 still hold good, but he has been allowed to visit Europe for medical reasons." [53]

Questions put by Sorensen dated 30th April 1936:

"Would it not be better for those who are taking an interest in the future of India to be acquainted with the nature of the charge made against this particular man and would it not be better that we should be acquainted with the actual text of the (intercepted) letters?"

To this, the reply given by Butler was not straight forward as he said that he was sending to the honourable gentleman a copy of the report of the debate of the Legislative Assembly which contained a great deal of material on this subject and the same information would be placed in the library of the House. Sorensen, then, wanted to know whether Butler was aware that by some 62 votes to 59, the arrest of Bose was censured in the Assembly as recently as three weeks ago. He further wanted to know how many terms of imprisonment had been served by Bose since 1921 and whether the Under Secretary of State for India was aware that in Bengal there was considerable perturbation regarding the arrest of Bose and that it was considered by many prominent officials in Bengal that, in view of the punishment which had been delivered and experienced by him, no further punishment was necessary.

It is evident from the above that even the British intelligentsia was perturbed by the way Bose was treated, as a result of which they wanted to know the grounds on the basis of which he was denied his basic human rights. When Butler stated that Bose was detained, as he was in January 1932, under Regulation III of 1818, a procedure which did not require trial on a definite charge, or the formulation of such a charge, Thurtle said on the 21st of April, 1936, :

"Is not the Hon'ble Gentleman aware that this prolonged detention without trial is quite contrary to British standard of justice and will he make strong representations to the Government of India to bring it to an end?"

Butler replied: "Mr. Bose's activities, connected as they are, and were with the Terrorist movement, are reasons which involve special methods such as are prescribed by this special Regulation."

Thurtle, it seems, was unstoppable as he continued asking questions about the specific reasons behind Bose's prolonged detention. If the person had committed a crime, it would not be impossible to prove it, and why no action was being taken to prove the crime, he wanted to know. To this, Butler said:

"The reason why this person was originally detained was referred to the scrutiny of two judges who thoroughly investigated the case against him."[53A]

To Maxton's query whether Mr. Bose was actually accused of terrorist activities, Butler replied that Mr. Bose was associated closely with one of the main terrorist parties and this was the reason why he was detained. [54]

The Years of Exile (1933-1938)

The two judges mentioned by Butler, were K.C.Nag and A.C.Blanc who had given a report on the 9th of December 1932 on Bose and his revolutionary activities. According to that report, Bose had crossed the limits of advanced politics and his activities were "directly and seriously endangering the security of the British Dominion from internal commotion.".[55]

Krishnadas Roy, who was Gandhi's personal assistant at Sabarmati, sent a letter from Bengal to Gandhi on Bose highlighting his intimacy with the Bengal revolutionaries. In that letter, which the British Government did not share with Gandhi for whom it was meant because the letter was intercepted by the IB, Krishnadas alleged Bose's close association with the Jugantar group of extremists. This also infuriated the Government further, which led them to detain Bose for a longer period of time and obviously without trial. Krishnadas's letter was actually the result of an intra-party intrigue in which some of the Congress members were involved. Krishnadas Roy explained on 27th March 1936 that he had no direct knowledge of "Sjt. Subhas Chandra Bose's complicity with the Jugantar Party" and that what he had reported for Gandhi's eyes had been based on hearsay or gossip".[56]

The fact that was revealed when Bose was rearrested by the British on arrival from Europe in Bombay on the 8th of April 1936 should be narrated because it explains Gandhi's attitude towards C.R.Das and his compatriots especially Bose who was probably the most charismatic nationalist leader of the country at that time. The British Intelligence seized the said letter probably in 1930 and used this intra-Congress information as an additional ground of their allegation that Bose was the leader of Jugantar revolutionaries.

When the Government in 1936 disclosed the letter and the identity of the writer, Dr. L. V. Paranjpye, a *Hindu Maha Sabha* leader who was opposed to Bose's political convictions, issued a statement alleging " a conspiracy" to entrap Bose "whose probable domination of the Congress was discountenanced by some orthodox Congressmen".[57] Gandhi, it was said, sent Krishnadas Roy who belonged to the anti-C.R.Das group, to Bengal for reporting against Bose and also on Nehru whose advice Bose sought before he decided to come back from Europe in the full knowledge that he was returning to another term of imprisonment. Nehru tried to manage the situation arising out of the said letter and accordingly sent a statement to Nagpur's *Daily News* on the 23rd of April 1936 with a view to repudiate Dr. Paranjpye's accusation. "It is an absurd calumny to suggest that anyone connected with the Congress, least of all Gandhiji, or my humble self, had been conspiring to get Mr. Subhas Bose into trouble."[58]

Nehru further wrote :

"Even if there were some foundation for them (charging Bose with leading Jugantar revolutionaries as alleged by the Government), we could not approve of the vindictive action that Government continues to take against a person who is honoured and respected throughout India." Towards the end of the statement, Nehru disclosed that Krishnadas Roy, formerly personal assistant of Gandhi, "has severed his connection with the AICC". This information shows that Krishnadas was probably a member of the AICC or its staff when he wrote the said letter to Gandhi, which the British Government was citing to justify their decision to rearrest Bose under Regulation III of 1818, as soon as he arrived in Bombay.

However, there has not been any evidence till date, of any public statement from Gandhi on Krishnadas's letter. Krishnadas himself, however, in his statement to *Amrita Bazar Patrika* of 23rd March, 1936 confessed that there existed a deep rooted animus in certain Congress circles working against Bose even at that early stage, that is, 1930.

He wrote: "We, the Gandhites, started with a prejudice against Sjt. Bose, because of his opposition to Gandhi at the two sessions of the Congress held in Calcutta (1928) and

Lahore (1929) and his open criticism of Gandhi's policy." (Amrita Bazar Patrika, 27th March, 1936).[59]

The two sessions Krishnadas mentioned remind us of the efforts Bose made, initially supported by Nehru and quite a few others, to have *Purna Swaraj* (complete independence) instead of Dominion Status within the British Empire as the Congress Party's ultimate goal. In 1929, sometime between May and July, Motilal Nehru came into conflict with Gandhi on the policy of boycott of the legislatures, the policy that he and C.R.Das had rejected and defeated in 1923 by forming the Swarajya Party within the Congress. In August 1929, Gandhi refused to accept the nomination made by the majority of the Provincial Congress Committees that he should be the next Congress president and suggested, instead, the name of Jawaharlal Nehru for the Lahore session. On this episode, Bose wrote later:

"In accordance with the Congress Constitution, the vast majority of the Provincial Committees had nominated Mahatma Gandhi (to be the President of the Lahore session of Congress due to be held in Dec. 1929), but he declined to accept the nomination. The general feeling in Congress circles was that the honour should go to Sardar Vallabhbhai Patel. But the Mahatma decided to back the candidature of Pundit Jawaharlal Nehru. For the Mahatma the choice was a prudent one, but for the Congress Left Wing, it proved to be unfortunate because that event marked the beginning of a political rapprochement between the Mahatma and Pundit Jawaharlal Nehru and a consequent alienation between the latter and the Congress Left Wing. ....The Left-Wingers did not like the idea that one of their most outstanding spokesmen should accept the presidentship of the Lahore Congress because it was clear that ....the president would be a mere dummy."[60]

The Lahore session, it may well be presumed, brought Gandhi and Nehru closer to each other but it did nothing to reduce the prejudice the Gandhians nursed against Bose.

Another extract from Krishnadas Roy's statement in *Amrita Bazar Patrika* of 23 March 1936 would possibly explain how one particular section of the Congress, apart from the British, was collecting information prejudicial to this heir of C.R.Das's political legacy.

"The letter (Krishnadas to Gandhi), as its content showed, was a private communication to Gandhi. In a private communication no one is expected to write weighing words, as one would do in the case of a public statement. My relation with Gandhiji was such that I was expected to convey to him whatever I heard, or saw, without much critical examination. He had other sources of information...It was therefore not incumbent on me to be judicially careful before I conveyed my impressions or observations to him. Although by birth I am a Bengali, I had been out of touch with Bengal for thirteen years before I went there in 1930 in connection with the Satyagraha movement. The alleged facts about the existence of several schools of revolutionaries in Bengal were gathered by me in prison during the rush of the movement when all sorts of people were thrown together pell-mell. These included Satyagrahis, unsophisticated villagers, some revolutionaries and a host of government emissaries or agent provocateurs who were sent to create confusion...I cannot vouch that I was not misled by some belonging to the last group into forming my opinion about the political situation in Bengal...

"This opposition and criticism (by Bose of Gandhi's policy) might have been induced by the radical outlook of Sjt. Bose as opposed to what is considered to be Gandhiji's conservatism. But some people often whispered into our ears that Sjt. Bose's real opposition centered round the Congress creed of non-violence... This, however, is no evidence to prove that Sjt. Bose was an out and out advocate of violence."[61]

Krishnadas Roy, six years after he carried to Gandhi an uncorroborated accusation, gathered possibly from Government agents who must have been aware of his closeness to Gandhi and the predisposition of some Gandhians to mistrust Bose, tried not to be the Crown's witness against Bose. Gandhi, as Krishnadas wrote, had other informants beside himself. But Krishnadas was not an ordinary person. During the non-cooperation campaign he was the personal assistant to Gandhi and in 1923 he joined issue with C.R.Das when the latter in a speech in Madras blamed Gandhi for mishandling a crucial negotiation with Viceroy Reading at a time when there was still a chance of a respectable agreement, if not a settlement, before the unconditional cancellation of the much hyped Non-Cooperation Movement of 1920-22. Krishnadas's letter, the existence and the substance of which, as given out by the British Government, were not denied by Krishnadas himself, reflected an old failing in the nationalist movement of India which not even Gandhi's avowedly spiritualized politics could remove.[61A]

The Golden Jubilee session of the Indian National Congress, however, was held in Lucknow under the Presidency of Jawaharlal Nehru in April 1936. With a desire to attend the session, Bose came back to India but as soon as he landed on the Bombay port from his ship named Conte Verde on the 8th of April 1936, he was arrested under Regulation III of 1818 and taken to Arthur Road Outpost, wherefrom he was taken to Yarveda Central Jail in Poona. A *Hartal* (strike) was observed in Bengal on the 10th of May 1936, as mentioned earlier, under the leadership of the revolutionaries as a mark of protest because of his repeated incarceration and the whole nation responded to this call positively. 10th of May was celebrated as Subhas Day all over the country.[62] As Amalendu Ghosh, an ex-BV leader pointed out, it was the Bengal revolutionaries who declared 10th May as Subhas Day, a day of protest.[62A]

He was removed again to Kurseong on May 20, 1936 and ordered to be interned in the house of his elder brother Sarat Chandra Bose on the Gidda Hills. The Rules set forth by the Government to be observed by Bose while a state prisoner at Gidda Hills were as follows:

"I.   You shall reside at Sarat Bose's house at Gidda Hills, Kurseong and shall not proceed outside the boundaries given below without the previous sanction of the Government.

"Boundaries : -

You are permitted to take walks within a radius of one mile from the residence.

"II. You shall hold no communication written or oral with any person

   (a) Connected in any way to your knowledge with any movement subversive of Government authority;

   (b) Resident in or visiting Kurseong except as approved by the Superintendent of Police, Darjeeling.

"III. You shall not concern yourself directly or indirectly with the affairs of any public body or engage directly or indirectly in any public activity or political movement.

"IV. You shall not contribute to the Press nor will you cause to be contributed to, or expressed in the Press by any other person, your views on political or public matters.

"V.   Letters written or received by you shall be censored by the Superintendent of Police or by a Gazetted Officer duly authorized by him. You shall limit your correspondence to seven letters per week.

"VI. You shall not entertain, receive visits from or allow to reside in the house any guests, either resident or non-resident at Kurseong or any relative except with the permission of the Superintendent of Police, Darjeeling."[63]

On the 17th December 1936, he was brought to Calcutta and admitted in the Medical College Hospital as his health was deteriorating considerably. He could not attend the Lucknow Congress for which he came back from abroad but his message was "Keep the flag of freedom aloft". He was, however,

The Years of Exile (1933-1938)

unconditionally released after five years of suffering, on the 17th March 1937 and went to Dalhousie to stay with Dr. Dharamvir at his residence. En route to Dalhousie, Bose was feted at Lahore by the Punjab Depressed Classes Young men's Association. While addressing the crowd, he said on May 12, 1937:

"In this land of ours, we are all depressed – because we are all enslaved. The difference between one Indian and another is only in the degree of degradation that has overtaken us....only through our national freedom can we hope to bring about an all-round upliftment of our countrymen. Freedom for us means not merely political liberty, but also social and economic emancipation."[64]

On the 6th April 1937, Bengal celebrated Bose's unconditional release by declaring the day as "All Bengal Subhas Day" and greeted him with flowers, garlands and band played by the volunteers at a huge gathering in Shraddhananda Park in Calcutta. Addressing the gathering, Ramananda Chattopadhyay, the well-known journalist and editor of *Modern Review*, said,

"the Government has put on his head a crown of thorns whereas his countrymen is honouring him today with a crown of flowers."[65] Bose spoke about the state prisoners, who were in the dark cells of the different jails, interned or deported elsewhere, and living life in sub-human conditions. He cited his experience in the Calcutta Medical College where a state prisoner, next to his cabin, expired and the Police was present there all through with their watchful eyes, following the dead prisoner to the burning ghat and was on guard till the body got totally burnt. He said he would try his best to rouse sympathy in the minds of the people for those martyrs who became victims of this repressive regime. In that meeting he paid homage to the memory of V.J.Patel, Dr. Ansari, Birendra Sasmal and J.M.Sengupta.

The system of provincial self-government, however, was introduced in the year 1937 in accordance with the provisions of the Government of India Act 1935. Accordingly, Indian National Congress took part in the election and got a majority in most of the provinces and after a lot of dilly-dally agreed to accept ministry. In Bengal, however, Congress did not get the majority and Fazlul Haque's proposal of a coalition between the Congress and his *Krishak Praja Party* was rejected due to the stubborn attitude of the Congress Party authorities. The non-acceptance of Haque's proposal paved the way, to a great extent, for the partition of the country after a few years.

However, a disappointed Haque joined the Muslim League and under his leadership, the League ministry made the life of the people in Bengal unbearable due to its reactionary nature. The imprisoned revolutionaries did not get release whereas in the other provinces, the prisoners were set free by the Congress ministries without delay.

Bose, in a statement issued from Dalhousie, on the 24th July 1937, said that Bengal was being governed by the most reactionary ministry in India. He also mentioned that whenever a liberal constitutional system was introduced in any part of the world, the political prisoners received amnesty but in Bengal, where more than two thousand detenus were imprisoned without trial, where many political prisoners were serving sentences after trial, many of whom were deported to the *Andamans*, it was difficult to believe that provincial self-government had been introduced there. Bose further pointed out that the continued detention of the prisoners was the most disappointing thing in Bengal and Fazlul Haque, the person who once was a pro-people leader, was now trying to keep the political prisoners under detention without trial. He made an appeal to Sir John Anderson, the then Governor and the bureaucracy in general by saying that in the Irish Rebellion of 1916, several thousand Englishmen were killed whereas in Bengal, just one secret revolutionary movement had taken place so far, as a result of which only a few dozens lost their lives. He said it because Anderson tried to draw a parallel between the Irish Rebellion and the revolutionary activities of the Bengalis. To Anderson, the situation in Bengal was not different from that of Ireland. Bose reminded him and his permanent bureaucrats that secret revolutionary activities were a thing of the past in Bengal as he had learnt from several sources that the youth in Bengal were no longer thinking in terms of a revolution, rather they were planning to launch an open mass movement.

Bose argued strongly for the release of the political prisoners who were detained only on the apprehension that they were associated with revolutionary campaigns. He wanted to know whether Anderson would repeat what he had done in Ireland where he transferred power, as he claimed, to the hands of the people's representatives and released all political prisoners before leaving the country.[66]

The Government of India categorised the political prisoners into two groups, violent and non-violent. Obviously, the non-violent political prisoners were not considered harmful by the Government. In a press release issued on the 24th of August 1937, Bose commented that only in India, this kind of a categorization existed. The statesmen, he stated, in Germany, Russia, Italy, Spain, Irish Free State and many other countries, were imprisoned during their struggle for freedom, for committing acts far more serious than the offences of the Andaman prisoners. To refute the comment of the bureaucracy that the death rate of the Andaman prisoners was much less than the others, Bose said that it was the sturdy youngsters who had been kept in bondage in the Andamans, they survived the torture inflicted on them because of their youth and good health whereas the prisoners elsewhere, mentioned by the bureaucracy, were non-political and criminals of the worst kind, alcoholics and sick.[67]

Bose came back to Calcutta on the 24th October 1937

from Kurseong when All-India Congress Committee was preparing for its meeting at Wellington Square in the city. It was at this meeting of the Working Committee where the well-known song entitled *Bande Mataram* created by Bankim Chandra Chattopadhyay, was mutilated under the presidency of Jawaharlal Nehru. *Bande Mataram*, which meant, "hail the mother" was the battle cry of the Bengal revolutionaries and by 'mother' they meant the motherland. This song became extremely popular during the movement against the partition of Bengal in 1905. Prior to that, the song entered into the life of the nation when Rabindra Nath Tagore, in 1896, sang it in his own composition at the Calcutta Congress and gradually the song became the *Mantra* of the revolutionaries. Incidentally, this song and the utterance of the term *'Bande Mataram'* was prohibited by the Government in 1906 as a result of which it became a challenge for the nationalist Indians against the colonial masters and in course of time, it became a symbol of patriotism and the slogan of the revolutionaries not only in Bengal, but in India as a whole. Although *Bande Mataram* came to be recognized as the National Anthem by the nationalists, the question of its official recognition in the Indian National Congress did not arise. After the formation of the Congress ministries in a number of provinces, *Bande Mataram* started being sung in the formal functions of the Congress as the national anthem. Muslim league, however, objected to it vehemently (Anandabazar 24th Sept. 1937) and adopted a resolution against it in its Lucknow Conference. Hindustan Standard dated 19th October 1937 wrote:

"The fifth resolution strongly condemned the attitude of the Congress in foisting *Bande Mataram* as the national anthem upon the country in callous disregard of the feelings of Mussalmans and considered the song as not merely anti-Islamic and idolatrous in its inspiration and ideas but definitely subversive of the growth of genuine nationalism in India

"The meeting further called upon Mussalman members

The Years of Exile (1933-1938)

of the various Legislatures and public bodies in country not to associate themselves in any manner with the 'highly objectionable song'." It may be pointed out here that the national flag visualized and subsequently designed by Madam Cama, the well-known Indian revolutionary abroad, was also tri-colour in green, yellow and red with the words *'Bande Mataram'* scripted at the centre. As stated earlier, Cama unfolded this flag at Stuttgart, Germany in August 1907 at the International Socialist Congress. Prior to that, she had presented the flag at the Conference of the Socialist Revolutionaries in Berlin in 1906 and said:

"This is the flag of Indian Independence. Behold! It is born. Gentlemen stand up and salute it."[68] A specimen copy of the said flag was preserved by absconding revolutionary Shyamji Krishnavarma who died in 1930 in Berlin. After his demise, the flag came to be possessed by his compatriot S.R.Rana who sent it to G. V .Khotkar, the editor of *Maratha*, a Maharashtrian newspaper. Even Sister Nivedita had visualized a national flag for India, which depicted *'Bande Mataram'* at the centre. She displayed the flag at the Congress exhibition in the year 1906.[69]

Madame Cama, who was "the notorious Parsi lady of 25, Rue de Ponthieu, Paris" to the British imperialists,[69A] used to help the Bengal revolutionaries at home and abroad. She said in the Stuttgart Congress that 35 million pounds were taken away annually from India to England without return and in consequence people of India died of poverty at the rate of half a million every month.

Cama wrote to the editor of *The Indian Sociologist* in September 1907: "I am terribly moved by the telegrams in the papers about comrade Babu Bepin Chandra Pal getting six months' imprisonment. This fact emphasizes the importance of having a central press in Paris (beyond the reach of the tyrannical English) where we can publish all necessary circulars etc. in different Indian vernaculars. It is high time now that you should take up this most pressing matter in hand first of all. Every Indian must be convinced that if Russian methods are carried on in our country rigorously by our oppressors, the so-called British rulers, we must meet it with measure for measure. The Russian people are getting everything printed in Switzerland, and thus they do not risk the freedom of their most valuable hands like Mr. Pal.

"I wish I could go to Calcutta and take up the thread where he has left it, and keep up giving the open-air lectures to the masses while he is absent."[70] On November 24th, 1908, Cama attended a usual Sunday meeting at India House, 65 Cromwell Avenue, London, presided over by Mrs. Krishnavarma where Bepin Chandra Pal, the renowned "extremist" Congress leader, spoke on "Hindu Politics". Cama, in that meeting, advised her hearers to follow the self-sacrificing example of the Bengal revolutionaries (whom she named and each name was greeted with loud cheers) and to be prepared for death. On December 19th, 1908, she attended a lecture on Indian Nationalism by Bepin Chandra Pal where she delivered a fiery speech that was afterwards reprinted in the *Free Hindusthan* and copies of the speech in the form of a leaflet entitled *"Bande Mataram"*, were sent to India in large numbers, posted, to avoid interception, from nearly a dozen different postal districts of London.

That Madame Cama used to give financial support to the Indian revolutionaries, particularly of Bengal, was confirmed by the reports that in April 1909, she contributed 10 Pounds towards the funds of Bepin Chandra Pal's Swaraj magazine. According to a confidential report of the Home Department, Cama was, in those days, regarded by the Bengal revolutionaries as a reincarnation of some deity, presumably the Goddess *Kali*.[71]

Virendranath Chattopadhyay, better known in the history of the Indian revolutionary movement as Chatto, (Jawaharlal Nehru called him by that name in his letters) was a well-known

The Years of Exile (1933-1938)

Bengali revolutionary abroad who also received whole-hearted cooperation from Cama while in Paris. In 1910, a Congress of Indian Nationalists was held in Paris, the Reception Committee of which consisted of Cama, V.V.S.Aiyar and Chattopadhyay. Their intention was to pass some resolutions on the subject of Indian Independence in order to impress the Indian question on the mind of Europe. A National Fund was also started in Paris of which Cama and Chattopadhyay were the treasurers and the former subscribed 5000 francs to it at the outset. Cama, however, devoted most of her time to the publication and distribution of *'Bande Mataram'* as its editor and other revolutionary literature. Chattopadhyay, later a Communist and a Comintern activist in the Soviet Union, was arrested in 1937 by the Leningrad NKVD on suspicion of espionage and sentenced by the Military Collegium of the Supreme Court of the USSR to death by firing squad.[72]

Not surprisingly therefore, it came as a shock for the Bengal revolutionaries when the Congress High Command decided to mutilate *"Bande Mataram"* due to the pressure exerted by the Muslim fundamentalists in 1937. The song and the battle cry *"Bande Mataram"* was, undoubtedly, a great contribution of Bengal to Indian nationalism and considered a part of the revolutionary ethos particularly in Bengal. There was protest from the aggrieved revolutionaries against the proposed mutilation and attempt was made to organize movements against the decision of the Congress stalwarts but the movements were not violent as the revolutionaries felt that on the question of national anthem, violence and bloodshed was to be avoided.[73]

Bengal could have done something substantial to change the decision if, instead of sending so many patriots to the gallows and deportations, it could supply more heads to the Congress Working Committee. Even a person like Bose had to accept the decision because he found that not only the fundamentalists, also the nationalist Muslims objected to it as they were pressurized by the former. Bose had a serious difference of opinion with the revolutionaries over the *"Bande Mataram"* issue because he insisted on the general acceptability of the national anthem without hurting the sentiment of any particular community. His pragmatism made him do so to the dismay of the revolutionaries of Bengal.

Bose, however, was permitted to set foot on the soils of England at long last in the year 1938 and stayed at 112 Gower Street, London, W.C.I. as a guest of the Indian Students' Union, Ceylon's Students' Association, and the Federation of Indian Students' Societies of Great Britain and Ireland. He addressed many public meetings and was given a public reception by the Labour leaders. Because of his progressive ideas and radical stance in public life, Bose was held in high esteem by the Labour Party leaders of England. Attlee, the then President of the Labour Party, Sir Stafford Cripps, the leader of the Socialists, and Harry Pollitt, the leader of the Communists met him at the public meeting in the Conway Hall presided over by the veteran Labour leader George Lansbury.

Arthur Greenwood, the Deputy Leader of the Labour Party, said in his welcome address that they were giving him warm welcome not only as the first President of the Trade Union Congress but also as one to whom great responsibilities were coming. Surely they were all aware of the fact that Bose was going to be the next President of the INC. The kind of adulation he received in England was, probably, beyond his imagination. He came to be globally recognized as a popular political leader of India as soon as he was selected the President of the INC. *Daily Worker*, the newspaper of the Communist Party of Great Britain greeted him and wrote:

"The people of this country will welcome Subhas Chandra Bose on the occasion of his visit here, as the ambassador of the Indian people. Prospective President of the Indian National Congress whose candidates won twenty million out of the thirty million votes at the recent elections, he can speak with authority on behalf of the Indian national movement.

"In the speech of the reception meeting in his honour at the St. Pancras Town Hall, he dwelt with special emphasis on the unity of India's national struggle with the struggle in China, in Spain, in Abyssinia, with the world struggle against Imperialism and Fascism."[74]

Bose met De Valera who was in London at that time, at the Piccadilly Hotel and discussed matters relating to Indian independence. Earlier, Bose, while in Dublin, said in a public lecture under the auspices of the Indian-Irish Independence League that as in Ireland, the British Imperialists tried to enforce their language and culture on the people of India so that the latter would become completely de-nationalized. But so far as the cultural domination over India was concerned, the worst was over. He said :

"In India today, we have a revival of our own culture adapted to modem conditions. We are told now that all is quiet on the Indian front, but that is not true. That is British propaganda. In fact the movement for independence in India is going on different lines from those of the past. The day is not far off when we would have in India a bigger upheaval than was witnessed at any time in the last 100 years."[75]

After the Haripura session of the Congress, Bose went to Bombay and addressed a meeting organized by the Bombay Congress Socialist Party, presided over by Jawaharlal Nehru at the Kawasji Jehangir Hall on the 25th of February 1938. There, he spoke of the Irish Rebellion of 1916 where 800 revolutionaries fought against fifty thousand British soldiers. At the outset, he said, popular support was not there in favour of the revolutionaries, but they were desperate and prepared to sacrifice themselves for their country's independence, many of them including John McBride were hanged. Bose mentioned also the activities of the Sinn Fein Party and its leaders and praised De Valera highly, narrated his achievements, how he escaped from the British prison, took shelter in USA, won the minds of the Americans in favour of his countrymen which ultimately acted as a pressure on the British Government to come to terms with the Irish. He also spoke of Valera's concept of 'external association', a remarkable contribution of the said leader, by means of which the Irish Free State could never be used as a military base by the British Government in case of an armed attack on it.[76]

Evidently, Bose acknowledged his indebtedness to the Irish freedom movement in spite of his leanings towards the progressive ideas of the Soviet Union. As said earlier, Irish freedom fighters exerted enormous influence on the Bengal revolutionaries. Even behind the formation of the *Swarajya Party* of C.R.Das, the Irish freedom fighters were the source of inspiration.

Bose never claimed to be a trend-setter in his ideas or strategies. He was aware of the fact that some leaders were driven by their egoism which made them sacrifice collective interest at the alter of self-interest. He had only one mission in life, winning national liberation for India; hence he studied meticulously the methods, the successes and failures of leaders of various countries with similar missions in life. The history of the Irish movements against England was the history of a relentless revolutionary struggle. India in bondage was placed in a similar situation and Bose felt that there was no reason not to follow the Irish methods in order to compel the alien rulers to accept the Indian demands, if no other method became fruitful.

Bose, however, met Rajni Palme Dutt, the well-known Communist leader of England, in 1938, when he visited that country. Dutt requested him to make some comments on his view of Fascism. Bose said that when he wrote his *Indian Struggle*, fascism had not started on its imperialist expedition and hence he was under the impression that it was just another extreme form of nationalism. Dutt wanted to know also his

The Years of Exile (1933-1938)

views on Communism. To this he said that Communism as it appeared to be demonstrated by many of those who were supposed to stand for it in India seemed to him anti-national and this impression was further strengthened in view of the hostile attitude which several among them exhibited towards the Indian National Congress, but the position now, had fundamentally altered, he mentioned. [77]

It may be mentioned in this connection that Bose, in his early years, was very much impressed by the success of the Bolshevik revolution and he welcomed it on Swami Vivekananda's terms. Perhaps he saw in the Soviet Union a reflection of Vivekananda's principle of equality irrespective of caste and class distinctions.

Bose got himself involved in the trade union and youth movements with the purpose of organizing a broad based front against the British imperialists. He wanted the Congress to be open to all and restructured so that alternative decision-making bodies could emerge within the Party to face newer challenges. He was certainly not a Marxist although there was an allegation contained in the history sheet submitted to the Central Government by the Bengal Government in 1932 that he had connections with a Russian emissary in Japan who was negotiating the supply of arms and money for a revolution in India.[77A]

Bose was not anti-communist either although he could not accept the claim of the Marxists that their ideology was indisputable. He considered the communist movement as an important force in India's struggle for independence and tried his best to secure their support. But he was not willing to accept blindly the Soviet model of socialism for the economic restructuring of India nor was he ready to follow the dictates of the CPGB (Communist Party of Great Britain) unlike the Indian communists of his time. Besides, the concept of proletarian internationalism was in conflict with his faith in the resurgent Indian nationalism personified in Vivekananda. As a result, an unbridgeable distance was created between Bose and the Indian communists, which neither of them could ever get over.

It will not be irrelevant here to mention that in those days the Indian communists used to communicate with the CPSU (Communist Party of Soviet Union) through the CPGB. From a letter dated 23rd March 1936, found in the Russian Archive by some researchers of Asiatic Society, it becomes evident that the CPGB was very much against the return of Bose to India during his years of exile. The letter goes like this:

"Dear Charlie

Enclosed is Report No.8. This contains some important information in connection with Bose. We have ever since heard that Bose has been refused permission to return to India and there is some effort to whip up a big campaign in his support. I think that the information contained here would justify us in not very seriously supporting this campaign. A question has been formed for the House of Commons and I think that from the information it is a good job that Bose is not allowed to return to India to further complicate a difficult situation for our comrades.

Sd/- Gordon" [78]

It is still unknown who these Gordon and Charlie Johnson were. But it is quite evident from this letter that neither they themselves nor their comrades in India wanted Bose to return to his own country. It may be assumed that the comrades belonged to the Communist Party of India. Probably they were under the apprehension that Bose, with his overwhelming popularity in India might jeopardize their chances of winning mass support in their favour.

Bose, however, wanted to have 'Samyavada' – an Indian concept that means literally 'the doctrine of synthesis or equality' based on the ideal of nationalism and made some prophecies about the future of Communism in his *Indian Struggle*. He said:

"Communism today has no sympathy with Nationalism in any form and the Indian movement is a Nationalist movement – a movement for the national liberation of the Indian people. Secondly, Russia is now on her defensive and has little interest in provoking a world revolution, though the Communist International may still endeavour to keep up appearances. The recent pacts between Russia and other capitalist countries and the written or unwritten conditions inherent in such pacts as also her membership of the League of Nations, have seriously compromised the position of Russia as a revolutionary power. Moreover, Russia is too preoccupied in her internal industrial reorganization and in her preparation for meeting the Japanese menace on her Eastern flank and is too anxious to maintain friendly relations with the Great Powers, to show any active interest in countries like India. Thirdly, while many of the economic ideas of Communism would make a strong appeal to Indians, there are other ideas, which will make a contrary effect. Owing to the close association between the Church and the State in Russian history and to the existence of an organized Church, Communism in Russia has grown to be anti- religious and atheistic. In India, on the contrary, there being no organized Church among the Indians and there being no association between the Church and the State, there is no feeling against religion as such. Fourthly, the materialistic interpretation of history, which seems to be a cardinal point in Communist theory will not find unqualified acceptance in India, even among those who would be disposed to accept the economic contents of Communism."[79]

Unfortunately, however, Report Number 8 stated to be enclosed with the letter of Gordon mentioned above, containing interesting information about Bose, was missing in the Russian Archive from where the Asiatic Society researchers recovered the document.

Bose, with his pragmatic, ideology-free stance and the image of a rebel, received allegiance from the revolutionaries of Bengal who looked upto him as their undisputed leader. They knew that he preferred uncompromising militancy of a mass movement as he said in June 1933 that the citadel of British rule no longer could count on a submissive and friendly civil population to sustain it.

Krishnadas's letter occupied a very important place as regards British accusations against Bose. Some of the accusations were false and blown out of proportion to justify the severity of persecution to which no Congress leader except Bose was subjected as long as he was within the control of the British power. Later, when Gandhi, rising above petty factionalism, could comprehend the totality of Bose's contribution to India's independence, it was already too late to heal the wound the estrangement had caused over a considerable period of time.

REFERENCES

1. Bose, Subhas Chandra, *Indian Pilgrim*, cited by Leonard Gordon, in Brothers against Raj, Penguin Books Ltd., India, 1990, p.64.
2. Bose, Subhas Chandra, *The Indian Struggle 1920-'42*, Oxford University Press, New Delhi, 1997, p.191
3. Ibid., pp. 259-260.
3A. Ibid. p. 358
4. Hindustan Times Sept 3, 1995.
4A. Das, Sitanshu, Subhas : A Political Biography, Rupa & Co., p. 147.
4B. Silvestri, Michael, "The Sinn Fein of India", The Journal of British Studies, Vol. 39, No. 4, (Oct. 2000), pp. 454-486.
5. Wood's Private Papers, National Archives, New Delhi.
5A. Ibid.
5B. File No. 749/1930, Home (Poll), State Archive, Govt. of West Bengal.
6. Private Papers of Subhas Chandra Bose, National Archives, New Delhi.
7. Wood's Private Papers, National Archives, New Delhi.
8. The combination of black police uniforms and tan army outfits gave

The Years of Exile (1933-1938) 183

rise to the term Black and Tans for the ex-First World War soldiers used by the British to crush the revolutionaries in Ireland.

9. Mosley, Sir Oswald, *My Life*, Thomas Nelson and Sons Ltd., 1970, Britain, pp.160-161.
10. *A Bridge of Words* (Letters exchanged by M.K.Gandhi and G.D.Birla), G.D.Birla Centenary Publications, Calcutta. 1994, p. 28.
11. Samanta, Amiya, *Terrorism in Bengal*, Vol. 1, (A compilation of documents), Government of West Bengal, 1995, p.748.
11B. Sykes, Christopher, Tormented Loyalty, Harper and Row Publishers, New York, p. 352.
12. *Collected Works of M. K. Gandhi*, Vol. LVI, p. 137
13. Ibid. pp.150-151.
14. Parikh, Narahari D., *Sardar Vallabhbhai Patel*, (the original in Gujrati), Navajiban Publishing House, Ahmedabad, first edition 1956, p.48.
15. Parikh, Nathalal, "Reminiscences", included in *Life and Works of Netaji Subhas Chandra Bose*, edited by P.D.Saggi, Overseas Publishing House, Bombay.
16. *Collected Works of M. K. Gandhi*, Vol. LVI, [letter in Gujrati language] dated 9th Nov. 1933, Publications Division of Government of India, © Nava Jivan Trust, Ahmedabad, pp.199-200.
17. Gandhi, Rajmohan, *Patel, A Life*, Navajiban Publishing House, Ahmedabad, 1990, p. 238.
18. Bose wrote to Gandhi on 6th April 1939 from Jealgora: "May I say in this connection that if there is anything in life on which I pride myself, it is this that I am the son of a gentleman and as such a gentleman. Deshabandhu Das often used to tell us, 'life is larger than politics'. That lesson I have learnt from him, I shall not remain in the political field one single day if by doing so I shall fall from the standards of gentlemanliness, which are so deeply ingrained in my mind from infancy and which I feel are in my blood." Netaji Subhas Chandra Bose, Correspondence and Selected Documents 1930-1942, edited by Ravindra Kumar, Inter-India Publications, New Delhi 1992, pp. 297-298.
19. Private Papers of Woods, National Archives
19A. Netaji : Collected works, Vol. II, p. 365.
20. Ibid. (letter written by Bose from Geneva on 20/2/1934).
21. Private Papers of Bose, National Archives
22. File No. 44/56/34, Home Poll., National Archives
23. Ibid.

24. Ibid.
25. IOR, File No. LIP & J/7/793, p. 275, Question no. 5, dated 9/12/1935, cited by Nanda Mukherjee in *Subhas Chandra Bose, British Press, Intelligence and Parliament*, Jayasree Prakashan Calcutta, 1981, pp. 110-111
26. Ibid.
27. File no. 44/56/34, Home Poll., National Archives
28. Ibid.
29. Ibid.
30. Ibid.
31. Majumdar, Nepal, *Rabindranath O Subhas Chandra*, (in Bengali), Saraswat Library, Calcutta, pp. 34-35.
32. Ibid.
33. File no. 44/56/34, Home Poll, National Archives
34. Ibid.
35. Ibid.
36. Ibid.
37. Ibid
38. Ibid.
38A. Ibid.
38B. Das, Sitanshu, A Political Biography, Rupa & Co., p. 164.
39. Interview of the author with Leonard Gordon in Ballygunge Place, Calcutta on 25th January, 2004
40. Woods Collections, National Archives
41. Private Papers of Bose, Sl. No. 14.1
42. Ibid. Sl No.1 0
43. Ibid.
44. Ibid. Sl.No. 11, N A
45. Ibid. Sl No. 13
46. Ibid. Sl. No. 15
46A. Silvestri, Michael, The Journal of British Studies, Vol. 39, Oct. 2000.
47. Private Papers of Bose, p. 56.
48. Bose, Nimai Sadhan, *Desh Nayak Subhas Chandra*, (in Bengali), p. 177
48A. Bose, Nimai Sadhan, *Desh Nayak Subhas Chandra* (in Bengali), p.183.

The Years of Exile (1933-1938)

49. IOR, pp. 206-207, cited in Subhas Chandra Bose, *British Press, Intelligence and Parliament* by Nanda Mukherjee.
50. *Who's Who in British Parliament*, Vol 4, A Biographical Dictionary of the House of Commons, ed. Michael Stenton, Stephen Less, the Harvester Press, Sussex 1981.
51. IOR, p.189
52. Ibid. p. 157-158
53. Ibid. File No. *L/P* & J/7/793, P. 189, cited by N. Mukherjee (Ibid.) p. 117.
53A. Ibid. p.157-58, cited by N. Mukherjee in *Subhas Chandra Bose British Press, Intelligence and Parliament*, p.119.
54. Ibid. p. 157-158, in Mukherjee, (Ibid.) p. 119
55. Basu, Krishna, *Prasanga Subhas Chandra*, (in Bengali), Ananda Publishers, Calcutta, 1997, p.112
56. *Selected Works of Subhas Chandra Bose*, Vol. 3, chief editor Ravindra Kumar
57. Das, Sitanshu, *Subhas Chandra, A Political Biography*, Rupa & Co. New Delhi, 2001, p. 89
58. *Daily News*, Nagpore, 23/4/1936.
59. *Amritabazar Patrika*, 27/3/1936
60. *Collected Works of Netaji*, Vol.2, pp.187-188
61. Ibid. Vol. 3, Appendix 9, pp. 186-187
61A. Op. cit. Subhas Chandra : A Pol. biography, p. 92.
62. Basu, Nimai Sadhan, *Desh Nayak Subhas Chandra*, (in Bengali), p. 177
62A. Interview of the author with Amalendu Ghosh, a veteran Bengal revolutionary (Bengal Volunteers), at his residence in Calcutta on 8/11/1997
63. File No. 22/92/1936-Home Poll, National Archives, New Delhi
64. Markandeya, Subodh, p. 107
65. Basu, Shankari Prasad, p. 200
66. Ibid. pp. 203-204
67. Ibid. pp. 205-206
68. *Amrita Bazar Patrika & Hindustan Standard*, 29/1 0/ 1937
69. Basu, Shankari Prasad, p. 257
69A. History Sheet of Madame Cama, National Archives, New Delhi
70. Ibid.

71. Ibid.
71A. Mitrokhin, Leonid, "A Triple Trap" in *Soviet-Land*, May 1991, No.5
72. Mitrokhin's Leonid, in Soviet Land, April 1991, no. 4,
73. Interview of the author with Amar Chatterjee, a veteran Bengal revolutionary (BV), on 31/1/1998 at his Calcutta residence, also with Amalendu Ghosh (BV) on 22/11/1997 at his Calcutta residence.
74. *Daily Worker* January 1938, cited by Shankari Prasad Basu, p. 292
75. *Subhas Chandra Bose Papers*, Sl. No. 15.2, National Archives, New Delhi
76. Basu, Shankari Prasad, *Samakalin Bharate Subhas Chandra*, Vol. 2, Mandal Book House, Calcutta, 1998, pp.287-288
77. Bose, S.C., *Indian Struggle*, Vol. 2, Appendix (Reprint of a Report of an interview of Bose with Rajni Palme Dutt, the well-known Communist leader in London, published in the *Daily Worker*, London, January 24, 1938).
77A. IB Report dated 24/6/1930 mentioned in the History Sheet of 1932, Home Poll., 1932, National Archives, New Delhi
78. *Indo-Russian Relations 1917-1947*, Part 2, edited by Ray, Vasudevan and Dutta Gupta, Asiatic Society, Calcutta, p. 256
79. Bose, S.C., *Indian Struggle*, pp. 352-353.

5
THE UNCOMPROMISING LONER (1938-1941)

The Presidentship of the Indian National Congress was the most coveted honour that any freedom fighter could hope for in India before Independence.

Bose was one of the youngest persons to be elected President of the Congress.

His election was in every way a fitting climax to his 17-year old public life, six years of which he spent in exile in Europe and more than five years in different jails in India. During this short span of time, he held several high offices, like those of the Chief Executive Officer and also the Mayor of Calcutta Municipal Corporation, the Secretary of the Swarajya Party, the President of the Bengal Provincial Congress Committee, the General Secretary of the All India Congress Committee, the President of the All-India Trade Union Congress and the General Secretary of the Indian Independence League. But more than the posts Bose held, it was his relentless struggle, self-sacrifice and an indomitable spirit that brought him to the forefront of Indian freedom movement. There is no doubt about the fact that Bose was hell-bent on the task of destroying the British regime in India. The then Secretary of State for India, Lord Zetland once commented, "Mr. Bose is a man who, while of great ability, has always directed his ability for destructive purposes". Quite obviously Bose was the most dreaded enemy of the British during those days.

When Bose was set free on 17th March 1937, Gandhi's secretary Mahadev Desai was one of the first important visitors to meet him in Calcutta. Gandhi sent a letter to Amrit Kaur on the 17th March 1937 in which he mentioned that "Desai had gone to Calcutta to see Subhas Chandra Bose."[1]

On the day of his release, Bose was brought from the Calcutta Medical College Hospital where he was admitted for treatment, to his Elgin Road residence to meet his mother. When he reached home, one of the Deputy Commissioners of Police came with the order for his unconditional release from detention.[2]

Gandhi sent Desai on 16th March 1937 to Calcutta to pay a visit to Bose, that is, before the latter was released. Probably Gandhi had prior information regarding Bose's release, or Desai was instructed to meet Bose at the Hospital where he was interned. Whatever might have been the case it proves that Desai was asked to see Bose because Gandhi wanted to obtain a status report on Bose's mental and physical health conditions. It may be assumed that Gandhi had Bose in mind at that time for the Congress Presidency for 1938. As a matter of fact, he could feel the pulse of the people who wanted a young and dynamic leader in the post of the Congress president to lead the country. Among the younger Congress leaders Bose was the most popular in those days. It may also be noted that in keeping with the Government of India Act 1935, Congress ministry was set up in seven out of eleven provinces generating in the minds of the people hopes and aspirations for a bright future in the years to come. They had a feeling that these ministries, composed of their own deputies, would surely fulfil their hopes and aspirations.

After the withdrawal of the Civil Disobedience movement, a feeling of resentment was growing towards Gandhian policies and programmes within the Indian National Congress itself mainly due to the criticisms by the Leftists. It may be noted here that in October 1934, Congress Socialist Party came into being under the leadership of Acharya Narendra Dev, J.P.Narayan, Achyuta Patwardhan, Minu Masani and Asok Mehta. Bose in March 1935 greeted the advent of this party in a statement issued from Vienna in which he said that he wanted this party to shoulder the responsibility of reconstructing India of the future. Since he was a believer in socialism, he welcomed the formation of the CSP wholeheartedly and there was a remarkable reawakening noticeable amongst the peasants, workers, students and intellectuals in those days and the All India Kisan Sabha came into being under the leadership of Swami Sahajananda Saraswati. Needless to say that behind all these developments, Bose's charismatic appeal was the main catalyst.

In September 1934 a disheartened Gandhi wrote to Ballavbhai Patel that he had decided to sever all connections with the Congress in the interest of the Party and the nation as a whole. He said that although he knew that Jawaharlal Nehru's love for him would never welcome this decision but since there was a growing difference of opinion between him and many other Congressmen, with the number of the socialists ever- increasing within the party itself, leading the organization from the forefront in spite of serious differences, would mean some kind of violence which ought to be avoided. Accordingly, in October 1934, at the Bombay session of Indian National Congress, Gandhi severed all formal relations with the organization and announced that from then on, he would keep his watchful eyes on the party from a distance. But even after this, there was virtually no change in the way he led the party. In fact, his main purpose here was to tackle his critics and opponents in a novel way and strategically he wanted to fulfill his purpose keeping Jawaharlal Nehru, supposedly the leading socialist within Congress, in front. He wanted to direct Congress in a reform-oriented way based on certain Acts of Parliament and obviously far removed from any kind of militancy.

In August 1935 the Government of India Act was passed by the British Parliament. Prior to that, when the broad outlines of the said Act were indicated in a White Paper in March 1933, the well-known industrialist G.D.Birla started giving assurance to the important dignitaries in the Government both in England as well as in India that Gandhi would no longer take recourse to any popular movement, rather he was more anxious than ever before to implement the ensuing constitutional reform proposals. Gandhi, obviously, had tacit consent behind this assurance.[3] But it was kept a secret before the countrymen and the Congress. Only the staunch Gandhi-loyalists like Patel, Rajagopalachari and Rajendra Prasad knew about it. With the initiative of Birla, Patel discussed the matter with Mr. Craik, Home Member of the Executive Council of the Viceroy and Gandhi was satisfied with this discussion.[4]

G.D. Birla was the channel of communication between Gandhi and the British ministers and politicians as he was a regular visitor in England during those days.

They did not, however, inform Nehru about this plan because they knew that Nehru would follow none other than Gandhi and his followers no matter what he said or preached as a radical. When Lord Halifax, in 1935, wanted to know from Birla, while in London, whether Nehru was inclined towards the Left, he said that he did not really know although Nehru was always found to be talking in a progressive and radical way.[5]

Although his promise to the British was kept a secret, Gandhi's preference for a constitutional reform was not incomprehensible to anyone. From July 1933, he had been advising Satyamurthi, Dr. Ansari, K.M.Munshi, Asaf Ali, Nariman and a few others to form a legislative party in order to enter the legislature. He even wanted to revive the Swarajya Party, which he opposed during the 1920's for its strategy of council entry. Now he felt that it had to be revived for the sake of participating in the election for the provincial legislatures.

Hence, it became quite clear before the Lucknow Congress of 1936 that come what may, Gandhi would certainly go the constitutional way against the wishes of the leftists. Sensing the probability of a conflictful situation in the ensuing Lucknow Congress, he felt the necessity of selecting Nehru once again as the President of the party. When Nehru accepted the offer, Gandhi felt relieved and at the same time the leftists became hopeful about the possibility of a renewed struggle against imperialism under Nehru's progressive leadership.

In Lucknow Congress, Nehru expressed, in unequivocal terms, his admiration for socialism, opposed the Act of 1935, emphasized the necessity of having a broad-based anti-imperialistic united front; in other words, whatever the leftists wanted, was largely reflected in his speech. But what happened in practice was rather disheartening for the leftists. Nehru, as per Gandhi's wishes and also due to the pressure of the rightists like Patel, Prasad and Rajagopalachari, retreated from his progressive stand. In his working committee, he selected fourteen members out of which ten were known to have been opposed to his professed socialist principles. Apart from Bose, three other well-known socialists, namely, Narendra Dev, Jayprakash Narayan and Achyuta Patwardhan were included, although it was Gandhi's decision as the latter thought that the inclusion of a few socialists in the working committee would help minimize the influence of the revolutionaries on the youth.[6]

Socialism, however, was nowhere to be traced in the resolutions adopted in the Lucknow Congress. Nehru did not change the content of his speech although these resolutions had been adopted before he read out his presidential address. He had an opportunity of directing the freedom movement from the forefront in collaboration with the left forces in an uncompromising way, but he did not want to get himself involved in any direct confrontation with the Government to avoid the wrath of the Gandhians. Nehru's biographer S.Gopal commented that it was kind of an intellectual opportunism reflected in the quest for contentment to be found in some vague idealism.[7]

The Lucknow Congress, about which the leftists were extremely hopeful and enthusiastic, proved to be a victory for the rightists. A letter written by G.D.Birla to Purushottamdas Thakurdas, another industrialist, on the 20th April 1936, just a few days after the Congress session, gives an assessment of the role of Nehru in the Lucknow Congress. It says that Gandhi kept his promises and made an arrangement so that no new promises were made. Nehru's proposals had been thrown into the waste paper basket because the resolutions passed were all against the major policies indicated in his presidential address. He was eager to hold his idealism in high esteem but he realized that it was not possible to implement it and hence never pressurized anyone for its implementation.[8]

During the presidentship of Jawaharlal Nehru, who always tried to project himself as a progressive intellectual, the provisions of the Act of 1935 dealing with provincial autonomy, could be implemented with the formation of Congress ministries in several provinces. Gandhi wanted, now, to implement the controversial recommendations of the said Act for a federation. If federalism could be introduced under the presidentship of Bose, a formidable leftist, then the opposition coming from the side of the leftists in general might be counteracted, he thought. He also assumed that Bose would give up his non-compromising stance and become a loyal Gandhian on being elected President of Congress but soon he was proved wrong. Bose was made up of a different mettle altogether, which even a veteran politician of Gandhi's stature could not guage at that point of time.

When in England, Bose told Lord Zetland on the 17th of January, 1938, that the federal scheme could not be accepted under any circumstances. He said the same thing to Rajni Palme Dutt, the leader of the Communist Party of Great Britain in the same year in an interview in London which was

The Uncompromising Loner (1938-1941) 193

published in the 24th January issue of *The Daily Worker*.

On 26th April 1937 Bose came to Allahabad to pay a visit to Gandhi before the meeting of the Congress Working Committee there. It was their first meeting in six years. In June 1937 Gandhi asked Miraben (Madeleine Slade) to be a guest of Dr. and Mrs. N.R.Dharamvir at Dalhousie with whom Bose was staying at that time for his recuperation. The Dharamvir family was very close to Bose from his days in London. Bose, it may be assumed, was aware of Gandhi's desire that Miraben should go to stay with the Dharamvir family in Dalhousie for change. He sent a wire to Miraben inviting her to come and stay at Dr. Dharamvir's house. There was another invitation for Miraben from a friend at Dalhousie but Gandhi advised her to put up with the Dharamvirs while Bose was there. On 20th June 1937, however, Gandhi wrote to Amrit Kaur to say that Bose should not leave Dalhousie in a hurry before his complete recovery. "He should be thoroughly restored for the task in front of him."[9]

From November 1937 to January 1938, Bose was in Europe and he received the news, while in London that he had been nominated President of the Indian National Congress. The proposal, to that effect, was initiated by none other than Gandhi himself.

At Haripura, the fifty-first session of Congress was held on February 19-23, 1938 on the banks of river Tapti in Gujarat, the venue was named Vithal Nagar in memory of Vithalbhai Patel.

To Bose, the goal of *Swaraj* always meant complete severance of the British connection. He said,

"The ultimate stage in our progress will be the severance of the British connection. When that severance takes place, and there is no trace left of British domination, we shall be in a position to determine our future relationship with Great Britain through a treaty of alliance voluntarily entered into by both parties. What our future relations with Great Britain will or should be, it is too early to say. That will depend to a large extent, on the attitude of the British people themselves."[10]

The most remarkable part of his Presidential address was his plea for planned economic development along socialistic lines. There was no ambiguity ever in his thinking. When family planning was unheard of, Bose pointed out that unchecked growth of population might pose a danger to planned development. Even the British writers admired his perceptions, as Gerard Corr observes:

"Bose was ahead of his time, for the people were not ready for this sort of direct, to the point bluntness about the Indian condition....He spoke what was on his mind, not always with due regard to the consequences."[11]

Bose decided to seek re-election as the Congress President in 1939. As a matter of fact, he was nominated by a number of Provincial Congress Committees. But his decision evoked a violent reaction amongst members of the High Command including Gandhi who wanted Pattabhi Sitaramayya as the next President. Bose was so confident about his victory that on the day of the election, he told the media people :

"I am mathematically certain that I shall beat Sitaramayya", and he was proved right as he won the election held on the 29th of Jan. 1939, with a lead of 205 votes. Bose got 1580 votes out of which 404 were from Bengal and the rest from the other provinces of India. His victory was due to the unified support given to him by the revolutionaries and the Leftists in the Party. A disheartened Gandhi declared Pattabhi's defeat as his own and the events that followed Bose's victory led ultimately to his resignation from the post of the President. Gandhi could not adjust his exalted ideal of non-violence with the ground realities and did not hesitate to trample all democratic norms only because of the apprehension that Bose might take the path of militancy for achieving independence. He was very much aware of the support of the uncompromising revolutionaries at the back of Bose which annoyed him the most.

It may be pointed out here that although Gandhi-Subhas conflict was mainly due to their difference of opinion on the question of non-violence, but Gandhi, if one may recall, was actively involved, during the Ist World War, in the British war-efforts. He recruited volunteers for the British Indian Army. Was this act in keeping with the doctrine of non-violence ?

Bose's effort, however, for a Left-wing consolidation within the Congress movement did not meet with success due to various reasons. At times, it seemed as if it was Bose, not the alien rulers against whom the struggle was going on.

In March 1939, at the 52nd session of the Congress at Tripuri, the Gandhian leaders became very active against Bose who was seriously ill at that time. Gandhi did not attend the session. Sarat Bose read out the Presidential address on behalf of his younger brother, in which Bose said that within the next six months, another world war was going to start and the Congress should give the British Government an ultimatum regarding independence. An alternative government would be formed if the demand of the Congress was not fulfilled by the foreign rulers and the final phase of the freedom movement would commence which required at least one lakh well-trained volunteers. Bose's Tripuri address marked a departure from the routine anti-war position the Congress had taken for more than a decade. Although war did not break out, he felt that the unstable balance in the European situation offered India an opportunity which Congress should immediately grab. He was willing to prepare for the "final advance" in the direction of *Swaraj* before the old imperial powers and the Axis countries reached a new state of equilibrium which could pave the way for the continuance of status quo in India. Bose wanted to avoid that possibility by all means. He had an extra-ordinary foresight which no other political leader in those days possessed.

Earlier the British politicians had talks with important Indians like Jawaharlal Nehru, M.A. Jinnah and G. D. Birla on the European crisis. Their purpose was not far to seek. Since the First World War, apart from the nationalist revolutionaries, most of the Congress leaders gave Britain unconditional support. Indian leaders, for historical and linguistic reasons, used to gather knowledge about world developments from British sources. It was therefore easy for the British to influence the nationalist intelligentsia of India through talks. Bose obviously belonged to a different category altogether and the British was well aware of it.

Bose, due to the British ban on his entry to their country, spent 1933-1936 in Europe largely as a scholar and an unofficial ambassador of India abroad. He acquired a thorough knowledge of the European situation unequalled by any other leader in the Congress hierarchy at that time. His first-hand knowledge about the international affairs led him to believe that very soon another world war was going to start and he considered socialist USSR as a dependable source of support for India's freedom struggle.

Bose said in his presidential address: "there is no doubt that once there is stable peace in Europe, whether through a Four-Power Pact or through some other means, Great Britain will adopt a strong Empire policy. She is now showing some signs of trying to conciliate the Arabs as against the Jews in Palestine. ...In my opinion, therefore, we should submit our national demand to the British Government in the form of an ultimatum."[12]

The leaders in the Tripuri session did not have the mentality of pondering over the address of the President. Instead, they were engrossed in the thought of reinstating Gandhian leadership in the Party by hook or crook. Govind Ballav Pant brought forward a resolution that the Working Committee should be selected by the new President, in consultation with Gandhi. It is difficult to accept that Gandhi did not know anything about the Pant Resolution when it was moved in the A.I.C.C. and then at the open session at Tripuri. As a matter of fact, the power to form the Working Committee was solely of the President; hence, the rule of consultation with Gandhi did not have any justification whatsoever. The point was made amply clear by the Chairman of the Reception Committee, Seth Govindadas, and a well-known Gandhite, who said:

'The position held by Mussolini amongst the Fascists, Hitler amongst the Nazis, and Stalin amongst the Communists, is also held by Mahatma Gandhi amongst the Congressites. It is true that in the written Constitution of the Congress Party, there is no specific position for him as such, but nobody will be able to dispute the fact that choosing the nominee of Mahatma Gandhi as the President of the Congress and most of the members of the Working Committee to be chosen from his candidates, has become a custom."[13]

Incidentally, the way Seth Govindadas and his compatriots hailed Gandhi by shouting, "Hindusthan ka Hitler ka Jai" shocked Rabindra Nath Tagore enormously. Nehru, who was always very much vocal against Fascism, did not utter a single word in protest against this kind of a delirium. Besides, a pertinent question may be raised here. Bose, the duly elected President of the Congress, was suspended from the Party on disciplinary grounds. The act of Seth Govindadas and his followers seem to be more serious and offensive calling for the same punishment, if not more. But no action was taken against the latter for openly hailing Fascism from the Congress platform. The reasons why Rabindra Nath Tagore, who had enough confidence in Nehru's leadership, lost his faith in the latter and conferred on Bose the revered title of 'Desh Gaurav' are not far to seek.

Pant resolution was passed in the AICC by 218-135 votes. The followers of M. N. Roy backed out already, now it was the Congress Socialist Party that preferred, very conveniently, to remain neutral. In all probability, the Socialist Party, that had been supporting Bose in all matters prior to Tripuri, opted, this time, to stay by the side of the larger group for their own safety. The CPI decided to support Gandhi on this crucial issue. They had supported Bose's re-election as Congress President in January 1939, but at the Tripuri session, they stayed away from him. In fact before the Communists arrived at Tripuri, they received an instruction from the CPGB leader Harry Pollitt asking them not to support any move that might create a rift in the Indian National Congress. This was the same policy Jawaharlal Nehru pursued when Bose decided to contest for a second term against the wishes of the Patel-led group of Congress Working Committee members. The CPGB's instruction was later explained in terms of the Soviet foreign policy requirements in Europe where the British government was still hoping for a settlement with Mussolini. It was said that Bose's move might jeopardize Congress unity in India and thus weaken the 'Popular Front' line against Fascism, which the Comintern demanded from its allies.[14].

Since Bose himself was very cautious about any move that might lead to a split in the INC, it may be deduced with certainty that the Indian Communists must have had other reasons behind their decision not to support Bose than the fear of a split in the INC.

He wanted Gandhi's approval without fully foregoing the interest of the Congress Left-wing and the radicals who had voted for his second term as the Congress President. Already the Communists (or the 'National Front') were maintaining a safe distance from Bose who was then the foremost leader of the Congress Left. Whether their action was prompted by their old prejudice or dictated by the CPGB, acting on behalf of the Comintern, or both, remains a mystery till date. P. C. Joshi, the General Secretary of the CPI, who refused to approve Bose's plea for non-violent, anti-British Satyagraha, said that Bose's Forward Bloc had to be opposed not because it was "too Left" but because it was "the disruptive agency of the bourgeoisie". "The proletarian technique" of struggle was already introduced in India, and there was therefore no reason why the communists should go with Bose's suggestion of non-violent non-cooperation if the British refused to concede India's national demands.[15]

Thus to withdraw support from Bose at a crucial hour before the outbreak of war, the CPI swerved to an ultra-Left position when they were in fact pursuing the National Front policy of not alienating the Congress stalwarts who were opposed to Bose. The crux of the matter is that the communists, for a long time, saw him as a political rival whose increasing popularity in the years 1938-1940, they did not like at all. In fact Bose's stance of not being guided by any imported ideological "ism", was incomprehensible to the Indian communists. Bose focused on the issue of national liberation only, for the achievement of which he was ready to tread any path or follow any device without any prejudice against or leaning towards any particular "ism". The Communists found him unamenable to the policies they prescribed from time to time. Bose wanted them at his side within the common platform of the Congress Party, particularly the Left wing, but he was conscious of their limitations. He was aware of the fact that the communists lacked mass support and they were in need of "a proper national perspective". He wrote in his *Indian Struggle*:

"When in September 1938, it appeared to the intelligent observer that Mahatma Gandhi for some reason or other, had lost dynamism and initiative, the following possibilities for developing an alternative leadership existed in India:

(1) Through Pandit Nehru

Pandit Nehru deliberately neglected this opportunity largely because of his internal weakness, lack of self-confidence and lack of revolutionary perspective.

(2) Through M.N.Roy

M.N.Roy did form a party and did talk of alternative leadership. But there was some defect in his character owing to which within a short time, he made more enemies than friends. Nevertheless, he still had a future but with the outbreak of the present war, he began to advocate unconditional co-operation with the British Government and that brought about his political doom.

(3) Through the Congress Socialist Party

Between 1934 and 1938, this party had the best chance of developing as the future national party of India, but it failed. ..The C.S.Party lacked a clear revolutionary perspective from the outset. It began to function more as a parliamentary opposition within the Congress than as the spearhead of a revolutionary movement. After September 1939, the leaders of this party were won over by Gandhi and Nehru and that blasted the future of the Party.

(4) Through the Communist Party

When the CSP failed to rise to the occasion, there was an opportunity for the Communist Party then functioning under the name 'National Front' to come to the forefront. But the Communist Party, besides being numerically small, lacked a proper national perspective and could not develop as the organ of national struggle. Not having its roots in the soil, this party very often erred in estimating a particular situation or crisis and consequently adopted a wrong policy."[16]

Bose tried hard to convince the Congress Socialist Party about the necessity of forming a Left bloc for rallying all the radical and progressive elements in the Congress but unfortunately the CSP did not pay heed to what he said. According to Bose, the CSP talked too much about Socialism, which was not the need of the hour. The country's immediate requirements were an uncompromising struggle against British imperialism whereas Gandhism was wedded to non-violence, not at all an effective method of struggle. It contemplated a compromise with Britain, which would ultimately lead to partition of the country, he thought. Bose lamented over the lack of understanding on the part of the Gandhians, of the importance of the international crisis created by the War for achieving Indian independence. He felt the necessity of a party, which would remedy these defects and bring about total liberation of the motherland.

After a few months of controversy and correspondence, Bose, the President, had to resign from the post. It was good for the Old Guard, the hard core Gandhians as well as for Bose himself who could explore a new avenue for service and self-sacrifice for the motherland.

On the 3rd of May, 1939, Bose announced the formation of the Forward Bloc at a large public meeting in Calcutta. This was to be an association of all Left-wing parties and the revolutionary groups functioning within the Congress. Prior to that, on the 28th April, 1939, the Congress leaders, at the AICC session of Calcutta, had accepted his resignation hurriedly without making any request to him for a reconsideration of the decision. Bose did not resign from the Indian National Congress though, he only formed a radical group within the Congress itself naming it the Forward Bloc.

At the AICC session in Calcutta, Rajendra Prasad was designated the new President against the norms of the Party. Sarojini Naidu, who was the chairperson of that session, announced that although she knew that she might have to face the charge of norm violation but the office of the President could not, under any circumstances, lie vacant.

It was in 1939 only that the Freedom Bloc of Burma under the leadership of Dr. Ba Maw came into being. Ba Maw was the prime minister under the Act of 1935 from March 1937 to February 1939. During the war, he was in prison under the authority of the British Government. When Japan, having ousted the British, granted Burma independence on the 1st of August 1943, Ba Maw became the Head of the State. The Freedom Bloc of Burma was formed several months after Bose's Forward Bloc. Burma was a part of India under the British at that time and connections between Calcutta and Rangoon (now known as Yangon) were very close in those days. Probably Ba Maw saw in Bose's Forward Bloc a model he could introduce in his own land to bring together different nationalist groups on a common platform. The immediate objective of the Forward Bloc "was an uncompromising struggle with British Imperialism for winning India's independence. To this end, all possible means should be employed and the Indian people should not be hampered by any philosophical notions like Gandhian non-violence or any sentimentalism like Nehru's anti-Axis foreign policy. The Bloc stood for a realistic foreign policy and a post-war order in India on a Socialist basis."[17]

Bose became the President of the Forward Bloc with Shardul Singh Caveesher and Lala Shankar Lal as the Vice Presidents and Pundit Bishhambhar Tripathy, K.F.Nariman and Satya Ranjan Bakshi as the General Secretaries. In Bombay at the All India Forward Bloc Conference, he stated the three main objectives of the Party, such as, to unite all the Leftists, to achieve unity in Congress through the Left coordination, and thirdly to start a movement for complete independence after having achieved Congress unity and a favourable atmosphere. Only the primary members of Congress could join the Forward Bloc and the Bloc would accept the Congress Constitution and its programmes, but the kind of constitutionalism and reformist tendencies that had developed in Congress, needed to be eliminated and it would be the duty of the Bloc to generate a revolutionary spirit in the minds of the people in general and to start a movement for uprooting the British regime from India utilizing the war situation and subsequently introduce socialism in the country.

Realizing the fact that it would not be possible for all the

Left parties to join the Forward Bloc, Bose formed the Left Coordination Committee in which J. P .Narayan, Acharya Narendra Dev of the Congress Socialist Party, P .C.Joshi and Somnath Lahiri of the CPI, Swami Sahajananda and N.G.Ranga of the Kisan Sabha, M.N.Roy and Karnick of the Roy group, Satya Bakshi and Tripathy of the Forward Bloc joined. A weekly magazine Forward Bloc started getting published from 5th August 1939 edited by Satya Bakshi, Gopal Haldar and Binay Ghosh. Somnath Lahiri and Panchugopal Bhaduri of the CPI, who were also members of the Bengal Provincial Congress Committee, used to cooperate with them wholeheartedly. The Communists were on the side of Bose at that time. As the Communist Party, in those days, lacked organizational strength and public support, it had to work in a clandestine manner, within the Congress and the CSP for its survival. When Germany attacked the Soviet Union during the War, their attitude towards Bose underwent a massive change that led them to go against him to the extent of calling him names. Their blind devotion to Soviet Union annihilated their political foresight and the nationalistic spirit. It would be relevant to point out here that in Presidency College, Calcutta, at that time, a "*Communist Thengao*" (Thrash the Communists) Party was formed by the patriotic students who were ready to beat up the Communists to give them a good lesson.[18]

Ironically, Bose still considered Gandhi 'the Man of India's Destiny', that is why immediately after the Nagpur Conference of the Forward Bloc, he went to Wardha to make his last appeal to Gandhi for giving a clarion call to the masses for the final assault on the British utilizing the opportunity presented by the Second World War. But he was disappointed with the attitude of Gandhi who, in unambiguous terms, expressed his inability to even bless him for a movement which he considered to be inopportune at that moment. Bose realized that no help could be expected from Gandhi and his followers. He met the Muslim League leader Mohammad Ali Jinna whom he found obsessed with his demand for Pakistan, which he thought could be attained with the help of the British. That Jinnah was not wrong had been proved a few years later at the cost of India's unity and integrity, but that is a different story altogether.

By the time Bose reached Calcutta from Wardha where he met Gandhi, he resolved with a strong determination to start a movement with the help of the revolutionaries on the basis of a new plan. He started holding meetings and organized rallies in various places on a regular basis to motivate people in favour of an uncompromising freedom struggle.

Bose resigned from the Presidentship of the INC, not from the INC itself as is commonly believed even today. As the *Swarajya* Party was formed in the past within the Congress itself by C.R.Das and Motilal Nehru to press their demands for complete independence, in the same way, FB was formed by Bose within the mother party itself to move forward with the demand for complete independence without any compromise formula. The Bengal revolutionaries, particularly the Bengal Volunteers and Anushilan Samity gave him assurance that come what may, they would not budge an inch from their revolutionary stand and fight till the end shoulder to shoulder with Bose.

The Congress High Command suspended the Bengal Provincial Congress Committee for reasons best known to themselves but this action could not destroy the indomitable spirit of Bose and his followers. An S.B. report states:

"In a meeting (4000) at Shraddhananda Park on 2.6.40, organized by the suspended BPCC, under the Presidentship of Prof. Jyotish Chandra Ghosh, the speakers, while explaining the resolutions of the last Dacca Conference, laid stress on the question of the release of political prisoners, the removal of the Hallwell Monument and the formation of a Defence Corps on a non-party basis and bitterly criticized the policy of the Gandhians with regard to the national struggle.

"Subhas Bose vehemently attacked the Press Censor Officer and threatened to expose him if he failed to correct himself within a week. As a protest, the newspapers should close down till the normal conditions returned and suggested that people should depend on verbal report for local news and on the radio for foreign news. He remarked that the loss of strength of British Imperialism ̄ their only enemy ̄ really counted towards their success. He bitterly attacked the shortsightedness of the British politicians, which, he said, was responsible for their continued 'gallant retreats' and the advancement of the Germans with terrific speed. Criticizing the attitude of Gandhi and the other Rightist leaders for not embarrassing the British, he remarked that it showed signs of their mental and moral paralysis. The Leftists with warm blood in them, wanted to take advantage of the situation and so have started the struggle in right earnest. Referring to the Citizens' Defence Corps, Subhas said that it would work separately from the Satyagrahis having no connection with the Congress and could not cooperate, in any way, with the Defence Army formed by the Government for the safety of British Imperialism ̄ the only enemy of India. Volunteers, some of whom wore uniforms, were present."[19]

Bose wanted to have a very strong Volunteer Corps composed of the young militant nationalists and the Leftist elements of the Congress, militarily trained and prepared to face any challenge for the achievement of freedom.

According to the same confidential report, entitled "Volunteer Corp of Subhas Bose", a volunteer rally was held at 6 Bhabani Dutta Lane, the office of the suspended B.P.C.C. in the evening of 6.6.40 attended by 40 men in plain clothes.[19B] The records of what they discussed or deliberated on, are not available but it may be assumed that the ensuing movement for the removal of Hallwell Monument might have been planned in that meeting.

On July 2, 1940, Bose led a popular demonstration for the removal of Hallwell Monument that stood as an index of defamation to Siraj-ud-daullah, the last independent Nawab of Bengal. Bose was arrested by the Fazlul Haq Government of Bengal and thrown into the Presidency Jail. The Provincial Government, however, after this incident, removed the Monument. In Bose's own words:

"The writer was then confined in prison without any trial. Long study and deliberation had convinced him about three things. Firstly, Britain would lose the war and the British Empire would break up. Secondly, in spite of being in a precarious position, the British would not hand over power to the Indian people and the latter would have to fight for their freedom. Thirdly, India would win her independence if she played her part in the war against Britain and collaborated with those powers that were fighting Britain." The conclusion he drew for himself was that India should actively enter the field of international politics.[20] He had already been in British custody eleven times, but now he felt that it would be a major political blunder if he stayed inactive in prison, while history was being made elsewhere. The British Government was determined to keep him in the prison, so long as the war lasted. As it is, they were very much perturbed by the fact that Bose, their "enemy number one", had returned from Europe to India to give the revolutionaries a fresh lease of life.

It is to be noted that Bose was not committed to any particular political ideology. He believed in the ideal of humanitarian nationalism, as did his spiritual guide Swami Vivekananda whom he considered 'the spiritual father of modern Indian nationalism'. Perhaps this is the reason why the protagonists of various ideologies, in and out of India. were antagonistic towards him. A few dates should be mentioned here to make an objective assessment of Bose's ideology-free stance. Soviet Union and Nazi Germany signed a non-aggression pact on the 23rd August 1939 and the Second World War started with the attack of Germany on Poland on the first of September, the same year. The Pact between the

Soviet Union and Germany ended on the 22nd June 1941 when the German army launched an attack on the Soviet Union violating the terms of the pact. Almost overnight, the war, which was, so long, being considered an imperialist war, became People's War to the communists. Russia attacked Japan on the 8th of August 1945, prior to which they were friends. When Bose went to Germany in 1941, the country was a good friend of Russia and Japan. Germany and Japan were hostile towards Britain but the latter was in good terms with Russia. It was, therefore, not possible for him to get help from Russia in his fight against Britain. He reached Germany on 3rd April 1941 at a time when the imperialist war was going on between the Axis and the Allied powers and there was no harm, according to the communists, in asking for help from Germany at that time. The evaluation of Bose by the Indian communists changed all on a sudden and he became a traitor and an enemy of the people in their eyes as soon as Russia was attacked by Germany. *Kirti Kisan Party*, the Punjab wing of the Communist Party, also changed its perspective totally.

During November-December 1941, a letter written by Harry Pollit, the Secretary of CPGB, was circulated with the help of the Government, amongst the inmates of the Deoli camp in which the theory of people's war propagated by the Party was explained [21] From that time onwards, the Communist Party started collaborating with the British imperialists in every possible way. Bhagatram Talwar who accompanied Bose from Peshawar to Kabul, on behalf of the *Kirti Kisan Party*, was arrested on 29th November 1941 but was released soon after presumably on the basis of assurance he gave to the Government regarding all kinds of help. After this, Bhagatram engaged himself wholeheartedly in his espionage work as a quadruple spy for Italy, Germany, Britain and Russia. He had a codename *Silver* and was known by his cover name *Kishen Chand* to Delhi Intelligence Bureau and Peter Fleming, Lord Wavell's clandestine informer sent by London.[21A]

Blind adherence to a particular ideology perhaps annihilates one's conscience and dampens one's rationality. During the 1930's and '40's, Bose's freedom struggle was evaluated in the light of an ideology by a section of the population. Each according to his own ideology tried to assess his role in the liberation movement. A particular ideological mindset may be nothing but a false consciousness within which one tries to take shelter in order to reach his goal. An individual or a party that succumbs to an ideology, refuses to accept facts which are not supportive of their mindset. Ideologies or *isms* like Nazism- Fascism, or Leninism-Stalinism are largely responsible for most of the disasters in the world. Civil society, that would hopefully be based on humanism, may be established only in an ideology-free environment and that is why the concept of de-ideolisation has been able to draw intellectual attention all over the world and strengthen itself towards the end of the 20th century.[22]

To some extent, Bose's thoughts resembled those of Kamal Ataturk of Turkey who was absolutely free from any ideological bias and ruled his country according to the requirements of his people. A strict disciplinarian, Ataturk made sure that after his death, Turkey would have a democratic government. As a result, his compatriot Ismet Inonu established subsequently a democratic government in Turkey in keeping with the liberal ideas of his predecessor.

Needless to say that in none of the writings of Bose, can one find a trace of advocacy of despotism or violence. But unlike Gandhi, he did not consider non-violence a basic or an unalterable principle to be followed at any cost or under any circumstances. As a matter of fact, no leader in those days, except the staunch Gandhians, considered non-violence as the only right method. The Marxists raise a question very often, whether Bose supported Fascism or dictatorship; they simply fail to comprehend the nature and magnitude of his ideology-free patriotism, which led him to seek help from the Axis powers.

Bose, as mentioned earlier, wanted wholeheartedly, to form a National Defence Militia, with the help of the revolutionaries, which would have a secret organization within itself. According to a secret report of the Special Branch, Calcutta,

"The leaders of the Bengal Labour Party think that the National Defence Militia proposed by Subhas Chandra Bose, will have a far-reaching role to play in the national struggle for liberation. They have also discussed the question of setting up a secret organization within the militia and keeping the different branches of the militia informed with news and orders from headquarters sent by means of invisible link."[23]

The same file mentions a report of *Ananda Bazar Patrika*, dated 11/5/1940, which says that Subhas Chandra Bose made an appeal to the people for the organization of a non-partisan volunteer brigade for the purpose of maintaining peace in the wake of the prevailing crisis generated by the war situation. Realizing the gravity of the situation, it was decided that volunteers would be taken from all sections of the population. The responsibility of recruiting volunteers had been given to Santosh Kumar Banerjee, the report said. With this purpose in view, a centre had been opened at 59A Durga Charan Daktar Road. The age of the applicant should be in between 18 to 35. The person who signed the note was named Santosh Kumar Banerjee.

The above-mentioned report shows that Bose was very much active in mobilizing the youth for any challenge that would come their way. He expected them to stay prepared with proper training and motivation for an uprising that might take place in near future.

Bose wanted to make the most of the war situation by striking the final blow to the British for the attainment of Independence. He also wanted to get the womenfolk to participate actively in the national freedom struggle, as he had enormous faith in the capability of the Indian women.

According to a secret file of the Special Branch of the Calcutta Police, women volunteers were being recruited in his Volunteer Corps under the leadership of Hemaprova Majumdar and Leela Roy.

"Subhas Bose's attempts to organize a Volunteer Corps have met with very little success. So far not more than 150 volunteers have been enlisted. Women volunteers are being recruited at the *Balika Shakti Sangha*, at 49, Mahim Haldar Street, Kalighat. Here too, the response has been poor.

"Under instructions from Subhas Bose, Mrs. Hemaprova Mazumdar M.L.A. (ex-convict), is endeavouring to enlist at least 50 girl volunteers in South Calcutta who will be ready to join the *Satyagraha* Movement and thus court arrest.

"Mrs. Hemaprova Mazumdar (ex-convict), M.L.A. and Mrs. Leela Roy (nee Leela Nag, ex-detenu) have succeeded in enlisting about 50 female volunteers. These two ladies recently collected about Rs.75/- from some public men of Howrah towards the funds of their volunteer corps."[24].

Another SB report of the Calcutta Police mentions the speeches delivered by the revolutionaries in 1940 in which the speakers insisted on the necessity of following the leadership of Bose in the days to come.[25]

The speeches, as recorded in the said file, follow a report given in page 5 on the Bengal Congress Volunteer Corps. It says, "All the volunteers of Bengal Congress Volunteer Corps are requested to fall in at BPCC office (6, Bhabani Dutta Lane) at 5 p.m. today (Tuesday). Sd/- Ramkamal Das, Adjutant, B.C.V.C."

As the speeches follow this report, it may be assumed that the volunteers of BCVC delivered them. The report narrates the gist of the speeches as follows:

"the Government was afraid of arresting Subhas Bose

on account of his international reputation and his arrest might lead to international propaganda and intensification of the struggle. The workers, peasants and youths were asked to attend the Dacca Conference on the 25th and the 26th May 1940 in large numbers and that this conference would be held in defiance of any ban imposed by Government. That they must take advantage of the war situation in their struggle for independence. That in the present war, the mass tendency was towards Germany as they considered the British their enemy and could not have any faith in what they uttered in respect of India. The report of the 'Floud Commission' as it could not redress the grievances of the exploited Kisans and the policy of Gandhi and the Congress High Command for their attitude to compromise with the British Imperialists, were both condemned. The audience was urged to follow Subhas Chandra Bose who had given a lead to the national struggle."

The above report is indicative of the fact that the Bengal revolutionaries, even during the 2nd World War looked up to Bose for guidance and leadership in their fight for freedom. They wanted the people to follow him as their undisputed leader.

However, in 1938, many detained revolutionaries including quite a few Bengal Volunteers, had been released from jail. The B. V. always considered Bose as the most trustworthy leader who alone could wrest freedom for the country. Kamakkhya Ray came to Calcutta and put up in a mess in Ballygunge that served as a shelter for the party activists. In the wake of the Second World War, the British Government did not want to take any risk by keeping the extremists out in the open, hence twenty-five leading members of the BV, the most dreaded revolutionary organization at that time, were arrested on the 13th of April, 1940 and thrown into prison. The Police was under the impression that the BV must have moved away from sporadic violent outrages and would get itself associated with a revolutionary movement on a wider scale. As a result of this sudden arrest, Bose lost his close contact with the BV at least temporarily. But he wanted to communicate with some reliable comrades of the BV through Sudhir Ranjan Bakshi, the younger brother of Satya Bakshi. Sudhir Bakshi was introduced by Amalendu Ghosh to Jatish Guha of BV, the main architect of the Anderson shooting (Darjeeling) and Burge murder (Midnapore).[26]

Jatish Guha met Bose at his Elgin Road residence and was instructed to organize secret societies in Northern India on behalf of Forward Bloc. While working there, Jatish Guha was suspected by the Police, nabbed at the Nausera station in the North-West Frontier Province and sent back to Calcutta immediately.

On July 2, 1940, Bose gave leadership to a popular demonstration for the removal of the Hallwell Monument that stood as an index of defamation to the memory of Siraj-ud-daullah. He was immediately arrested by the Fazl-ul-Haq Government and thrown into the Presidency jail. As a result of the movement, the Monument was removed by the provincial Government, as has already been pointed out.

The arrest of Bose created a nationwide uproar but the Congress stalwarts including Gandhi, seemed unconcerned. The latter was asked by many why he did not protest against the arrest. In an article published in *Hariijan*, Gandhi gave an explanation:

"I have no doubt that hundreds, if not thousands, must have asked this question. ..It is true that Subhas Babu is a Rashtrapati of the Congress twice elected in succession. He has a record of great sacrifice to his credit. He is a leader born. All these qualities alone will not warrant a protest against his arrest.. .Hundreds of issues of greater importance can be discovered."[27]

Bose, in a letter written from Presidency Jail to his elder brother Sarat Bose, observed:

"The more I think of Congress politics, the more I am

The Uncompromising Loner (1938-1941)

convinced that in future we should devote more energy and time to fight the High Command. If power goes into the hands of such mean, vindictive and unscrupulous persons, when Swaraj is won, what would happen to the country?"[28]

While in detention, Bose was elected Member of the Central Legislative Assembly. It would not be irrelevant here to point out that it is an established convention in the constitutional system of Great Britain that while the Legislature is in session, its members are immune from arrest, and if under arrest, the members are set free during the period when the Legislature is in session. But no such constitutional niceties weighed with the British Government in keeping their arch enemy Subhas Bose behind bars even during the session of the Legislature.

In the solitude of the Presidency Jail, however, Bose met two of his most trusted lieutenants—Hem Chandra Ghosh and Satya Ranjan Bakshi, both of the BV, who were also imprisoned there at that time.

Though imprisoned more than ten times, Bose felt very much restless this time because when the freedom movement required him very badly, whether at home or abroad, he was sitting idle doing nothing as a captive in prison. He was quite sure about the fact that the British Government would not release him before the end of the war. He gave an ultimatum to the Government that it had no legal or moral justification for keeping him imprisoned and if he was not set free, he would undertake fast unto death. At the outset, the Government did not take his ultimatum seriously and the Home Minister of Bengal informed his elder brother Sarat Bose, the then Congress Legislative Party leader, that his younger brother should be apprised that it would be foolish of him to think of a release at this juncture. Accordingly Sarat Bose visited his brother in his cell at the dead of night and gave him the Minister's message.

Bose wrote a letter to the Home Minister on the 30th of October 1940, a letter also to Fazl-ul-Haq, the then Premier of Bengal, and a couple of letters to the Presidency Jail Super in which he urged the Government to preserve his letters in the archives since they consisted of his messages to the countrymen. He pointed out in these letters that he was arrested without any warrant or any official explanation under Rule 129 of the Defence of India Rules. The official justification that followed later was related to the demonstration led by him for the demolition of the Hallwell Monument. The Secretary of State for India gave the explanation in the House of Commons to that effect. All the others who were detained on that ground, were released one after the other, hence there was no real justification for keeping him and his close associate Narendra Narain Chakrabarty in custody any longer.

British justice seemed to be rather weird as the Government issued release orders for the other prisoners detained in that connection, simultaneously an order for the permanent detention of Bose was issued under Rule 126 of the Defence of India Rules which said that a prosecution under Rule 38 before two Magistrates would commence on the charges of having delivered seditious speeches and for writing an article which he did long time back. He pointed out that while the Central Legislature was in session, he, as a member of the said Assembly, enjoyed immunity from imprisonment. He also pointed out that without the approval of the Central Legislature, war was declared unilaterally by the British which a Government could not do under the existing system of law. Furthermore, he said that his detention was absolutely vindictive and therefore he took a decision to go on a fast unto death in the same manner as Terence MacSwiney, the Irish patriot, and Jatin Das, the well-known Bengal revolutionary did. Bose, in elaborating on the cause of his decision to fast unto death, said:

"It is through suffering and sacrifice alone that a cause

The Uncompromising Loner (1938-1941)　　　　　　　　　　215

can flourish and prosper and in every age and clime, the eternal law prevails¯the blood of the martyr is the seed of the church.

"What greater solace can there be than the feeling that one has lived and died for a principle? What higher satisfaction can a man possess than the knowledge that his spirit will beget kindred spirits to carry on his unfinished task?"[29]

Bose started his fast unto death on November 21, 1940, as stated earlier. The British Government was deeply involved in the war which was in full swing at that time; hence it was not possible for them to take the risk of letting such a well-known leader of international repute, die in police custody. As a result, Bose was released on Dec 5, 1940 but kept interned at his Elgin Road residence with sixty-two plain-clothed I.B. agents keeping round- the- clock vigil on him as well as on all the guests entering the house and coming out of it. The British plan was that as soon as Bose recovered from illness (caused by the week-long fast), he was to be arrested again. He was supposed to appear before the court on Jan 27, 1941 for the alleged seditious speeches and writings. It is obvious from above that Bose had a very short span of time to take decision regarding his future course of action. Fortunately, Satya Bakshi, his close associate and one of the stalwarts of the B.V., was released from jail on ground of ill health almost simultaneously with Bose and Bose confided in him on his future course of action.

Bakshi in his well-known article *'Keno Netaji'* (Why Netaji) published in the Bengali daily *Basumati* (Calcutta) in the year 1968, on the occasion of Bose's birth anniversary, explained why the Bengal Volunteers considered him the leader of the revolutionaries. He wrote:

"Why Netaji Subhas Chandra Bose was considered *Neta* (the leader) acceptable to all the revolutionaries? Forty years ago, a few leaders of the Bengal revolutionaries asked the same question. Netaji, then, had just returned from Mandalay and been elected the President of the Bengal Provincial Congress

Committee. To which revolutionary group I belonged, everybody knew. I used to follow Netaji like a shadow under all circumstances. Beginning from 1921 till the period before partition, the revolutionary groups (Anushilan, Jugantar or the other revolutionary organizations) were in the majority in the Bengal Congress. The Congress had chosen its leaders and formed the committees with their votes only.

"The revolutionary friends asked: Subhas Chandra did not belong to any particular revolutionary group. Why did we accept Subhas Chandra as our leader instead of any member of the revolutionary groups? I remember having said we could have had any Tom, Dick or Harry (*Ram, Shyam or Jadu* in the original version) as the President of the Congress by way of election. But the country is above the politics of votes. Would the country accept Tom, Dick or Harry? De Valera, Sun Yat Sen were leaders of a revolutionary group, still they were the leaders of their countries too...Leaders are not born out of votes. Question came, out of what else, then? I said, educational qualifications, personality, strength of character, aristocracy, perseverance and actions that make one an undisputed leader outshining the others. History has things in store that cannot be evaluated by numericals, difficult to understand, imponderable."[30]

Having failed to motivate Congress in favour of an immediate uprising with a demand for complete independence, Bose formed the Forward Bloc within the Congress Party itself as has already been pointed out. Sardar Shardul Singh Caveesher of the Forward Bloc, wrote in an article entitled "Netaji and India's Fight for Freedom", in the Puja special number of the daily called *Hindusthan Standard*, in 1962:

"Subhas Bose wanted a general uprising in the country at the opportune moment to throw off the foreign yoke. Gandhi was as anxious as Subhas Bose for the independence of the country but wedded to non-violent methods, he could not agree to Subhas Bose's programme and policy."[31]

This was a common theme in Bose's agenda since 1928, particularly since 1933, to be more precise. In his Presidential speech at Maharashtra Political Conference (Poona, 3rd May 1928) and at the Third Indian Political Conference (London, 10th June, 1933), he had acknowledged Gandhi's contribution to the awakening of the people but criticized the wrong application of the method of non-violent mass action. In the history of mankind, no country had ever achieved national liberation without militancy, he pointed out.

Bose was not an adventurous militant, recklessly pushing for action, but he preferred hitting the iron while it was hot. He believed that occasional compromises could lead to consolidation of the Indian nationalist position if the terms of settlement were favourable. But neither the path of periodical political compromises with the British Government nor the alternative course of uncompromising militancy was being followed with consistency, he felt. They alternated, giving the Government all advantages. Bose would, as he said in June 1933, prefer uncompromising militancy of the nature of a mass movement, well-organised and if necessary, prolonged. The British Empire existed in India like a well-equipped fortress standing in the midst of a territory, which had suddenly become hostile. Bose pointed out that all these years, the civil population of India was found by the British, submissive and weak. Now the citadel of British rule in India could no longer count on the peace- loving, docile native population for its sustenance.

The role the state would play in national reconstruction under various political conditions was bothering Bose very much during the 1930's. He was actively involved in organizing the youth of India and in motivating them for a movement that would lead to complete independence. As a matter fact, he was the motivator of the youth movements under the Congress banner almost all over the country. If Italy's youth movements impressed Vijay Lakshmi Pundit in 1927 when she was there as a tourist, the same youth movements in the 1930's might have impressed Bose too. It is possible that initially he had "some illusions" about Italy's youth movements. Actually, when he visited Italy, Mussolini had not yet invaded Abyssinia. "Fascism had not started on its imperialist expedition, and it appeared to me merely an aggressive form of nationalism", Bose explained later during an interview with CPGB ideologue Rajni Palme Dutt, which was published in the *Daily Worker*, London, on 24th January, 1938.

Bose left no stone unturned to win sympathy from the other countries of the world for India's freedom struggle. He travelled tirelessly from Turkey in the East to France and Ireland in the West also with a view to understanding which direction the European situation was moving towards and how new nations were coming into being out of the old Austro- Hapsburg empire. He encouraged the formation of Friends of India Societies in different countries, which might be utilized occasionally to further the cause of India's independence.

He had a long-standing interest in Ireland, its relentless struggle and the methods its leaders employed not only against savage repression but also to out-maneuver the imperial power in the British Parliament and occasionally at the conference tables. That Ireland had lessons for India to learn was the belief shared by Bose with the other Bengal revolutionaries. According to a secret file, a book called *"The Irish Republic"* by Dorothy Maccardle became a cause of concern for the Government as it felt that the said book might create problems for the authorities. The government was worried whether the book should be prohibited entry into India under the Sea Customs Act. W.F. A.Hamilton writes on the 18th of December 1936:

"It strikes me as being very strong meat for nationalist India, providing a ready reference book on the way the Irish obtained their freedom. The price, however, is a factor likely to curtail its circulation and it may not therefore be necessary

The Uncompromising Loner (1938-1941)

to prohibit it. At the same time, however, I think that the I.O. should be asked to read the book and cable to the Government of India its views thereon."[32]

Hamilton writes again to the Home Department on the 13th of April 1937:

"...One copy of the book has come to notice in the U.P. and has been sent up to us for examination and advice.. .Five copies of the book have also come to notice in Calcutta and addressed to a book shop well known to us as dealing in doubtful literature. As the book is likely to appeal more strongly to Bengali youths than to others, the Calcutta Police have been advised to withhold the books under Section 26(1) of the Post Office Act as provisionally we considered it objectionable.

"The whole of the book has not been read in this office but examination of it shows that it is mainly of historical value and while written in a partisan spirit (the British Government invariably being shown in the wrong), it is less bitter than at first seemed probable. There is, however, a most objectionable chapter...in which the need for assassination of Police officers is stressed. That the assassination of the Royal Irish Constabulary was a feature of the *Sinn Fein* trouble is ancient history, and is as well known to the Indian revolutionaries as to the Irish themselves.

"The book cannot be regarded as a textbook of instructions in republican or revolutionary methods but its contents are such as to be strong meat for impressionable students. .."[33]

Another note with the signature of H. S. Stephenson of the Home Dept. dated 2-5-37, says:

"It might be possible to object to the book on two grounds, first, from the point of view of the dangerous parallel which might be and no doubt has been drawn between the Irish 'struggle for freedom' and the course of events in India, and second, from the narrower point of view of terrorism.

"The superficial parallel between events in Ireland and the Congress struggle is remarkable. There is the parallel executive, which Congress tried in some places to set up in the last Civil Disobedience Movement and the parallel legislature of recusant elected delegates of which there is talk at the present time. The Declaration of Independence... the Truce with England corresponding partly with Delhi Pact, and finally the treaty, leading upto the split in Sinn Fein ranks into pro-Treaty (or office acceptance) and anti-Treaty parties. Throughout there is an appeal to America and the outside world. It is I think tolerably clear apart from terrorism that the Congress have modelled their policy largely on the Irish troubles." Although the national leaders of Congress were vocal about the avowed principle of their party being non-violence, to the British, Congress and Bose with the revolutionaries behind him appeared to be synonymous and the most annoying cause of concern. The note goes on to say:

"Secondly there is terrorism and actual fighting. The account is written throughout on the supposition that a state of war exists. Not for a moment does the writer admit that the Sinn Fein fighting against the British or the Republicans, after the Treaty, fighting against the Irish Provisional Government were rebels...Persons killed on either side in ambushes are 'killed in action'. When it comes to executions of captured men, the execution of rebels is termed murder, those of Government men are as often as not justified...

"Again there is De Valera's speech among many others on pages 454 and 455... The general attitude is summed up in De Valera's words quoted on page 512. Apart however, from this attitude there is a great deal which terrorists in their organizations and working, must have taken from the Irish example. The taking and shooting of hostages (which I believe was contemplated in Chittagong) and reprisals (see page 972) are matters in which objectionable instructions might be drawn from the book. There are three incidental references to India,

The Uncompromising Loner (1938-1941) 221

to the Amritsar shooting on page 330, to the mutiny of the Connaught Rangers on page 578 and an extract from a speech of Lenin follows on page 657 in which he talks of the 'emancipation of India and the degradation of Egypt' I share D.I.B's doubts about this book and am inclined to agree with the India Office that proscription is undesirable."[34]

The Government was always under the apprehension that if a book with rebellious contents were proscribed, then it would become more popular than before, with the revolutionaries. The Chittagong uprising itself was modelled on the Easter Rebellion that took place in Ireland under the leadership of the *Sinn Fein* Party.

Surya Sen was the elected secretary of the Chittagong District Congress Committee for two terms. He organized groups of Satyagrahis to defy the ban on private collection or manufacture of natural salt. While Gandhi was striding along the coast lines of Gujrat during the Civil Disobedience Movement, revolutionaries under the leadership of Surya Sen seized control of Chittagong, the port city (now in Bangladesh) on the 18th of April 1930 to coincide with the anniversary of the Easter Rebellion of 1916 in Ireland. This was the most remarkable revolutionary outrage in India after the 1857 Revolt that shook the foundation of the Empire under the British. Surya Sen, having been inspired by Bose's Bengal Volunteers in the Calcutta Congress of 1928, trained his volunteers with military discipline and planned meticulously the whole operation. The Government was desperate to crush the Chittagong revolutionaries by hook or crook. Anderson, as the Governor of Bengal tried to increase military involvement in police operations against terrorists in Bengal. He incorporated military officers into the civil administration and provided the impetus for the recruitment of military officers into the Intelligence Branch of the Bengal police. These military Intelligence Officers (MIOs) served as plainclothes inspectors in the IB and in Chittagong, they led the search for Surya Sen and other members of the Raid. The DM and MIO in Chittagong developed a system of cordoning off villages for search by troops in which houses were ransacked in a search for arms.

One of the closest disciples of *Swami Vivekananda*, *Sister Nivedita* was an Irish lady with *Sinn Fein* connections. She was deeply involved in the revolutionary activities in Bengal as a supporter of the *Anushilan* and *Jugantar* groups.[34A] It was on her insistence only that Aurobindo Ghosh came to Bengal from Baroda in 1906, to kindle the spirit of revolution in the minds of the young Bengalees. Aurobindo sowed the seeds of militant nationalism here in Bengal in that paleolithic age of revolution when actions against Government were not at all organized by militant groups under proper leadership.

Vivekananda, the spiritual Guru of Bose, must have realized that liberation of an exploited and starving people in bondage was necessary but it was like ploughing the sands on a desert. Thus, when he gave a clarion call to his countrymen 'Arise, Awake', the listeners could not miss the inner implications that they could not rise without dislodging the usurpers. An ascetic and a practical Vedantist, Vivekananda did not offer any ready recipe for political revolution, but he was reported to have said to a well-known disciple of Ramakrishna Paramahansa, Swami Saradananda: " Even a cow tied to a rope makes all kinds of efforts to get free." Annie Besant, another Irish lady, spoke of Vivekananda's influence as one of the leading causes of the emergence of Indian nationalism. She mentioned it in her Presidential address at the Indian National Congress in 1917.[35]

An IB file (No 749 of 1930), of the State Archives, Calcutta, mentions a note sent by Wilkinson, District Magistrate of Chittagong to Tufnell Barret, the Second Additional Deputy Secretary to the Government of Bengal, Political Department, dated 10th October, 1930, in which the former expressed his worries about a book called *"My fight for Irish freedom"* by

Dan Breen, published by Talbot and Company Pvt. Ltd. Dublin. Wilkinson quoted particular portions from the said book, which he found to be dangerous for the British Imperialists. Dan Breen was in the Violence Party of Ireland, later on he joined the *Sinn Fein*. His book was full of revolutionary ideas and strategies and the copy seized by the Police had some fiery lines specially marked by unidentifiable people. Wilkinson, therefore, wanted to proscribe the book and put a ban on its import into India under the Sea Customs Act.

Bose however, was a born rebel, a hard-core revolutionary, but certainly not a terrorist as the British preferred to call him. Vivekananda's writings exerted profound influence on him and developed in him a sense of pride in the culture and civilization of his own country. As he writes in *Indian Struggle* about Vivekananda,

"With him religion was the inspirer of nationalism. He tried to infuse into the new generation a sense of pride in India's past, of faith in India's future and a spirit of self-confidence and self-respect. Though the Swami never gave any political message, everyone who came into contact with him or his writings developed a spirit of patriotism and a political mentality. So far at least as Bengal is concerned, Swami Vivekananda may be regarded as the spiritual father of the modern nationalist movement."[36]

Needless to say that the Bengal revolutionaries belonging to the *Anushilan* and *Jugantar* groups as well as the Bengal Volunteers were simply mesmerized by the towering personality, youthful image, fighting spirit, political dynamism, and the rebellious character of Subhas Chandra Bose that attracted them towards him. Generally speaking, Bose also had faith in the dedication and sincerity of the revolutionaries belonging to different groups but the Anushilanites and the Bengal Volunteers were more close to him than the others. Although initially he was associated with the *Jugantar* group very closely and his name was often mentioned in the Police records as a

'Jugantar terrorist' but later on, when *Jugantar* was merged with the Gandhian Congress in 1938, Bose moved away from it and started working in collaboration with the other revolutionary groups, particularly the Bengal Volunteers. It is to be noted that he was not in favour of individual killings or unplanned violence. To oust the imperialist usurpers, he believed, it was necessary to have proper mental and physical preparation for the final assault on the strong and well-armed opponent. He had been insisting on it, it may be recalled, since the Amarabati Conference in 1929. Even in the Lahore Congress held in that year, Bose called upon the leaders to give up all hesitation and form a parallel Government that would be Indian in every way.

However, the Tripuri session of the Congress was held in March 1939, and the Second World War began in September, just six months later. The Gandhians, who thought that their immediate mission was accomplished with the virtual expulsion of Bose from the national platform called Indian National Congress, were now faced with a problem: which way to go, if they oppose the British which as a nationalist and patriotic organization they should do, but that would be nothing but going the Bose way, or they should support the colonial masters in their war efforts against the Axis. "Here is Nehru's version of the Hamletian dilemma ('To be or not to be, that was the question'), "how to reconcile the two dominating trends in our policy: Opposition to British Imperialism and opposition to fascism and nazism?"[37]

After a lot of discussions, their think-tank came to the formidable conclusion that they would offer their support to the British Government and in return, they would demand freedom for India and the subsequent establishment of a national government at the Centre. Nehru and Rajendra Prasad even met the Viceroy who, to their utter disappointment, promised nothing. At this juncture, Gandhi, as always, launched his movement of individual Satyagraha. Sampuram Singh, an unauthorized Satyagrahi of Punjab, put up a resistance by mistake, or by instinct which was not in keeping with the Gandhian principle of non-violence. The Magistrate immediately imposed a fine of one anna, (in those days, one rupee was equivalent to sixteen annas) which he paid from his own pocket. This particular incident made the whole affair look somewhat ridiculous.

Gandhi and the Congress, however, decided not to embarrass the British Government as Britain was then engaged in a deadly struggle for survival. Bose, on the other hand, thought that Britain's predicament was India's opportunity. Hence, instead of helping the colonizers who had exploited India for nearly two centuries, the country should range itself on the side of Britain's enemies to ensure its own freedom. Congress was planning to have a National Government for the period of the war, which Bose had already demanded at the Tripuri Congress, calling it an 'ultimatum'. But at that time, the Old Guards of the Congress were more keen on ousting Bose from national politics than winning freedom or forming a National Government for that matter. He had very clear idea about the intention of the rulers, that they would never part with their 'Jewel in the Crown', come what may, war or no war. He also had great apathy for the "politics of mendicancy", as he was basically a man of transparency with a very strong sense of self-respect. His argument was that India should not beg for her freedom when freedom was her birthright.

Although Bose was in the Congress Party under the leadership of Gandhi for more than fifteen years, he was at this time seriously thinking about developing an alternative leadership in the face of the impending war, which he, unlike many other politicians, could foresee much earlier, clearly. He did not want to come out of the Congress, but he planned to bring it out of the clutches of Gandhi and use the platform as a strong base for an anti-British onslaught. He knew that he had a huge following in and outside Bengal. The peasants, the workers and the revolutionaries were with him as always, but he had to resign from Congress Presidentship in 1939 (29th April), as the situation was made unbearable for him due to the opposition of the top leadership in Congress. He then, proceeded to form a new group with the massive support of the revolutionaries and the other like-minded people to give Congress a fresh lease of life.

Bose had to fight on more fronts than one, with the Right Wing of the Congress, the communists and above all, the foreign imperialists whom he considered his arch enemy. He also had to sort out the differences that cropped up occasionally between the Bengal Legislative Party and the *Anushilan* members of the Forward Bloc.

It may be pointed out here that as per the provisions of the Government of India Act 1935, election took place for the first time in January 1937 and Congress got majority in 7 provinces. Power was granted to the elected representatives of the people all over the country. There was hope in the minds of many that now the repressive Acts of the Government would be withdrawn and the political prisoners would be released. But soon they realized that that were grossly mistaken. As a result, the Andaman prisoners went on a fast with the demand that they should be sent back to India without delay and to express their sympathy for the Andaman prisoners, the inmates of Deoli camp also went on a hunger strike. These fastings yielded some results as the Andaman prisoners were gradually brought back to India and before 25th August 1938, 2304 detenues without trial were released. In all the provinces except Bengal and Punjab, the ministries, in keeping with the provisions of the said Act, released the political prisoners. Ultimately Punjab also gave in to the pressure of public opinion and released the imprisoned revolutionaries. Only the Bengal revolutionaries remained behind bars as a result of which the inmates of Alipore jail started fasting unto death with the demand of release. The inmates of Dumdum Central jail joined them with the same demand. But they put an end to their protest when Bose requested them to do so and promised them that he would do his utmost to set them free. But soon after, the 2nd World War started from 3rd September 1939 and the jails started getting filled once again with the detenues without trial.

Anushilan Samity, under the guidance of Trailokya Chakrabarty (commonly known as *maharaj* in those days) wanted to utilize the war situation as did Bose and they considered him the only leader with a national stature who would be acceptable to all the revolutionary groups. It may be recalled that way back in 1924, Bose was imprisoned in the Mandalaya jail along with Chakrabarty and this proximity developed into a close friendship in course of time. In his prison memoir, Chakrabarty wrote that in the jail once he fell down and got badly hurt while playing tennis. Bose used to wash his wound everyday himself with water boiled with *Neem* leaves. Whenever somebody fell sick in the jail, Bose stayed awake the whole night by his side.

In 1939, it was decided by the revolutionaries that an armed resistance would be put up on a massive scale under the leadership of Bose. Bhulabhai Desai, the well-known Congress leader stated in London that the INC wanted a compromise with the Government. Against this, the anti-compromise movement started under Bose's leadership and simultaneously preparations for the resistance were going on. It was decided by Bose and the *Anushilan* leaders that if Congress launched any movement, that would be made to turn into an armed resistance. At this juncture, Bose, under pressure of circumstances, resigned from Congress presidentship and his ties with the *Anushilan* became stronger than before after that incident.

Bose, however, went on a tour of North India with Trailokya Chakrabarty, met a few veteran revolutionaries in various places. Akbar Shah of the North-West, Bhai Paramananda of Hamirpore and many others agreed to join them. They tried to establish contact with the army through

Akbar Shah. Bose had already discussed with Pratul Ganguli the prospects of his moving out of India and organizing an armed force abroad. Help was sought in this regard from the workers in the frontier areas. It was decided that after the Ramgarh Congress, Chakrabarty would go absconding and start preparation for the revolution staying somewhere in Punjab. Following the instructions of Bose, he went to Madhya Pradesh and met Keshav Hedgewer of the *Rashtriya Sayam Sevak Sangh* and the latter assured him help and assistance by joining with them with his 60000 volunteers. Trailokya Chakrabarty met also Ganesh Damodar Savarkar, the elder brother of Veer Savarkar in Kashi. He along with Sachin Sanyal agreed to join the movement for revolution as whole timers. During those days, Anushilan's Delhi cadre Sushil Bhattacharya told Chakrabarty that he could procure arms from the Delhi Fort with the help of funds. As soon as Bose came to know about it, he agreed immediately to give Rs 10000/- and assured further monetary help in future. But unfortunately arms could not be procured from the Red Fort as expected.

The Sikh leader Niranjan Singh Talib told Rabindra Mohan Sen, a well-known Anushilanite, that the Sikh Regiment stationed at Alipore was willing to establish contact with the Bengal revolutionaries and it transpired from discussions with them that they were not willing to fight for the British any more and wanted to join the revolutionaries in their struggle for freedom utilizing the war situation. After the preliminary talks, a meeting was held at Bose's house where the leading members of the Regiment and *Anushilan* were present. It was decided that preparation for an armed resistance in the nature of the uprising planned by Rashbehari Basu and his compatriots in 1915, had to commence immediately. But within a few days, this Regiment was ordered to move towards the front. When they refused to oblige, the leaders were shot dead and the others arrested. Trailokya was also arrested unexpectedly in the beginning of 1940 along with many other Anushilanites as a

The Uncompromising Loner (1938-1941) 229

result of which the possibility of an armed resistance within the country was nipped in the bud.37A (*Bharater Swadhinata Sangram O Anushilan Samity* by Kshirod Kumar Dutta, Anushilan Samity Pachattartama Pratistha Barshiki Udjapan Committee, pp. 126-132).

Japan did not join the War at that time and Bose planned to go out to East Asia to make the most of the War situation along with Rashbehari Basu. With the help of Jiten Basu of the *Anushilan* who was an employee, at that time, of the Japanese Consulate in Calcutta, the Vice-consul was contacted for help. Soon after it became clear that Japan was going to declare war against the Allies. Bose, therefore shelved his original plan of moving towards the East and decided to take the North-West frontier as his escape route to Moscow.

During the War period, things were developing at a very fast pace on the domestic front. In two of Bose's letters sent to Gandhi he offered the proposal for a United Front and participation of Forward Bloc members in the *Satyagraha* campaign. At the same time he indicated that this movement (*Satyagraha*) was limited and thought that only mass struggle could result in victory.(Appendix II).

Nehru's speech on 20th March 1940, at Ramgarh was rather harsh on Bose and his followers for wanting an immediate start of a Civil Disobedient Movement. Nehru said: "I am surprised that people ask us to immediately start civil disobedience, but I ask them, why are they indulging in tall talk instead of direct action if they have the courage to do so."[38]

He went on to say:

"Misguided enthusiasm of a few people to go head-on for any objective has often caused disruption in fighting forces. Such enthusiasts are counter-revolutionaries and rebels. Our objective should be to get the entire army moving and not a few headstrong people who can be described as adventurers. They are no better than terrorists."[39]

The Government continued to make preventive arrests especially in Bengal and Punjab, the two most 'troublesome' provinces. Incidentally, Nehru wrote to Krishna Menon about the campaign Bose was making against Congress passivity:

"Subhas Bose is going to pieces and has definitely ranged himself against the Congress", Nehru wrote it on the 2nd of March, 1940.[40] Ironically, he admitted that the war was being waged by two blocs of Imperialist Powers, but he was unwilling to extend to Bose, the kind of support he gave to many other leaders whose views were closer to that of Bose.

According to a secret file of the Home Political Deptt, Calcutta, numbered C 616/40, the old rivalry between the Bengal Labour Party and the *Anushilan* members of the Forward Bloc found expression in a fight in the Dacca Political Conference as the latter did not like the distribution of Bolshevik leaflets by B.L.P. men in the Conference. Subhas Bose was trying to pacify them. His main purpose was to unite all the revolutionaries and the leftists on a common platform under the banner of Forward Bloc. The Report states:

"The members of the recently formed Forward Bloc Labour Sub-Committee will try to co-ordinate the different labour organizations and cooperate with the B.P. T. U .C. The Forward Bloc will set up a rival peasant organization on a provincial scale because the Bengal Provincial Kisan Sabha is controlled by the C.P.I.

"At the meeting of the Congress workers of Ward 1, held at 1/1, Shyampukur Street on 2.6.'40, it was resolved to enlist Congress members forthwith and to organize Ward 1 Forward Bloc. The resolutions of the Bengal Provincial Congress at Dacca were endorsed. The formation of a Defence Corps under the name of *'Desh Raksha Bahini'* and also the enlistment of volunteers for carrying on propaganda to remove the Hallwell Monument were decided upon.

"Hemanta Bose, Amar Bose (ex-detenu), Kalipada

Bagchi (ex-detenu), Ramkamal Das, Baidya Nath Ghosh, Ramapati Bose, Shanti Sinha Roy, Arun Dutta, Kanugopal Banerjee, Sudhir Kumar De and Biswanath Mukherjee met together at 6, Bhabani Dutta Lane on 4/6/1940, and decided to move in ten batches in different wards of Calcutta and make house to house propaganda for the enlistment of volunteers and collection of funds in connection with the proposed Hallwell Monument agitation."

The same file contains a paper clipping entitled 'Central Calcutta Forward Bloc Defence Corps.' It runs like this:

"Volunteers are being recruited for the Defence Corps in response to the appeal made by Sj. Subhas Chandra Bose. Young men between the ages 18 and 35 are requested to enlist their names as early as possible, in view of the urgency of the situation. Applicants are to see the undersigned at the given address.

Sd/- Arun K. Dutta

Commander

C.C.F.Defence Corps

62, Bowbazar Street,

Forward Bloc Office

Second Floor."

It is evident from the above that Bose was trying hard to organize the masses particularly the youth of Bengal in the form of volunteers not to support the British in its war efforts but to stay prepared for a militant onslaught upon the usurpers. Even the members of the 'depressed classes' were summoned to join the freedom struggle as volunteers. Dr. J.P .Sarkar, Secretary, All Bengal Depressed Class Karmi Sangha of 15, Harrison Road, stated to have said that Subhas Bose asked the youngsters of the country to join the national movement as volunteers. So the work of enlistment started in the Sangha office. Every nationalist depressed class worker was invited to join as volunteers.[41]

Even the women were being recruited in the volunteer forces, as has already been pointed out. Women volunteers were being recruited at the *Balika Shakti Sangha* at 49, Mahim Haldar Street, Kalighat. Under instructions from Bose, Mrs. Hemaprova Mazumdar M.L.A., (ex-convict) enlisted 50 girl volunteers in South Calcutta who would be ready to join the *Satyagraha* Movement and thus court arrest.[42]

Mrs. Leela Ray (ex-detenu and wife of Anil Ray of Sri Sangha), was working with Hemaprova in organizing women volunteers all over Bengal. According to confidential reports, these two ladies succeeded in enlisting quite a few female volunteers with a militant bent of mind to fight for freedom. They collected funds from some resourceful men of Howrah towards the financial resources of their volunteer corps. Both Leela Ray and Anil Ray joined the Forward Bloc with all their revolutionary associates after the Tripuri Congress. Bose gave the responsibility of editing the weekly *Forward Bloc* to Leela Ray who, thus, became the second editor of this weekly after Bose.

At Madaripur (in the Faridpore district of East Bengal), a revolutionary group was very active at that time, under the leadership of Purna Das, the ex-State prisoner. This group was known as '*Purna Daser Dal*' (the party of Purna Das). The Home Political records called this group 'Madaripur Jugantar' and put it under the general category of Terrorist Groups. The Faridpur Congress Workers' Conference at Madaripur under the presidentship of Bose ended smoothly, to the disappointment of the British Government, which was carefully watching every move of the leader.

A remarkable incident took place in Faridpur when Bose came to preside over the above-mentioned conference. Santosh Dutta and Bidhu Mazumdar, both ex-detenu, had instructed sixty persons to demonstrate against Subhas Bose, but

The Uncompromising Loner (1938-1941)

according to the police records, they dared not do so, for fear of ex-state prisoner Purna Das and ex-detenu Prafulla Chowdhury who had under their control 800 trained volunteers. Bose put up at the house of Bijoyananda Dutta, an ex-detenu. He was given address of welcome by several organizations of Madaripur...and was entertained at a tea party by Suren Saha (ex-detenu). Before leaving Madaripur, he presided over a public meeting at Charmuguria, (Madaripur). All these ex-detenus were revolutionaries who could not think of any leader other than Bose to guide them in their freedom struggle.

Through the Forward Bloc, Bose tried to give the liberation movement a new lease of life by convening district conferences all over Bengal and by contacting other revolutionary groups outside Bengal with the sole purpose of organizing volunteer corps in the form of a national militia. He wanted to

(1) popularize the Dacca Conference Resolutions,
(2) to coordinate the labour, peasant and student movements all over the country,
(3) to hold a series of meetings in Calcutta and the industrial areas to mould public opinion, and
(4) to convene immediately a conference of leading political and public men in order to organize volunteer corps and to raise the necessary funds.[43]

Bose launched the Forward Bloc to be a common forum for all Left-wing Congress adherents. Many of the Indian Communists were functioning in the Congress Socialist Party within which they were a distinct group. Bose was very much aware of it and was keen on a broad based Left consolidation of which a mention has already been made. Although a strong believer in Socialism, he never wanted to join the CSP because he preferred to place importance on retaining the all-inclusive and composite character of the Congress as the premier anti-imperialist front for Indian independence. The primary task of the nation at that time was to get rid of the foreign power and it had to be done under the leadership of Congress, he felt. Since the CSP failed to draw to itself "all progressive, radical and anti-imperialist elements in the Congress ", the idea of a Left Bloc within Congress originated, according to Bose, at Haripura Congress. The paramount purpose was obtaining a Left consolidation to push the Congress from 'constitutionalism' to the path of an uncompromising struggle, no matter how tenacious it might have been, for achieving Indian independence. "But the attainment of political independence will not mean the dissolution of the Bloc. It will only mean a new phase in its life and activity. And that phase will undoubtedly be a Socialist one."[44] It should be noted that he always referred to his new formation as a bloc, not as a party.

Bose recalled that Gandhi in 1919, broke the hold of a previous generation of national leaders and transformed the Congress into a mass organization. "After a number of skirmishes, the left-wing under the leadership of Mahatma Gandhi succeeded in capturing the Indian National Congress in 1920. That was the signal for several of the erstwhile leaders like Messrs. Jinna, B.C.Pal, and B.Chakraborty to walk out of the Congress. The left-wing became the dominant party in the Congress... With the suspension of the Civil Disobedience Movement in 1922, a rift occurred within the majority party and, over the issue of carrying the fight into the Legislatures, it split into two groups the Swarajists and the No-Changers. After a time, the differences were made up through the Congress accepting the Swarajist plan of extending the fighting front to the Legislatures."[45]

In the nationalist freedom struggle then, there were clearly two groups, the Rightists and the Leftists since 1919 only, but these terms were not in vogue at that time. The circumstances might have changed, as they always do, but difference of opinion would inevitably be there between the older and the younger generations and Bose preferred to call the more radical and progressive section of the movement as the Left Wing to which he himself belonged. He was also aware of the fact that yesterday's radicals become today's rightists and examples were not far to seek.

The Indian Struggle that gives an idea about his experiences in the struggle for India's independence during the period of 1920-'34, was banned in India. In the book, he commented about Nehru :

"his popularity in India today is, according to the writer, second only to that of Mahatma Gandhi". It shows that he did not nurture any ill feeling towards his political rival Nehru. He formed the Forward Bloc with the sole purpose of rejuvenating the Congress and not to discard the parent body as moribund. Even in the mid-1930's he had seen the probability of a Leftist revolt in the Congress that might have led to a new political formation, a more radical Congress in the same way as it happened under the leadership of Gandhi in 1919-'20 a mention of which has already been made. Bose thus wanted now to revitalize the Congress to lead in the final phase of the freedom struggle discarding the politics of compromise, which he never supported because he knew that compromise would invariably lead to conditional independence, *i.e.*, transfer of power with a rider.

It is clear from official records that Bose was preparing the ground for a reformed Congress to face the challenges of the War, for which he was travelling all over the country, sometimes on his own initiative, sometimes having been invited by the regional Congress leaders with a Left orientation. As a Calcutta SB record shows:

"There is a move to invite Mr. Subhas Chandra Bose to Sind and in all likelihood, he will be asked to preside over the Sind Political Conference, whose venue may probably be Karachi. The correspondent further writes,

'I also understand that Mr. Subhas is likely to be invited to Hyderabad and Sukkur where there is a growing body of Congressmen owing allegiance to the left wing creed.

'The Hyderabad Municipality has already voted a civic address to Mr .Subhas Bose when and if he visits that city.

'Swami Govindanand of Karachi is convening a conference of Congressmen belonging to the Left Bloc, in his house very shortly.'

Cover addressed to:

The News Editor

Ananda Bazar Patrika

No.3, Burman Street, Calcutta."[46]

Bose insisted on the fact that the way the Congress was radicalized by Gandhi and his followers in 1919, they could certainly be regarded as leftists from the perspective of their time. Even before them, radical leaders like B.G. Tilak, Aurobindo Ghosh and Bipin Pal led the protest against the moderate policies of the right wingers, e.g. Sir Phirozeshah Mehta and Surendra Nath Banerjea at the Surat Session of Congress in 1907. Bose in the introduction to *The Indian Struggle*, (first published in London, January 17, 1935), described Tilak, Ghosh and Pal as the 'Left Wing leaders' and the others like Mehta and Banerjea as the 'Right Wing leaders'. Although leaders like Tilak, Ghosh and Pal were better known, in those days, as 'extremists', Bose preferred to consider them the Left-wingers. To him, evidently, the word 'Left Wing' stood for more radical, more progressive and certainly non-conservative section of a particular group. In his post-Tripuri letter Nehru criticized Bose for introducing these terms, which he found to be vague, and meant to be laudatory for some and pejorative for others.

C.R.Das, the political Guru of Bose, who was the President of the Gaya Congress way back in 1922, had a plan for council-entry, which was defeated by the so-called no-changers in the Party. He was, then, thinking of resigning from the Congress to implement his plan with the help of a new political formation. As a result, the Congress was divided into two groups, and Motilal Nehru announced at the open session the launching of the *Swarajya Party* within the parent body, as has been stated earlier. After the Tripuri Congress fiasco, Bose also decided to launch a new formation within the parent body as a part of his Left consolidation move to strengthen the struggle for independence. Nehru, the avowed socialist, deserted him at this stage. Bose observed:

"Nobody has done more harm to me personally and to our cause in this crisis than Pundit Nehru. If he had been with us-we would have had a majority (at the Tripuri session of the Congress). Even his neutrality would have probably given us a majority. But he was with the Old Guard at Tripuri."[47]

It is to be noted that after the demise of Tilak of Maharashtra, C.R.Das of Bengal, and Lala Lajpat Rai of Punjab, the three most 'troublesome' regions, where militant nationalism frightened the alien rulers the most, gradually lost their former importance among the Gandhians. As Calcutta, the former capital of India, was abandoned by the Government largely due to the trouble caused to them by the so-called 'extremists', the centre of nationalist politics too, moved from Bengal to the areas where Gandhi's personal influence was beyond anybody's challenge.

The militant nationalism of Bengal was looked down upon also by quite a few pre-Gandhi Congress leaders. Nehru, while a student at Cambridge, having heard a speech delivered by Bipin Chandra Pal who was visiting the University, wrote to his father Motilal Nehru, a letter that expressed his negative feelings about Pal's oratory. It was the first decade of the 20th Century. At that time, Bengal, Punjab and Maharashtra became the nerve centres of revolutionary activities. Nehru was quite young at that time and he wrote to his father that he did not like Pal's speech at all, which was full of fiery words, and "this pleased him (Senior Nehru) for he had no liking in those days for the fire-brands of Bengal."[48].

Motilal Nehru, a moderate leader at that time, presided over a provincial conference in his own province and took up a strong line against the 'Extremists' of Bengal and Maharashtra.[49].

It may be recalled that Lord Minto used to be advised by Gokhale through his PSV James Dunlop Smith, on how to deal with the extremists generally and of Bengal in particular, although it was Maharashtra, not Bengal that was the first to use the method of vidence against the local British officials. For a long time, the British blamed the *Chitpawan* Press that stood for journals owned by the *Chitpawan Brahmin* leaders of Maharashtra's early extremist resurgence of the late 19th Century. Gokhale, the moderate Congress leader told Dunlop Smith on 15th January 1908:

"the Extremists will cease to be a factor of any importance in the country. They have never had any hold in the United Provinces and Madras: they have ceased from troubling in the Punjab. ..in Bombay and the Central Provinces their influence and actions are confined to narrow limits. Their only strength is in two Bengals (the province of Bengal had been partitioned by Lord Curzon, Lord Minto's predecessor), and their centre is in Eastern Bengal. It is quite a mistake to suppose that the agitation is worked from Calcutta. The directing power is in Eastern Bengal just as the racial feeling is the bitterest there."[50]

Smith somehow had an impression that "Mr. Gokhale is somewhat tired of the Bengalis." The alien rulers were also very much tired of the Bengal 'extremists' as a result of which Gokhale's impressions were soon communicated to Lord Minto by Dunlop Smith.

The idea of violent protest against the colonial rule might have been transplanted from Maharashtra to Bengal. It would not, perhaps, be untrue to say that the pathfinders of the Bengal revolutionaries whom Gokhale disliked, were the *Chapekar* brothers who, as Lala Lajpat Rai wrote, were the real founders of the revolutionary movement against the British rule in India. W.C.Rand, the special plague officer of Pune, and Lt. Charles Eagerton Ayerst were killed in Pune on 22n June 1897, thus paving the way for a violent trend in the blooming nationalist movement. The *Chapekar* brothers were hanged, Damodar, the eldest one, mounted the gallows with the Gita in his hand, which was a gift from B.G. Tilak.

If Tilak was 'the Father of Indian Unrest', then Aurobindo Ghosh must be viewed as the new prophet for the Bengal revolutionaries. His initiation into revolutionary creed occurred when he was working in a Baroda college under the Gaekoad. It might be recalled here in this context that in 1911, Delhi Durbar was held to celebrate the coronation of King George V who came to India to grace the occasion. The native kings came in large numbers to show loyalty to the Monarch and gave him '*Kurnish*' in a very special way, i.e. they came forward, bent their heads and moved backwards without showing their back to His Majesty. When his turn came, Sayaji Rao, the Gaekoad of Baroda, walked straight to him, shook hands, turned back and proceeded towards his seat. This incident created a lot of hue and cry everywhere around and it was being shown in cinemas as a mark of audacity on the part of a native king. But the revolutionaries of Bengal felt very proud by this act of the Gaekoad and when he came to Calcutta, Satish Sen, a revolutionary from East Bengal, met him and addressed him as the 'Victor Immanuel of India' (King Immanuel participated in a big way in the freedom struggle of Italy led by Mazzini and Garibaldi). The king of Baroda wanted to know who and where their Garibaldi was. In 1870, Italy achieved independence and Garibaldi was the Chief of the Liberation Army who was already the source of inspiration for the Bengal militants.

The revolutionaries believed that in order to have a successful uprising, three things were essential, namely,

(a)   a philosopher who could see beyond, a Seer
(b)   a competent statesman, and
(c)   a military leader to guide the revolutionaries along the road to freedom.

According to Jadu Gopal Mukhopadhyaya, a revolutionary from Bengal, certain rules were framed by the *Anushilan* group to be strictly applied for the recruitment of youngsters, the qualifications necessary being, a spirit of sacrifice, inexhaustible energy and non-impulsiveness. The revolutionaries considered Aurobindo as the philosopher-visionary; Tilak as the competent statesman, but their Garibaldi was missing. At last in 1915, they found him in Jatindra Nath Mukherjee, commonly known as 'Bagha Jatin' who sacrificed his life fighting directly against the British at Balasore, Orissa. His gallant fight inspired the youngsters not only in Bengal, but also in the other parts of India to rise in revolt against the oppressors, as a result of which the country got a leader like Surya Sen who organized the famous Chittagong Armoury Raid and a few years later, Subhas Chandra Bose, whose army the Azad Hind Fauj (Indian National Army) fought the last battle for independence at Kohima.[51]

According to a confidential report of the Government, the *Anushilan* group was trying hard to frustrate the chances of restoration of harmonious relationship between the Bose brothers and the official Congress. The *Anushilan* group was with Bose in the post-Tripuri phase of his life. The report states:

"It is reported that Sarat Bose has promised to explain his conduct in the recent Congress bye-election to Maulana Abul Kalam Azad by 6-9-'40. Kamini Kumar Dutta has requested Maulana Azad to settle the matter, as it was impossible to carry on Congress work in the mofussil in opposition to the Forward Bloc members."[52]

The above report shows that Forward Bloc became very popular since its inception in Bengal, especially in the mofussil areas. The report goes on to say,

"Subhas Bose had told Sarat Bose not to yield to Maulana Azad but to create a division amongst Congressmen and then to secure from His Excellency, the Viceroy, recognition as the leader of the Bengal Congress. On the assurance of the support of Pratul Ganguly, the leader of the *Anushilan* Group, Sarat Bose is said to have decided to follow Subhas Bose's advice. It is said that the *Anushilan* Group is trying its best to frustrate any rapprochement between the Bose brothers and the official Congress... The BPCC members who are being hampered in their work in the country by the false propaganda of the *Anushilan* Group, feel that this rupture will be for their good. Dr. B.C.Roy has, under the influence of Kamini Kumar Dutta and N.R.Sarkar, consented to lead the Bengal Congress once more."[53].

According to the Hallwell Monument Movement File of the Special Branch, Calcutta, leaflets were printed and distributed by the Indian Red Army all over the province, describing Bose as the supreme leader of the movement and calling him *'Deshgaurab'*, the honorific title conferred on him by Rabindranath Tagore.[54]

The leaflet states

"Just in the hearts of the most civilized city of your country, stands the Hallwell Monument symbolizing the most bare-faced imprudence of British Imperialism in India. Look at the black words inscribed on the marble and you shall find there a disgraceful distortion of the history of Bengal, the mischievous myth of the "Black hole tragedy" spun out of the power-dizzy brains of the British Imperialists, and an unfounded scar in the acetylene life of Nawab Shirajuddowla, the last torch-bearer of freedom in Bengal. Today when we are marching ahead, Hindus and Moslems, Sikhs and Christians with triumphant peals for Complete Independence of our country, we cannot allow the darkest and the most inhuman untruth of our nation to stand there under the sun. On our way forward, we must trample that "MONUMENT" of lie, down under our feet and the marble slabs commemorating the victory of British Imperialism must be reduced to dust. The struggle has begun. The supreme leader of the movement, Deshgourab Subhas Chandra Bose, has courted arrest. Other leaders have smilingly welcomed imprisonment. ..Still, the ministers of Bengal, the shameless hirelings of British Imperialism, are issuing contemptuous statements challenging the strength and morale of the fighters. Let us grip the challenge in our iron clutch and hurl it back on the black faces of the incorrigible reactionaries." They appealed to the people to come forward in hundreds and thousands to demolish the Hallwell Monument from the heart of the city and to unfurl there with a chorus of *Bande Mataram*, the National Flag, which they considered to be the symbol of Victory, Truth and Freedom.[55]

The same file goes on to say that the 'Red Army' was a pseudonym for the *Anushilan* Samity, which was assumed with the object of making CPI look responsible for the objectionable leaflets. Probably the group wanted to keep itself unidentifiable by the Police.

Another leaflet on behalf of the Indian Red Army, congratulated the students of Bengal whom they called 'the revolutionary vanguard'. It gave an account of what actually happened on 22nd July 1940 in Calcutta. On the night of 21st July, the Home Minister Khaja Sir Najimuddin and the C.M. Fazl-ul-Haq wanted a deputation of their Muslim comrades but "these two impertinent gentlemen refused to pay patient hearing even to the legitimate demands of the students. Moreover, the Minister in charge of Law and Order was so much obstinate and rude that he did not hesitate even to threaten their comrades." He said it openly that if the students did not give up their plans of strike, demonstration and the removal of the ill-fated Hallwell, he would suppress it ruthlessly, by police violence and terrorism. On the 22nd July, "that lap dog of the Imperialists actually did what he meant."

Bose was very much worried about the future of the political prisoners and tried hard to secure their release from the jails and the various detention camps, as mentioned earlier. Muzaffar Ahmed, the well-known communist leader, sent a type- written letter to the convicts in the Alipore Central Jail in reply to the letter of a convict called Subodh Chowdhury on the 4th of Sept. 1939. In this letter, Ahmed mentioned the meeting of the Congress Working Committee and the subsequent disciplinary action taken against Bose that led to the formation of a virtually parallel Congress in Bengal. "Feelings were very high amongst the supporters of Bose. To them, provincial prestige was everything...so, for the time being, there was a little lull in the release movement.

"Mr. Subhas Bose promised to us that he would finish his outside Bengal tour by the 7th Sept. latest, and after that he would spend his whole time in the political prisoners' release movements."[56] The communists were well aware of the fact that Bose had a more popular image and was more capable than any other leader, of organizing mass movements against the autocratic Government. They were solely dependent on him for the release movement.

The Bengal revolutionaries, particularly *Anushilan* and the BV accepted Bose as their leader and relied on him for help and guidance in their struggle for freedom. Regarding the Bengal Volunteers, a police record shows that agent 243 (that is how the police referred to the spies employed for the collection of information) reported that ex-state prisoner Bhupendra Kishore Rakshit Roy wrote a letter to Madhu Banerjee (convict, Lebong case) saying that the BV group had decided to accept Subhas Bose as their leader and that they were following him wholeheartedly. The writer asked the convict to persuade the other prisoners to break the hunger strike if Bose requested them to do so. The convict was requested to inform Ganesh Ghosh, another convict in the Chittagong Armoury Raid case, about the contents of the letter.[57]

Another letter, dated 28-2-38, from Ambika Charan Chakrabarty, convict, Chittagong Armory Raid case, at that time, an inmate of Dumdum Central Jail, writing to Sasanka Shekhar Chowdhury (ex-detenu belonging to *Jugantar*), sent through a messenger stated that the writer was glad to receive the message from Sarat Bose but extremely mortified to know about the malady of '*Su Babu*' (Subhas Bose). He said that he was praying for his speedy recovery and long life. He asked Chowdhury to tender his "hearty reverence and love to him and *Su Babu*."[58] Letters of the imprisoned revolutionaries used to be intercepted by the Police, that is why Bose was mentioned as '*Su Babu*' in their correspondences.

In those days, the revolutionaries were considered to be leftists in their orientation with their progressive, anti-establishment ideas and they supported Bose as an uncompromising, anti-imperialistic leftist leader. The letter, mentioned above, further said that all the friends must be informed that it was the writer's humble request that leftists in general, particularly the volunteers of all groups of Bengal should pay special attention to effect the success of '*Su Babu*' at Tripuri in all respects.

"Let not the victory or defeat of Su Babu depend on individual liking and disliking. The success of Su Babu and the success of the anti-imperialists are cohesive and co-extensive. We submit that all should be unanimous on this point."[59]

Bose's sympathy for the political prisoners was overwhelming, as their patriotism, courage and the spirit of self-sacrifice impressed him the most. Even if he organized an army outside India, he had a firm conviction that it would not be possible for him to oust the British from the motherland without the active support of the revolutionaries inside. An SB report

The Uncompromising Loner (1938-1941)

shows that in his statement to the Press, Subhas Bose proposed to utilize the two month's time limit to make preparations for direct action or *Satyagraha* which, he said, would be necessary if the prisoners were not released by then. He also hoped thereby to create an all-India crisis on a large scale.

"Preparations for the threatened movement continue. Bimal Protiva Devi (ex-detenu) is reported to have given out that 3500 Satyagrahis, including 300 Sikhs have been enrolled. One Hopchand Kothari of 165 Bowbazar Street, had asked Subhas's permission to resort to sympathetic hunger strike."[60] Bose could feel the pulse of the common people and realized that most people wanted a mass movement which would ultimately lead to a war of independence and with this end in view he tried to awaken the whole nation with the help of the revolutionaries.

Police records show that the Bengal revolutionaries were aided also by Bose's elder brother Sarat Bose in many ways. An agent of the Directorate of the I.B. reported on the 12th of October 1939 that Purnananda Dasgupta (convict, Alipore Central Jail), wrote to Rabindra Mohan Sengupta (ex-state prisoner, *Anushilan* Samity), on 12th Oct.1939 informing him that there was no chance of a hunger strike at that point of time. The conditional offer of release by the Government had been rejected by the convicts...the writer "wants Subhas Chandra Bose to issue a statement regarding his discussion with the Hon'ble Home Minister over the question of release and urges the necessity of an interview between Subhas Chandra Bose or Sarat Chandra Bose and the convicts." The writer informed the addressee that Surendra Nath Sarkhel of the *Jugantar* group recently released from the Midnapore Jail had been working with the *Anushilan* members in jail and was willing to work with them outside also. The writer expressed his inability to understand how the addressee could start a struggle in face of the Ordinance that would lead to the internment of the revolutionaries.[61]

It is true that when the 2nd World War started, there was widespread and indiscriminate imprisonment of the revolutionaries. As Britain was involved in the War, she did not want to have further trouble within their most prized possession i.e. India and that led them to the spate of internment of the trouble-shooters almost all over India particularly Bengal.

Sarat Bose, it may be noted, though not in favour of sporadic acts of violence, nevertheless believed that armed revolution would be necessary in the final phase of the struggle for freedom for terminating foreign rule. At the same time, he, in common with the patriotic Indians, could not withhold his admiration for the spirit of self-sacrifice and courage of the young revolutionaries who attempted to physically liquidate torturous police officers like Sir Charles Tegart and his followers responsible for committing acts of indescribable brutality on political prisoners in police custody and in jails. Further, in his capacity as a lawyer, Sarat Bose had extended help for the defence of persons accused of complicity in the murder of oppressive bureaucrats. He volunteered to defend Ananta Singh, one of the principal accused in the Chittagong Armoury Raid case. According to a confidential report:

"Sarat Bose paid the expenses of some revolutionaries who went to Burma to see Subhas Bose and to organize a movement there."[62]

When Dinesh Gupta was hanged, the Corporation of Calcutta passed a resolution "recording its sense of grief at the execution of Dinesh Chandra Gupta who sacrificed his life in the pursuit of his ideal". A confidential IB record states :

"This disgraceful tribute to a political murderer still stains the records of the Corporation and there can be no question whatever that Sarat Bose was the moving spirit behind it."[63]

It may be recalled that Charles Tegart had written in a confidential note, in 1932 that Sarat Bose assisted the revolutionary movement for years by means of his Purse, his Press and his Prestige. He was not the man to throw bombs himself but he was ready to provide money for their manufacture. He would probably never shoot a European official as long as he lives, but he was eager to incite young men to commit murder. Few men in this Presidency (Bengal) had provided so much money for revolutionary enterprises. No man was more responsible for the prevailing cult of revolver. No man had done as much as Sarat Bose to instill into the minds of the youth of Bengal that poisonous creed which justified political assassination and canonized political murderers. This very dangerous individual should be dealt with under Regulation III.[64]

The British Government imprisoned the younger Bose under Regulation III several times on the same grounds. An extract from a Home (Poll) file states:

"as the brother of Mr. Subhas Bose, Sarat Bose has all along played a very prominent part in Congress politics and he has acted as Mr. Bose's right hand man for a number of years."[65]

Many of the Bengal revolutionaries felt that both the Bose brothers were their leaders in the militant nationalist movement for freedom. They looked up to them for moral support, guidance and funds. It is evident from the police records that even after the fiasco at Tripuri, the revolutionaries depended heavily on Subhas Bose and his elder brother for guidance. A letter, written to Sarat Chandra Bose, dated 30th March 1939, signed by Ambika Charan Chakrabarty, prayed for the success of the '*Rashtrapati*' (President of the Indian National Congress) and his elder brother in the freedom struggle. "We, behind the prison bars, here, cannot do anything but sympathize with you...the nation have abundantly manifested during the Tripuri session and in course of Rashtrapati's election that we should plunge headlong in the struggle for freedom having an unstinted conviction in our own strength and policy without depending upon Imperialism and idly killing time. Nobody can place an impediment to it."

The revolutionaries in the post-Tripuri days, wanted Bose and his elder brother to be at the forefront of the struggle. Within the Congress, they noticed two policies to be evident in those days. On the one hand, "there is a tendency to confine the struggle within parliamentary tactics after transgressing the mass revolution. On the other hand, to lead the mass revolution on the basis of your and Rashtrapati's policy and to utilize the Ministry and the Legislature tending towards mass struggle. A friction of these two policies is evident in every major issue."[66]

Bose was in constant touch with the revolutionaries, known as the "*Swadeshis*" in those days, with the help of whom he planned to mobilize the youth for a mass uprising. An ex-detenu Dhirendralal Das Sharma of Chittagong is reported to have shown Bose a letter written by convict Ambika Chakrabarty in which he instructed the members of the revolutionary groups to mobilize secretly. The letter was smuggled out of jail by them but evidently, through the police agents, the information reached the Special Branch. It was difficult in those days for the revolutionaries to organize a mass movement on a grand scale within the country against all odds in front of the ever-vigilant eyes of the Special Branch that considered them nothing but criminals.

However, the Forward Bloc formed by Bose was a source of inspiration and courage not only for the Bengal revolutionaries, but also for all the freedom loving people belonging to different professions all over the country. *Anushilan* had branches not only in Bengal, but even outside and this is evident from the police records. The police record entitled "Anushilan- Central Provinces" states that some R.Ranga Rao of the Robertson College, Jabbalpore had informed ex-detenu Ramesh Acharji that he was particularly glad about the formation of Subhas Bose's Forward Bloc which he described as the only party which would lead the way to immediate freedom. Referring to affairs in Hyderabad, he is reported to have said that all concerned were prepared for a greater sacrifice.⁶⁷ It may be deduced from the above record that *Anushilan* Samity had a widespread network that included even the Central Provinces.

The police kept its watchful eyes on the Forward Bloc activities as it was to them, the vanguard of the militant nationalists because Bose was its leader. They tried to collect information about its members through the various agents spread all over India. According to an SB report, a revolutionary called Abinash Bhattacharjee was "either an ex-detenu or an ex-convict employed in the Calcutta Corporation, immediately after his release, by Subhas Bose, and is working there for the Bloc."⁶⁸

Sarala Devi, one of the early exponents of militant nationalism, was also under the vigilance of the secret police. Report mentions that a man called Dipak Dutta Chowdhury "is a pet child of Sarala Devi and is actively connected with her political activities. The family has close association with the Bose family. Sarala Devi and Dipak are well-known to the Bose brothers."⁶⁹

During the War, the *Anushilan* leaders tried to motivate people by insisting on the non-violent character of the ensuing movement, as they were not prepared for an armed resistance. Their leader Pratul Ganguli said that the party must try to obtain "the cooperation of the Indian troops and procure fire-arms which they lack at present. When a mass revolution breaks out, arms should be collected by raiding small armouries and there would be arrangements to get assistance from the Indian troops."⁷⁰First and the foremost task ahead was motivating the people and winning their wholehearted support for a revolution and then the armed resistance would take place. The leaders knew that no revolution could succeed without a overwhelming mass support and no country had ever achieved independence without bloodshed. *Anushilan* Samity was trying to organize its members in a revolutionary army under the leadership of Bose. It is reported that a meeting was held at 7/8 Harrison

Road on 22-12-39, in which Pratul Ganguli said that the tactics to be adopted in the coming civil struggle would be entirely different from the tactics employed in the past. He advised *Anushilan* members to think well before joining the struggle as they might have to risk going to jail. "He reminded his hearers that the *Anushilan* was supporting Subhas Bose and if the movement was a success, their party would regain much of its lost influence in Calcutta."[71]

Bose was planning his escape from the country during this period as he realized that the Old Guards of the Congress would not allow him, under any circumstances, to use the party as a revolutionary platform and launch an attack on the imperialist usurpers who were in a difficult position due to the War. Simultaneously, he had to fight with the High Command for the shabby treatment they meted out to his elder brother Sarat Bose, the then leader of the Congress Parliamentary Party in Bengal, by taking disciplinary action against him. Bose took the whole thing as an attack on Bengal's home front and declared that if the High Command persisted in their present policy, there would be a parallel election not only in Bengal but throughout India at the next general election.

Bose was so close to his elder brother that when disciplinary action was taken against the latter by Maulana Azad as the Congress President, he was shocked and, fairly enough, issued a statement in protest. He suggested that all the Congress members of the Assembly should resign and seek re-election on this issue. He threw a challenge to Gandhi to set up the Working Committee's candidates to fight the elections as against candidates to be set up by the Bengal Provincial Congress Committee.[72]

Bose was very much perturbed on this issue and he said that it passed his comprehension how such a step could be taken by the Maulana when the country was passing through a crisis of that magnitude and the Congress leaders themselves had been making repeated appeals for unity. He commented:

"I need hardly say that we, on our part, desire national unity from the bottom of our hearts and we are fully prepared for an honourable solution of all outstanding differences and problems. But we cannot accept the position, which some Congress leaders have taken up, namely, that the offer of honourable compromise can be made to the British Govt., but not to one's friends and colleagues on the Left."[73]

Bose reminded the High Command that if any attempt was made to insult or humiliate or discredit the Congressmen of Bengal in the public eye, they would be under the painful necessity of not only resisting such an attack, but of counter-attacking wherever they found it possible to do so. The fact that they were preoccupied with larger issues, should not induce the Maulana and his friends to think that they would ignore the attack from the Right on their Home Front. [74]

Bose defended his elder brother by refuting the allegation of the High Command regarding breach of discipline. He said that discipline in an autocratic organization meant obeying the orders of one's superior officer or officers. In a democratic organization it meant abiding by the will of the majority. The Maulana and the Congressmen of his way of thinking demanded that since they were in the majority in the All-India Congress Committee, the Leftist minority should implicitly obey the majority's will and on their failing to do so, they should be punished. The same principle of rule by majority should naturally be applied in the Provincial Congress Committee as well but it was not done. "Here in Bengal, the Rightist minority want to defy the Leftist majority with impunity and when they do so, they are always supported by the Rightist High Command." [75]

He pointed out that one could not have it both ways applying a double standard. Rule by majority in the All-India Congress Committee and a rule by minority in the Bengal Provincial Congress Committee cannot exist simultaneously. Consequently the argument of 'discipline at any cost', which

Maulana advanced, could not hold water, he said. As a matter of fact, Maulana wanted to penalize the leader of the Bengal Congress Parliamentary Party for giving effect to a resolution of the Party viz. that the leader should issue the whip for the indirect election to the Upper House.

In Bengal, however, it was mainly the revolutionaries who constituted the Leftist majority in Congress and later, joined the Forward Bloc en masse. What the All-India Congress Committee was practicing in those days, according to Bose, was nothing but authoritarianism as they suspended the existing Bengal Congress Committee and introduced an ad hoc committee in its place. "Authoritarianism on the part of a dictator or a group, may be tolerated if either of them has the necessary following and position in a particular area. In the case of Bengal, neither the Maulana nor even Gandhi should be unaware of the real position.

"In the last analysis, if the Congress is a national organization as we all claim, the justification for that claim will depend on the degree of public confidence it can command. Since the ad hoc committee does not command public confidence in Bengal, no fiats from Ballygunge Circular Road (the residence of Maulana Azad in Calcutta) or from Wardha (where Gandhi stayed) can infuse life into it and convert it into a Provincial Congress Committee." [76]

Bose further said that no ukase from either place can kill the valid BPCC and that was the reason why even after the so-called suspension, they had continued to function under the name of the BPCC and would be continuing to do so in future. Bose and his followers did not resign from the Provincial Congress even after the formation of the Forward Bloc as the Congress was its parent body. The Bengal leaders, evidently, did not accept the order of the High Command for the suspension of the BPCC on a ground that they found to be unjustifiable. As a matter of fact, the Old Guard of the INC could not reconcile themselves with the step taken by Bose, i.e. formation of the Forward Bloc. Probably it appeared to them as an unpardonable offence which could not go with impunity.

Bose pointed out that those who had taken the oath of allegiance to His Majesty King George and his heirs, would not necessarily be bound by that pledge if a revolution took place... "Likewise a revolution has taken place within the Congress during the last two years which has altered the situation beyond all recognition."

He further said,

"There can be no question of going out of Congress because we are Congressmen and our organizations are Congress organizations. If in future we have to fight the High Command, in the elections throughout the country as we have fought in the extra-parliamentary sphere, we shall do so in the name of Congress and not by going out of Congress. The Congress is ours as much as it is anybody else's." [77]

He started his political career as a Congressman, and he knew that Congress was not just a political party at that time; it was a common platform from which any nationalist Indian could convey his message to the people and to the power that be. If Forward Bloc got separated from Congress, it would lose its credibility to the common people.

In spite of all this, Bose expected the Gandhians in Congress to accept the policies and programmes of the Bloc and he depended heavily on the support of the Leftists. But there was no reason for him to nurture such an expectation after the Tripuri fiasco. He was well aware of the fact that J. P. Narayan, for instance, no matter how much he believed in socialism, would never oppose Gandhi beyond a certain point and come close to him, as Narayan felt that without Gandhi's leadership, it was impossible for anyone to start a national movement whatsoever. Bose also knew that the other Left groups were disunited and weak whereas the Gandhians within

Congress were in a very strong position and it would be an uphill task for anyone to challenge the overwhelming popularity of Gandhi amongst the masses. He expected the Forward Bloc to have the same success as that of the Swarajya Party under the leadership of C.R.Das in 1923-1925, but in 1939-40, the whole political scenario changed beyond recognition. The nature of his conflict with Gandhi and the one between C.R.Das and Gandhi was completely different. During those years, Gandhian leadership was in its infancy which grew into a monstrosity in the late 1930s. Besides, there were the Rightist Gandhian leaders whose antagonism towards Bose was of an extreme kind, who indirectly forced him to resign from the Congress Presidentship and wanted to annihilate him politically. Surprisingly, Bose expected even these people to allow him and his Bloc to work within Congress and to change the existing Congress policy of compromise. Later on, of course, he was disillusioned.

It is possible to explain why Bose had these expectations from the Old Guards. Even after Tripuri, he did not give up the hope of unifying Congress. He thought that to fight against the British Raj, a united Congress was essential. After his resignation from the post of the *Rashtrapati*, the Gandhians would definitely cooperate with him, he thought. Secondly, he was overwhelmed by the spontaneous expression of anguish and sympathy for him all over the country after his resignation and the subsequent expulsion from the Party. The anxiety people showed during his illness, their concern for his health and their prayer for his quick recovery affected his political thinking to a great extent.

After the formation of the Forward Bloc, he travelled throughout the country and addressed almost a thousand public meetings. Everywhere he was received with hysterical expressions of applause and ovation that led him to believe that even if he started a movement against the wishes of Gandhi, he would be supported by the people. Thirdly, the

The Uncompromising Loner (1938-1941)   255

Forward Bloc was getting more and more popular which made him optimistic about the future of the party. Even Gandhi himself admitted that after his resignation, Bose had become more popular than before. Inspite of all the differences, Bose always gave importance to Gandhi's comments and observations.

Even Rabindra Nath Tagore was very much perturbed by the decision of the Congress to expel Bose from the party. He requested Gandhi and the members of the Working Committee to withdraw the order of expulsion for the sake of national unity. Dinabandhu Andrews also wrote a letter to Gandhi with the same request to which Gandhi replied :

"I feel Subhas is behaving like a spoilt child of a family. The only way to make up with him is to open his eyes...I am quite clear, the matter is too complicated for Gurudev to handle."[78]

For his political guru Deshabandhu Chittaranjan Das, Bose had great respect and he never hesitated to express it in unequivocal terms in front of the Old Guards. When he heard that Maulana described himself as more than a Bengali, he said, "If so, let him follow in the footsteps of our great leader Deshabandhu C.R.Das. Let him give up his policy of vendetta and through toleration and love that the Deshabandhu was able to convert foes into friends and present a united Bengal. No other gospel will appeal to this province." [79]

In his relentless struggle for independence, Bose never lost the support of the Bengal revolutionaries and towards the end, it was the Bengal Volunteers (BV) and the Anushilanites who were with him even in the final phases of his struggle. Although it is clear from the evidences that Bose was closely associated with the various revolutionary groups of Bengal, his closeness with the Bengal Volunteers was of a different dimension altogether. As Hemchandra Ghosh pointed out, since 1923, they were very close to each other and the message of revolution Bose wanted to internalize not only through his intellect, but also through his entire being as a result of which revolution gradually turned into his religion. "But because we were members of a secret society, our relationship was always kept a secret."[80]

During the period of 1939-40, Bose was unconditionally supported by the members of the BV in his struggle against the Congress stalwarts. A mention may be made of Satya Bakshi, Major Satya Gupta, Manindra Kishore Ray and Jyotish Joardar who joined his side openly. The office of the Forward Bloc and *Forward* newspaper was housed, at the outset, at 49 L, Dharmatala Street on the ground floor. Later the office was shifted to the 2nd and the 3rd floor of the Indian Association Hall in Bowbazar, Calcutta. Manindra Kishore Ray of the BV was the whole-time manager of the office and *Forward*, the daily newspaper, with BV's Niranjeeb Ray as its printer and publisher. Every week, almost 80,000 copies used to be printed from Popular Printing Press owned by BV's friends called Bijoy Dhar and Debendra Lal Basak of Calcutta. Niranjeeb Ray and Phani Majumdar used to bear the responsibility of supervising and directing the work of the daily under the instruction of Satya Bakshi, the party secretary. This goes to show that the Forward Bloc of Bose and the BV were in close connection with each other.

Seven or eight months after the shifting of the Forward Bloc office to the Indian Association Hall, on the 13th of April, 1940, twenty five leading members of the BV got arrested at dawn. As a result, Bose's connections with the BV were disrupted all on a sudden. Yet the very next day he contacted Sudhir Bakshi, the younger brother of Satya Bakshi and enquired about the other reliable BV leaders still not confined. Sudhir Bakshi met BV leader Jatish Guha, the man behind the killing of Burge, the District Magistrate of Midnapore and the attempted murder of Anderson, through Amalendu Ghosh (BV), and took him to Bose at his Elgin Road residence. Bose's plans for leaving the country was taking shape at that time and Jatish Guha became a reliable consort of Bose with regard to communications with the North West frontier region, Punjab Forward Bloc and the Kirti Kissan Party.

Bose always tried to do everything methodically and hence, meticulous planning used to precede all his actions. He organized the Hallwell movement with a definite purpose in view, i.e. he wanted the Government to focus its attention totally on this movement so that the bureaucracy could be kept in the dark about his larger plans of going out of the country and launch an attack on the Raj from outside.

On the 2nd of July 1940, the day before the starting of the movement, he was arrested and thrown into the Presidency Jail, where Hem Ghosh, Satya Bakshi and Manindra Kishore Ray were already kept imprisoned, all from the BV. They decided that the war had presented before them an opportunity which they must utilize to the best of their ability, and somehow or the other they had to come out of the prison to implement their plans. Bose commenced his fast unto death on and from the day of the Kali Puja in the month of November as a protest against his detention without trial and got himself conditionally released on the 5th of December 1940. The Government of India was very much annoyed with this decision of the Govt of Bengal as it was unwilling to see Bose outside prison walls.[81] He was, however, kept interned in his Elgin Road residence surrounded by IB agents.

The B. V. leaders like Jatish Guha, Binay Sengupta, Kamakshya Ray and Sasanka (Comet) Dasgupta under the leadership of Satya Bakshi were actively involved in his secret plans and their execution. They stood all along behind Bose's dramatic escape from India. It was with their financial help that Bhagatram Talwar of the Kirti Kisan Party (the North-west wing of the CPI) could escort him from Peshawar to Kabul and saw him off to go to Moscow. (Amalendu Ghosh of the BV said in an interview with the author at his own residence in Calcutta).

In 1941, when away from India, Bose sent a message written in pencil to his compatriots in India through his guide Bhagat Ram Talwar. Bhagat Ram came to Calcutta after Bose's departure from Kabul for Moscow and met Sarat Bose in his Woodburn Park residence on the 31st March 1941. Along with the message, Bhagat Ram brought an article written for the periodical named *Forward Bloc* entitled 'Forward Bloc-Its Justification'. The message was entitled, 'To My Countrymen' in which his own address was given as 'Somewhere from Europe.' In this message, he explained the reasons behind his escape from India, as a result of which the Bengal Volunteers took the initiative of circulating it everywhere. Jatish Guha, Binay Sen, Kamakshya Ray and many other leading members of the B.V. took an active part in printing and distributing the message in different parts of the country. To all the consulates in Calcutta, to the lawyers of the Calcutta High Court and other courts, to the well-known educationists and other celebrities, copies of the said message were sent in ornate envelopes commonly used for wedding invitations. As a precautionary measure, on top of the envelope, the word '*Shubho Bibaha*' (Auspicious Wedding) was inscribed to deceive the I.B.[82]

Bose, however, asked Bhagatram to contact the B.V. leaders in Calcutta for sending two reliable B.V. men to Kabul with the purpose of communicating with him and also for taking training from the Italian legation. He wanted at least one of them to be selected by Satya Bakshi. As per his instructions, Satya Bakshi took up the responsibility and sent B.V.'s Shantimoy Ganguli to Peshawar. Bhagatram, his associate Harmahinder Singh and Ganguli reached Kabul on the 1st of May 1941. The latter sent all the necessary information regarding the secret activities of the revolutionaries in Bengal to Bose in Germany through the Italian legation and took his instructions to be followed back home. Bose was happy to learn that Bakshi, one of his closest allies, was still outside jail.[83]

In the middle of June 1941, Shantimoy Ganguli and the

others came back from Kabul.[84]

The work Bose started in Germany required communications with India as a result of which a powerful radio transmission centre was set up near the Northwest frontier under the supervision of the German engineers. It was decided that as soon as the Indian engineers took charge of the same, the Germans would go back to their country.[84A] Satyabrata Majumdar of B. V. was assigned the responsibility of the centre, and if he were incapable, then the task would come upon another engineer Phani Chowdhury. Unfortunately, the plan did not materialize due to an unforeseen contingency as Germany launched an attack on Russia on the 22nd June 1941, which changed India's political scenario to a great extent. The Kirti Kisan Party changed its stand immediately, and the imperialist war became people's war to the Indian communists overnight following the instructions of the CPGB. It not only dissociated itself from the BV, also disclosed the names of the BV leaders to the police. As a result, Satya Bakshi, Jatish Guha, Binay Sen, Comet Dasgupta and Amalendu Ghosh, the leading BV men, were arrested immediately and thrown into the prisons. Satya Bakshi and Jatish Guha were kept in the Red Fort of Delhi, tortured mentally as well as physically. Shantimoy Ganguli escaped punishment by absconding.

It will not be irrelevant here to mention that the major burden of the funds required for the escape of Bose from India to foreign lands was shouldered by the B.V. men. Their contribution in this regard was remarkable.[85]

The Bengal Volunteers, it may be noted, however, considered themselves as Bose's 'Home Front' after his departure from India. They followed his instructions religiously as long as they could maintain contacts with him.[85A]

It may be mentioned that Jyotish Bose, an ex-revolutionary and one of the closest allies of Subhas Chandra Bose, maintained contact with him through transmitters after his departure from India. On the roof of his Deshapriya Park residence was kept a powerful transmitter through which Bose used to communicate from abroad with his people in Calcutta. This house was also a favourite hide-out for the Bengal revolutionaries during those days. Jyotish Bose, however, was captured by the police with hundreds of other followers of Bose. Most of them were exiled to the Andaman Cellular Jail while Jyotish Bose was kept at the Presidency jail, Alipore, to be hanged on 30th June 1945. The order was, however, revoked due to Gandhi's intervention[86]

REFERENCES

1. *Collected Works of Mahatma Gandhi*, Vol. LXV, Publications Division, Govt of India, Navajivan Trust, Ahmedabad, 1975, p. 4
2. Bose, Ashoke Nath, *My Uncle Netaji*, Bharatiya Bidya Bhavan, Bombay 1989, p.134
3. *CWMG*, Vol. LXI, op.cit. pp 253-4, and p. 310, see also G.D.Birla, *Bapu*, Vol 2, Bharatiya Bidya Bhavan, Bombay, 1977, p 106
4. *CWMG*, Vol LX, op.cit, 1974, P 227
5. Birla, *Bapu*, Vol 2, op cit. p 123
6. S.Gopal, ed., *Selected Works of Jawaharlal Nehru*, Orient Longman, New Delhi, 1974, Vol 7, p.210
7. Ibid, Vol 7, p. 206
8. *Purushottamdas Thakurdas Papers*, File 177, Nehru Memorial Museum Library, cited in S.Gopal, p. 209, Vol 7
9. *CWMG*, Vol LXV, p. 325
10. Presidential Address at Haripura Congress, February 1938 quoted in Markandeya, S. *Netaji S.C.Bose*, Arnold Associates, New Delhi, pp.116-117.
11. Corr, Gerard H., *The War of the Springing Tiger*, Bombay, 1975, cited in Markandeya, *Netaji Subhas Chandra Bose*, ibid., p.122.
12. *Selected Speeches of Subhas Chandra Bose*, edited by S.A.Ayer, Publication Division, Govt of India, 1962, p. 103
13. Ananda Bazar Patrika dated 11.3 .1939
14. Overstreet, Gene D. and Windmiller, Marshall, *Communism in India*, pp. 168-170
15. Ibid. p. 181

16. Bose, S.C., *Indian Struggle*, Oxford University Press, New Delhi, 1998, pp.376-377
17. Ibid. p. 377
18. De, Ramaprasad, Director, National Council of Education, Bengal, Cal. 32, to the author— oral statement recorded on 4th March 2002 at the National Council, Jadavpore, Calcutta
19. File No. C 616/40, Special Branch, Calcutta Police
20. Bose, S.C., *The Indian Struggle*, p.386
21. Overstreet and Windmiller, *Communism in India*, University of California Press, Berkeley 1959, pp 194
21A. Holt, Thaddeus, the Deceivers, Skyhorse Publishing, New York, 2007, P. 308.
22. Bell, David, *The End of Ideology*, Free Press, New York, 1965
23. File No. C 616/40, Special Branch, Calcutta Police
24. Ibid
25. Ibid, p. 6
26. Ghosh, Amalendu, formerly of the B.V.—oral statement recorded by the author on 30th January 1999 in Calcutta
27. Markandeya, S. *Netaii Subhas Chandra Bose*, Arnold Publishers, p. 138
28. Ibid, pp. 138-139
29. Ibid, p. 143
30. *Basumati*, a Bengali weekly, 1968, Calcutta
31. Caveeshar, Shardul Singh, article in the Puja No. of the Hindusthan Standard in 1962
32. File No. 41/7/37-Home Poll, State Archive of West Bengal
33. Ibid,
34. Ibid,
34.A Basu, Shankari Prasad, *Nivedita Lokmata* (in Bengali) Vol.2, Ananda Publishers, Pvt. Ltd., Calcutta, 1394 B.S. pp.184-197.
35. Sengupta, Subodh, *India Wrests Freedom*, Shishu Sahitya Samsad, Calcutta, 1982, p. 15
36. Op cit, *The Indian Struggle* p. 22
37. (Nehru, J .L., *Discovery of India*, pp. 504, 526), quoted by Subodh Sengupta, *India Wrests Freedom*, p. 245
37A. Dutta, Kshirod Kumar, Bharater Swadhinata Sangram O Anushilan Samity, Anushilan Samity Pachattartama Pratistha Barshiki Udjapan

Committee, Kolkata, PP. 126-132 (in Bengali).
38. Nehru, J.L., *Selected Works*, Vol. 2, p. 10, General Editor S.Gopal, Orient Longman, Delhi 1972
39. Ibid, pp. 11-12
40. Ibid,
41. C 616/40, Special Branch Calcutta Police
42. Ibid,
43. Ibid,
44. Bose, S.C., *Crossroads*. 1962, pp. 179-180, also his unsigned editorial in Forward Patrika, dated 12-8-1939,
45. Ibid, p.178
46. PM 522/38, Special Branch, Calcutta Police
47. Op cit, *Crossroads*, p.112
48. *Jawahar Lal Nehru, An Autobiography*, John Lane, The Bodley Head London, reprint February 1947, p. 22
49. Bose, *Crossroads*, op cit. p.23
50. Servant of India, A study of Imperial Rule from 1905 to 1910 as narrated on the basis of the letters and diaries of Sir Dunlop Smith by Lord Butler, Longmans, 1966, PP. 121-122.
51. Mukhopadhyaya, Jadugopal, *Biplabir Jibaner Smriti*, (in Bengali), Academic Publishers, Calcutta, 1982, pp.520-522
52. File No. CM 525/42, Special Branch, Calcutta Police
53. Ibid
54. PM 700/40, Special Branch, Calcutta Police
55. Ibid
56. PM 511/38, SB, Calcutta Police
57. Ibid
58. Ibid
59. Ibid
60. Ibid
61. Ibid
62. 31/XXVII- 32, Home Poll, Government of India, quoted in *Sarat Bose Commemoration Volume*, p.123, Sarat Bose Academy Calcutta, 1982
63. Ibid, p.131
64. Ibid
65. Ibid, p.133

The Uncompromising Loner (1938-1941)   263

66. Ibid.
67. Ibid, p.136
68. Ibid, pp. 141-142
69. Ibid, p. 142
70. Ibid, p.31
71. Ibid, p.147
72. Ibid, p.38
73. PM 511/38, SB, Calcutta Police
74. Ibid
75. PM/805/42, SB, Calcutta Police
76. Ibid
77. M 598/39, SB, Calcutta Police
78. Ibid
79. 516/40, SB, Calcutta Police
80. Ibid
81. Ibid
82. Majumdar, Satyabrata, formerly of the BV, oral statement to the author, recorded on the 16th June, 2000 at his residence in Sonarpore, near Calcutta.
83. File No. 516/40, Special Branch, Calcutta Police
84. Interview of the author with Mrs. Sneha Ganguli, the widow of Shantimoy Ganguli (BV), a close associate of Bose, at her Calcutta residence on 24/01/1998.
84A. Interview of the author with Satyabrata Majumdar on 16/6/2000 in Sonarpur, near Calcutta.
85. Author's interview with Amalendu Ghosh at his residence in Calcutta on 30th January 1999, also Speech delivered by Uma Mukherjee, at the Institute of Historical Studies, Calcutta on the 29th July, 2000
85A. Majumdar, Satyabrata, interviewed by the author on 16/6/2000. Also in *Netajir Homefront* (in Bengali) by Satyabrata Majumdar, Subodh Mitra, Calcutta, 1404 BS.
86. Author's interview with Jyotish Bose, an ex-revolutionary, at his Deshapriya Park (Calcutta) residence on 16th August 1997.

6
CONCLUSION

Militant nationalism was an outcome of a desire in the minds of the subjugated people of India for resistance. The spirit of self-sacrifice to put up resistance against the alien rulers facilitated the development of a revolutionary movement in India, particularly Bengal. Bankim Chandra Chattopadhyay gave a clarion call to the Bengalis and through them to all the Indians when he said that a patriot was not to have a mother, father, brother, wife or children, the country was his only mother, who was greater than the heavens, "*Janani Janmabhumischa Swargadapi Gariyasee.*" The mother in bondage, was immersed in the ocean of eternity, who was going to rescue her and reinstate her on a pedestal of glory? Bankim asked.

Nationalism was elevated to a spiritual level also by Swami Vivekananda whose practical *Vedanta* strongly urged for the socio-economic and political reconstruction of the motherland which would lead to the development of the spiritual life of everyone in society. The youth of Bengal was rejuvenated by the message of Swami Vivekananda who instilled in them a spirit of nationalism that paved the way for the emergence of a new India. At the Chicago conference on world religions, in 1893, he said that the need of the hour for India was not religion, the teeming millions were in need of food, a square meal a day but in stead, what they received was brickbats. In January, 1902, Japan organized a similar

Conclusion 265

conference on world religions and invited Vivekananda to attend it. In December 1901, *Kakasu Okakura*, the well-known painter from Japan, came to India for escorting Vivekananda to his country but the latter could not go due to ill health. *Okakura* was given felicitation in Suren Tagore's house where he said that the whole of Asia had one single culture and both China and Japan got united in their attempt to terminate western hegemony in this region. India had to be liberated to be drawn into this endeavour. When he criticized the lackadaisical attitude of the Indian people for being so inactive in this regard, young barrister P.N.Mitra who later founded the *Anushilan Samity*, felt deeply hurt and decided to do something worthwhile to facilitate the struggle for national liberation. As a result, on the 10th of March 1902, *Anushilan Samity* came into being on the auspicious day of *Dolpurnima*. The ideal of the society was not only physical exercise and training in lathi-charge, but a holistic development of human faculties with the help of practice that is *Anushilan* of potentialities following the ideal of Bankinchandra. P.N.Mitra became the president, with C. R. Das, Aurobindo Ghosh, Suren Tagore and Satish Basu as the vice-presidents, treasurer and secretary respectively. A National Council consisting of five members including Sister Nivedita, was formed to look after the revolutionary campaigns and 49 Cornwallis Street became the head office. The contribution of Sister Nivedita in this regard was remarkable but her role in the Indian freedom struggle has not yet been properly assessed.

One may point out here that it was Raja Ram Mohan Ray who was very much inspired by the ideals of the French Revolution, its battle cry of liberty, equality and fraternity. Young Bengal was charged with these slogans and it was Ram Mohan who initiated the celebration of the Bastille Day every year at the Calcutta Maidan. At this festival, the tri-colour of the French Republic used to be hoisted and it may be mentioned here that after a good many alterations later, the tri-colour became the national flag of India after Independence.

When we look back, we find that to suppress the mutiny of 1857, the British took recourse to unprecedented torture on Indian population. This was an eye-opener for the educated Indians who realized that the alien rulers were not their friends; the relationship was actually between a master and the slaves. Besides, the British officers who started coming in to India with a high and mighty attitude, following the change of administration from East India Company directly to the British Government, did not show any eagerness to befriend the Indian population. The Mutiny demonstrated that in the political arena there was a desire to break loose from Western fetters. From this consciousness, sprang up a nationalistic sense of self-respect the ground of which was prepared by Ram Mohan Roy, Ishwar Chandra Vidyasagar, Keshab Chandra Sen and their followers. The cultural movement, the Renaissance that started in Bengal at about this time was in every way nationalistic. According to Subodh Sengupta, Bankim Chandra was the greatest figure of the second phase of the Bengal Renaissance as Ram Mohan was of the first. In course of time, with the enlightenment of the *Renaissance,* Michael Madhusudan, Hemchandra, Nabin Sen and many other Bengali intellectuals appeared on the scene one after the other. Bankim Chandra may be regarded as the father of modern Indian nationalism, as he was the high-priest of *Bande Mataram,* our greatest national song. His novel *Anandamath* (1882) was the Bible for the secret revolutionaries who modeled their secret societies on the organization founded by Satyananda, the main character of *Anandamath.* Bankim Chandra reinterpreted the Western concept of nationalism as an intense love of motherland based on an awareness about its past greatness and future potentialities. The novel was based on the story of a band of selfless *Sanyasees* who regarded the motherland as the mother Goddess Durga, the source of great power and energy. With them devotion to motherland was a

Conclusion

religion and selfless service for reinstating her from the present degenerate conditions to the status of her former glory was the only form of worship to the deity. Bankim thus, raised the concept of nationalism to a level of divinity.

Bengal saw the arrival of Rabindranath Tagore in the world of Bengali literature and music, Abanindranath Tagore and Nandalal Bose in the arena of painting, Jagadishchandra Bose and Acharya Prafullachandra in the sphere of science. The last quarter of the 19th century and the 1st of the 20th may be regarded as the turning point in Indian history. The seeds of independence were sown during this period of time.

In the British Indian Army, there was no place for the Bengalis; the authorities armed every community except the Bengalis for reasons best known to themselves. Strangely enough, a community intellectually so advanced, mentally so progressive, were deprived of an opportunity to fight militarily against the enemy. While in England, P.Mitra tried to get into the Army but could not succeed, Brahmabandhav Upadhyay left home for getting into the Army but he too failed to fulfill his dreams. The Bengalis, therefore, had to take up arms in their own hands for national liberation which they believed, was the need of the hour. Pistols were the only alternative to rifles which they could not procure, and indigenous bombs served the purpose of arms in their fight for freedom. The two militant nationalists, who fought against such a formidable enemy as the British, by giving leadership to a well-organised army, were none other than Rash Behari Basu and Subhas Chandra Bose, both from Bengal.

The revolutionaries of Bengal, labeled "terrorists" by the British rulers, started their revolutionary campaign much before the commencement of the movement against partition of Bengal in 1905. That was the first phase of the revolutionary movement, which continued for several years.

Girija Shankar Raychowdhury, the biographer of Aurobindo Ghosh wrote that there was a society in Cambridge called *The Lotus and Dragon Society* the aim of which was to achieve Indian independence through militancy. This was the place where Aurobindo and C.R.Das, batch-mates in Cambridge, met and came close to one another. They used to deliver speeches in the *Mujlish*, the association of the Indian students abroad, on the misrule of the British in India. The ideology of the French Revolutionaries exerted influence also on Aurobindo. He came back to India in 1893 and joined the Gaekoad College in Baroda as the Principal on the request of *Maharaja* Sayaji Rao.

Towards the end of the 19th century, the ideal of national liberation took the form of certain festivals like the *Ganapati Utsav* and *Shivaji Utsav* in Maharashtra. Balgangadhar Tilak was the leader of these nationalistic festivities under the general supervision of Thakursahab, the ruler of a native state in Madhya Pradesh, who subsequently went to Japan and joined the Russo-Japanese war never to come back. The series of articles written by Aurobindo published in the periodical called *Induprakash* drew the attention of the group of Thakursahab who made him the president of his group's Gujrat branch when the former joined the *Anushilan Samity*. It was Sister Nivedita who went to Baroda in 1902 and requested Aurobindo to come to Bengal and join the revolutionary movement. In the account of Barin Ghosh, it is stated that Bengal went the revolutionary way from 1902 onwards, but five years earlier, the first militant spark was noticed in Poona arising out of a Hindu-Moslem riot. Due to the bureaucratic repression, that spark was extinguished with the hanging of the Chapekar brothers who killed two European officers (1897) and the imprisonment of Tilak, as a result Bengal had to take up the responsibility of rekindling that extinct flame with a new fervour.

In the early years, the centre of the revolutionaries was 108 Circular Road in Calcutta where rigorous training in mind and body of 'the political missionaries' (Kshirod Dutta), took place. Senior members gave honorary service as barrister

P.Mitra taught world history, Sakharam Deoskar gave detailed account of the prolonged colonial exploitation of India, Jatin Banerjee taught war techniques, and Suren Tagore was the teacher of the European Renaissance, the American War of Independence, and the history of the Irish liberation movement.

Aurobindo Ghosh published a booklet of sixteen pages called *Bhabani Mandir* which aimed at the establishment of a temple of Goddess Bhabani, worshipped by Shivaji, where an army of dedicated revolutionaries would be formed at the altar of the Goddess. About *Bhabani Mandir* the Rowlatt Committee Report stated :

"The central idea as to a given religious order is taken from the well-known novel Anandamath of Bankim Chandra. We find the glorification of Kali under the name of Shakti or Bhabani (two of her numerous names), and preaching the gospel of force and strength as the necessary condition of freedom. The necessity of Indians to worship Shakti or Bhabani, manifested as the mother of strength is insisted upon if success is desired. A new order of political devotees was to be instituted. A new organization of political sanyasis was to be started who were to prepare the way for revolutionary work. It was the liberation of India from foreign yoke."(Report of Rowlatt Committee, p 67).

It is true that Tilak raised his voice against the policy of mendicancy followed by the INC but it was Aurobindo who showed for the first time, an alternative device to put the alien rulers into trouble. Way back in 1906, he preached the cult of passive resistance and non-cooperation and in a draft resolution on this device was put forward in the first issue of *Bande Mataram* edited by him. The objectives were as follows:

"(a) By an organized and relentless boycott of British goods we propose to render further exploitation of the country impossible.

(b) By an organized judicial boycott we propose to make the bureaucratic administration impossible.

(c) We refuse to send our boys to Government schools, schools aided and controlled by Government

(d) We refuse to go to the Executive for help or advice or protection." (*Studies in the Bengal Renaissance*, pp 170-171).

It may be said in agreement with R.C.Majumdar that the new school of politics known as the Extremists as opposed to the Moderates showed in unequivocal terms, the aim of the Indian political struggle and the methods to achieve it long before the Gandhians appeared on the scene with their much publicized doctrine of *Ahimsa*.

Inspired by the newspaper *Sandhya* introduced by Brahma Bandhav Upadhyay in August 1905, the militant nationalists of Bengal brought out their publication *Jugantar*, in March 1906 with Bhupendra Nath Dutta as its editor. From the very first issue, *Jugantar* started spreading the message of revolution and in 1910, members of different militant groups (*Bagha Jatin* or Jatindranath Mukherjee as one of their leaders), who were being tried in the Howrah Conspiracy Case, were collectively termed by the prosecution as 'Jugantar terrorists.' *Jugantar* served as a rallying point for the Aurobindo-Barindra group and many others who gradually came to be associated with this weekly like Abinash Bhattacharya, Debabrata Basu, to name but a few. In course of time, several militant groups scattered all over Bengal stuck to the name *Jugantar* without getting themselves merged into a single whole. Hence Jugantar, unlike *Anushilan*, due to the lack of a strong centralized leadership, functioned like a federation of various revolutionary groups and interestingly enough, even Bose was labeled by the bureaucracy as a 'Jugantar terrorist'.

During the movement against the Partition of Bengal in 1905, *Anushilan Samity* of Dacca was established which became in course of time, so powerful that it gained popularity all over the country and came to be known as THE *Anushilan Samity* outside Bengal. Besides these two major militant organizations, there were many other smaller groups, particularly in East Bengal who believed in the creed of revolutionism and agreed on the methods and techniques of operation. But, as Gopal Haldar points out in his essay called *'Revolutionary Terrorism'* in the *Studies in the Bengal Renaissance,* except for two brief interludes, in 1914-1917 and in 1925-1928, the *Anushilan* and the *Jugantar* could never see eye to eye with each other and to some extent it is true that the history of revolutionary campaign in Bengal is a history of rivalry between these two major groups which even brought about a rift within the Bengal Provincial Congress leadership in the post-C.R.Das period manifested in the Bose-Sengupta bi-polarity.

The British bureaucracy, however, having studied the motives of the revolutionaries thoroughly, admitted that they were not just terrorists; they "waged war against the King established by law."

C.R.Das, it may be noted, opposed the proposal of dyarchy presented by the Government of India Act of 1919 and brought it on the verge of collapse by legislative non-cooperation of elected Swarajya Party members in the councils. He opposed Sir Surendranath Banerjee at this stage who lost his relevance in Bengal in spite of his pioneering leadership in the political awakening of India in the late nineteenth century and his uncompromising opposition to the partition of Bengal in 1905. Das, incidentally, secured in the capacity of a practicing lawyer, Aurobindo Ghosh's release from the Maniktala Bomb Conspiracy Case in 1908. Ghosh's *Bhabani Mandir,* basically carrying forward the nationalist thought Bankim Chandra Chattopadhyay's *Anandamath* represented, was published, in all probability, in August 1905 - a crucial year in Indian history.

The second phase may be said to have started from 1920-21, which culminated in the militant struggle for independence by the Indian National Army under the leadership of Subhas Chandra Bose. In the final phase of the struggle for independence, Bose provided an alternative leadership in national politics, which was dominated by the Gandhians. This alternative leadership showed an alternative path to the freedom fighters of Bengal who believed that freedom could only be wrested from the alien rulers by a revolution, not by prayer and petition as professed by the mainstream Congress leaders.

The Bengal revolutionary groups were looking for an undisputed leader whose credibility and dedication to the cause would be beyond anybody's challenge and their expectations were personified by Bose who believed that independence could not be achieved without active resistance on a massive scale. In spite of their rivalry and difference of opinion on various issues, the Bengal revolutionaries with all their subgroups agreed on the question of the necessity of a common leader who would guide them in their common struggle for freedom through all thick and thin and Bose was their first choice.

It is to be noted that revolution and rebellion are not the same, particularly in the context of the revolutionary movement in Bengal. A rebel aims at an immediate objective. By any means the mission must be accomplished without delay and that is the culmination of a rebellion. But revolution is something more than that. A revolutionary ideal or goal, based on a passionate patriotism and a spirit of self-sacrifice, cannot be confined to an immediate achievement of something craved for and the enjoyment of it to the heart's content. It moves further and there is no end of its onward march, and hence, there is no scope of complacence in the life of a revolutionary. He must be ready to sacrifice his life for the transformation of social, political, and spiritual life of his countrymen and the revolutionary movement might even cover his entire life to be continued by the following generations. Society might have newer problems to tackle with, new strategies might have to be innovated by the revolutionary as a result of which he might have to change his plans and programmes to keep pace with time. In spite of all this the purpose and the ideal of revolution remains unchanged. Even if he fails in his mission, he will have a moral victory when his venture proves to be selfless and truly patriotic.

Revolutionary Bengal believed in the rejuvenation of India after liberation but it never discarded the traditional Indian values and beliefs, the wisdom of the sages. At the same time it did not live in the past glories ignoring the ground realities of the present. Revolutionary Bengal never accepted any particular Western or Eastern political philosophy, old or new, without judging their respective merits and that is why it did not accept Marxism as the one and only infallible ideology, an absolute truth. It may be pointed out this connection that within the period of 1931 to 1937, many of the nationalist revolutionaries in different jails, particularly Buxa, Deoli, Baharampore and Hijli Camps as well as the Andaman Cellular Jail, turned into Communists and the role played by the British rulers was remarkable in this process of transformation. During this period, piles of books on Marxism and Leninism started getting access into the prisons having been 'censored and passed'. Interestingly enough, even Sir John Anderson, then Governor of Bengal, having visited the Andamans in 1936, sent two huge wooden boxes of books as a gift to the Andaman prisoners on which it was written clearly "A gift from the Bengal Governor to the political prisoners of the cellular jail."

According to Ganesh Ghosh, the well-known Chittagong revolutionary, most of these books were Marxist literatures, Marxist philosophy and Marxist economy.[1] Ganesh Ghosh, who, later, became a Communist, wrote that during those days, the political prisoners used to be supplied with books on Marxism probably because the Government was under the impression that if the revolutionaries turned into Marxists, they would give up their doctrine of militant nationalism in favour of internationalism, they would have a wider perspective in their analysis of social change.

Dr. Parimal Ray, a detenu of the Deoli Camp in 1934, narrated in his book *Down Memory Lane* his experience there. He was asked by an IB officer in an interview in the said camp whether he had read any 'communistic literature' so far. Although, in those days, he was attending classes on Marxism taken by a co-prisoner comrade Kali Sen, Ray's answer was in the negative as he thought that a frank admission might enrage the authorities. He wrote:

"I was surprised with his comments in this." The officer retorted instantly, "Oh, that is why your ideas remain so narrow and parochial. You must read communist literature".[2]

The rulers noticed carefully the way the Indian Communists stayed away from the Salt Movement (*Laban Satyagraha*) of Gandhi, started using foreign clothes instead of boycotting them on the ground that the boycott would render the workers of Lancashire jobless. The Indian communists developed a global perspective as desired by the Raj, with sympathy and concern for the workers of the world, nationalism pushed to the backseat. All this made the rulers joyous and welcome Marxism in this country with open arms as a result of which the bureaucracy tried its best to convert the revolutionaries into hardcore communists and labeled this change as a revolutionary transcendence.

The Jugantar revolutionaries, however, were with Bose till 1935 as an important factor in Bengal politics but from the mid-thirties, they started associating themselves with the anti-Bose camps and ultimately merged themselves with the mainstream Congress leaving behind all traces of militant nationalism. When, as a leftist leader within the Congress, Bose proclaimed that real and ultimate power to be given to the people, otherwise people would capture power by any means, the *Anushilan* and the Bengal Volunteers supported him wholeheartedly.

Conclusion

Before the Tripuri Congress of 1939, the revolutionaries assembled at his residence for a discussion on current affairs. It was decided that Bose had to be re-elected as the Congress President to prevent the rightist Congress leaders from surrendering to the conditions laid down by the British rulers by means of their clandestine compromise formula. Acharya Narendra Dev, the well-known socialist, circulated a memorandum in support of Bose's candidature on the request of the *Anushilan* leaders. Trailokya Chakrabarty, and Ashrafuddin Ahmad Chowdhury of the *Anushilan* group, spread the message of Bose far and wide. Chakrabarty travelled all over North India along with Bose after the latter's suspension from the Congress for mobilizing popular support for a mass upheaval against British imperialism.

After 1940, however, Bose and Pratul Ganguli of the *Anushilan* group, decided, while in Alipore Central Jail, that since most of the revolutionaries were imprisoned, it would not be possible for them to have a rising from within, hence Bose would leave the country for Russia and Ganguli would meet him there. Bose always had a liking for Russia and the way the country reconstructed her economy during the post-revolution era.

Earlier in 1938, he received a letter from Rashbehari Basu, an ex-Anushilanite, asking him to lead the nation from the forefront with a revolutionary spirit to be instilled in the Congress, which was, to him, an evolutionary body.

Bose, with his extra-ordinary political foresight, realized that a second imperialistic war was in the offing and hence it was necessary to consolidate, without delay, the revolutionary forces in the country. Trailokya Chakrabarty said that Bose was the ideal of the Indian youth and the revolutionaries of Bengal were inspired by his fearlessness, intense pragmatism and his dynamic and uncompromising leadership.[3] The Bengal revolutionaries were emotionally involved with Bose and hence, they had a firm conviction that come what may, they would surely achieve the much-coveted independence under his leadership.

Bose requested Rabi Sen of the *Anushilan* Samity to send a reliable person to him for an urgent work. Tridib Chowdhury of the *Anushilan* Samity was selected by Rabi Sen and brought before Bose who sent him to one of his friends in the north-west frontier province with a letter, to make an assessment of the tribal situation there and the possibility of his escape through that region to an unknown destination. Tridib Chowdhury performed this task eight to nine months before Bose's escape.[4]

The Bengal revolutionaries realized that in order to fulfil the revolutionary ideals that included restructuring of the economy, national liberation was essential. For the eradication of poverty, the teeming millions must be set free. Sri Aurobindo had said once during the first decade of the 20th Century:

"Our nationalism is a religion that has come from God". He further said that when the divine message came down, Bengal was prepared to internalize it. It seemed as if the entire community woke up from slumber and gave a clarion call to the whole nation to follow the path of freedom.

What Aurobindo said about the preparedness of Bengal to accept the divine message, may be exemplified by the great personalities of 19th century Bengal who enlightened the country during the British regime itself. It may be recalled that Vivekananda, Bankim Chandra, Vidyasagar and Rabindranath Tagore already prepared the ground for resistance, implicitly or explicitly, in various ways.

One may also recall what Bipin Chandra Pal had to say on the 16th of October 1905, that life of every individual was great but the life of a nation was even greater, it was divine. In 1906, he wrote in *New India*,

"Absolute national autonomy is the national goal, and the nation must attain it or perish in the national attempt."

Conclusion

Vivekananda, the spiritual Guru of Bose, inspired young Bengal with his message that emphasized man-making more than anything else. He said that only one God was awake, that was the nation itself. One should let all the other Gods go to sleep for the time being, it should be the duty of the youngsters to serve the nation in all possible ways which included an arduous fight for freedom. He asked the youth to rise above casteism, untouchability and all kinds of slave mentality, or else, freedom would remain a far cry. Vivekananda's message rejuvenated the youth of Bengal; they became ready to fight not only against the foreign rulers but also against the feudalistic discriminatory practices prevalent in society, to uplift the downtrodden. A revolutionary psyche developed in course of time, in the minds of the youngsters, which prompted them to revere humanity as a whole irrespective of caste, creed, language or social status. They realized that a revolution could be successful only when it brought about a drastic change in society and politics. The motherland in bondage was to be served by all means because the service to the country was actually a service to God, they felt. They also realized that political freedom cannot be fruitful without a sense of commitment to the social cause and that is why the energy and enthusiasm of the revolutionary groups in Bengal did not waver after the initial outbursts.

Pratul Ganguli wrote in a Bengali periodical called *Prabasi*, (1367 B.S.), that the revolutionaries were the role models for the youngsters so far as character building was concerned. Honesty, discipline, perseverance and patriotism were considered to be the values constituting the foundation of human life. Certain moral values were adhered to by the young revolutionaries who dreamt of a free India, prosperous and egalitarian to be the pathfinder for all the colonized countries of the world. There were members in many revolutionary groups in Bengal who never saw any pistols or bombs throughout their life. It was the spirit of self sacrifice, not the weapons to be used for the annihilation of the enemy, that mattered the most.

It was these qualities of the Bengal revolutionaries that impressed Bose to a great extent. There is no doubt about the fact that 'revolutionism' i.e. the philosophy of revolution that developed in India was actually a contribution of Bengal that spread gradually in the other parts of the country. Incoherent militant actions and instances of self-sacrifice were there in the other parts of India but a carefully nurtured revolutionary creed as such, was nowhere in existence except in Bengal.

The revolutionaries of Bengal, however, were of different mental compositions. Those who were philosophically oriented and ready to sacrifice their lives for their convictions never distinguished between patriotism and humanism. They internalized the revolutionary creed, craving for getting rid of subjugation and all forms of discrimination in society.

Secondly, there were the young activists, who wanted to enjoy the romance of revolutionary adventures. They had undaunted spirit and courage to face any consequence of their action.

In the third category, one may put the power-loving ones who fought with the others for leadership, and often indulged in factional politics. There was yet another type who associated themselves with the revolutionary activities for the purpose of promoting their own self interest. They were the enemies of revolution. As a matter of fact, it was the revolutionaries of the first two types who organized and participated in the militant campaigns in Bengal. It is to be noted that the religion of these revolutionaries was different from the orthodox Hindus. They were above all sorts of casteism and irrational superstitions, having faith in Ramakrishna Paramhansa Dev's doctrine of religious tolerance and Swami Vivekananda's ideal of man-making. They visualized an independent and prosperous India and were never looked down upon by society in which they lived. They followed the instructions of the Gita that asked one to perform one's assigned duties wholeheartedly without worrying about the results. These revolutionaries used to study the history of Irish and Russian revolutions from which they got inspiration.

It is true that the Indian National Congress did not have any nationwide organization whereas the revolutionaries had well-organized groups and dedicated workers in almost every nook and corner of the country and through them, they could obtain popular support far and wide. In Bengal, Congress was popular but the revolutionaries were closer to the people's heart at the grassroots level due to their tender age and strength of character. It was often found that they were working for the Congress particularly during elections. The younger members of the Congress in Bengal belonged either to some revolutionary groups or were very much influenced by them. The Congress leaders often sought help from the revolutionaries either to capture power or to retain power in the Congress organization at the provincial level. The revolutionaries too, due to their disunity and lack of experience as leaders of mass movements, associated themselves with this or that Congress leaders.[5]

The British rulers could not suppress the dedicated revolutionaries of Bengal with the help of innumerable conspiracy cases that were common in those days. Most of the Bengal revolutionaries never compromised with any consideration of self interest whatsoever.

Bose always held the revolutionaries in high esteem because he was basically an uncompromising revolutionary himself although he never believed that without mass support there could ever be a revolution for uprooting the alien rulers from India. He was a Congressman who adopted the avowed Congress principle of Gandhian non-violence as a strategy but he knew that the mighty colonial masters could be thrown out of the country only by means of an armed uprising. As a philosophical doctrine, non-violence was ideal to him, and he never condemned the doctrine on theoretical grounds. But his pragmatism never let him accept the doctrine as a workable device specially when on the other side of the fence there was a formidable enemy like the British Raj. As a result he tried, with the help of his elder brother Sarat Bose, to help the militant nationalists in all possible ways in their fight against the enemy. Congress was at that time, not just a political party, it was a common platform, a forum for the nationalists. Bose joined Congress with a view to reaching out to the people with his message of uncompromising struggle for India's freedom. In him, the qualities needed to be a revolutionary leader was abundant who had a widespread network for collecting secret information from the British Intelligence offices, and who used to spend about Rs.1000/- per month for this purpose.[6]

The ideal of revolutionism (*Biplab Baad*) gained popularity in Bengal amongst men and women alike who were inspired by the messages of the Renaissance- men of Bengal named earlier. Their historic sermons awakened the Bengali ethos and generated in it a hankering for freedom. Revolutionism then, may be said to be an inevitable bi-product of the spectacular reawakening of Bengal which transcended all barriers of caste, class or religion. This Bengali ethos reflected the regional variation of Indian nationalism with its focus on physical force which was different from the Gandhian nationalism considered to be the mainstream Indian nationslism.

Mazzini once said that there might be ups and downs for political organizations but there could never be any downfall for the religious organizations. This religion stands for neither any individual nor any particular religious sect or fanaticism, thriving on some prejudices, irrational customs and usages. This religion is humanism that preaches universal brotherhood and well-being of mankind as a whole.

The revolutionaries of Bengal struggled for freedom in the hope of a rejuvenated India but they did not want to achieve it at the cost of her ancient wisdom and the rich cultural heritage. They never tried to adhere to any particular political dogma either from the East or from the West without a careful scrutiny. Their progressive outlook made them look beyond and rise above all kinds of bigotry. 6A. Their mental make-up matched with that of Bose whose only mission in life was to achieve freedom for the motherland and undertake elaborate socio-economic reconstruction after the accomplishment of the mission.

Many revolutionary organizations came into being all over Bengal and Bose was to them the symbol of unadulterated patriotism and a role model to be followed. He was accepted as the leader of the United Revolutionary Party composed of the various revolutionary organizations during the 1920s. *Anushilan Samity*, *Jugantar*, the Bengal Volunteers and their various branches considered Bose the most dependable leader for the furtherance of their common cause. As a matter of fact, the Bengal Volunteers, the revolutionary brigade most feared by the British, came into being under the leadership of Bose during the early years of his political career. He had a distinct plan of providing the Congress with an alternative leadership along the line of militant nationalism for uprooting the alien rulers from India. Obviously, he was considered the compromise-candidate of both *Anushilan* and *Jugantar* groups for the post of the General-Officer-Commanding at the Calcutta Congress of 1928. These two revolutionary groups accepted only Bose as their common leader in their struggle for freedom. Further, it was Bose who inspired the revolutionaries of Chittagong and their leader Surya Sen to stage the historic uprising in April, 1930.

Successive British Indian Governments tried to brand Bose as a front-ranking Congress leader who was privy to all 'terrorist conspiracies'. But it is not correct to say that the British Government used to blow things out of proportion regarding his relationship with the militant nationalists labeled by them as the terrorists. There is ample evidence which points to the fact that Bose had a very close relationship with the Bengal revolutionaries and they, especially the Bengal Volunteers and the Anushilanites cooperated with him in every possible way to make him leave India for the erstwhile Soviet Union in 1941 for launching an armed attack on the Raj from outside.

Bose, certainly, was not the first Congress leader the British accused of consorting with the nationalist revolutionaries whom the British Indian bureaucracy preferred to describe as terrorists. Lokamanya Tilak was the first prominent Congress leader to be so branded.

There are documents to prove that Bose used to help the revolutionaries, as did his political guru C.R.Das, by providing them with funds, making arrangements of secret shelters for the absconders, providing employment to them under the Calcutta Municipal Corporation in the posts of primary teachers. On several occasions he paid homage openly to revolutionaries like Gopinath Saha, Bhagat Singh, Jatin Das and others. But it is also true that he never accepted the idea wholeheartedly that the alien rulers could be driven out of the country by the method of individual killings. He earnestly believed that an uprising was essential which would be possible only with massive popular support.

Although Bose was basically a Congressman, many revolutionaries happened to be his co-prisoners in different jails and prison camps all over the country and this gave him an opportunity to come into intimate contact with them and discuss his plans regarding an armed resistance.

He was well aware of the fact that the youth wanted him to lead them from the forefront and this awareness made him organize youth power as the Volunteers who would motivate and inspire the people in favour of an armed struggle against the Raj. There is no doubt about the fact that the model of Irish volunteers was in front of him as the driving force. During the INA phase of his life abroad, Bose, in many of his speeches, referred to the revolutionaries as great patriots of India.

The Gandhian hardliners were skeptical about the method of militancy which was in clear violation of their avowed non-violence dogma. They were also opposed to Bose's admiration for the martyrs who, they believed, were nothing but 'misguided youth'. Bose was not disrespectful towards the ideal of non-violence as has already been pointed out, but the country's freedom was more important to him than adherence to any particular dogma. Bose tried his best to stiffen the opposition of the Congress Party to any compromise with Britain as he knew that this kind of a compromise would surely lead to a partition of the country. That he was right in his apprehension was proved in 1947 when India was cut into pieces causing unprecedented suffering to the people relegated overnight to the status of a refugee.

After the Munich Pact in September 1938, Bose began an open propaganda throughout India in order to prepare the Indian people for a countrywide national struggle which would synchronize with the ensuing war in Europe. This move was resented by the Gandhians who did not want to be disturbed in their ministerial and parliamentary jobs.

Even after his suspension from the Indian National Congress, Bose sent proposals to Gandhi for a joint movement through a United Front. But the latter rejected the proposal saying that the trends of movement headed by Congress were quite opposite. (see appendix II). He formed the Forward Bloc within the Congress Party itself with the immediate objective of an uncompromising struggle against British imperialism for winning India's independence. The Bloc stood for a pragmatic foreign policy and a post-war restructuring of India along socialistic principles.

The revolutionaries, however, did not let him down during his hour of crisis after the suspension. They gave him unconditional support by assisting him as much as they could and continued with their assistance even after his departure from the country. The *Jugantar* leaders, who were close to C.R.Das, considered Bose as his real successor. They had the same strategy as that of Bose in so far as they took to revolutionism secretly and expressed their faith in the device of non-violence outwardly. Later on, as stated earlier, however, they turned into Gandhians leaving behind all traces of a revolutionary outfit.

Bose became the leader of the Left group within the Congress before he reached the age of thirty. Leftism in those days meant two things, viz. uplift of the downtrodden, and liberation of the colonized country by means of an uncompromising struggle. After the Gaya Congress of 1922, many Jugantar revolutionaries joined the Swarajya Party of C.R.Das which seemed to be the Indian counterpart of the Violence Party of the Sinn Fein of Ireland. Bose used to contribute regularly to the publications of the *Jugantar*, Swarajya Party and the periodicals of the other revolutionary groups.

The Bengal revolutionaries had an affinity with the Irish revolutionaries ever since the Easter Rebellion of 1915. They were inspired by the acts of European revolutionaries since the early 20th century, but in the 1920s and 1930s, the example of Ireland took precedence over all the others. As Michael Silvestri observes in his article *"The Sinn Fein of India"* in the Journal of British Studies, "the imagined bonds between Irish and Bengali nationalism were more important than any concrete linkages." According to Charles Townshend, "for Bengali nationalists, the inspiration of de Valera, Dan Breen, and Patrick Pears and the 'martyrs' of the Easter Rising helped inspire plans for revolution against the British Raj."[6B] It was as early as the 1920s that the Sinn Fein rebels attracted the attention of Bose as well for his uncompromising struggle against the British imperialists. In his book *The Indian Struggle*,

Bose referred to the freedom fighters of Ireland and their revolutionary strategies as a source of inspiration for the Indian freedom fighters.

While in Europe, Bose worked relentlessly as the unofficial ambassador of India abroad. Before he accepted the British offer of exile from India he made up his mind to make the most of the opportunity to learn more about Europe. He visited several European countries including Ireland the revolutionary tradition and spirit of which impressed him and the other like-minded people overwhelmingly. In the minds of the Bengal revolutionaries he noticed the same spirit and dedication as the members of the Sinn Fein. Wherever he went, he established or promoted friendship societies tying up the freedom-loving people of India in a bond of friendship with the people of those countries. He highlighted the needs and aspirations of the Indian people to the foreigners through these friendship societies so that the Indian freedom struggle could be strengthened with their sympathy and support.

The revolutionary *guru* of Bose was Rash Behari Basu of the *Anushilan Samity* who had formed a militant group in Chandannagore before joining the Samity. It was Rash Behari Basu who requested Subhas Chandra Bose to come to East Asia and take the leadership of INA for launching an armed attack on the British imperialists from outside. Basu wrote to him from Tokyo in 1938 that the fetish of non-violence should be discarded and the creed should be changed. According to him, the non-violence atmosphere was simply making Indians 'womanly men'. No nation in the present world, he wrote, should think of non-violence if it wanted to exist as a self-respecting member of the world.(see Appendix I).

Way back in 1939, it was decided by the Bengal revolutionaries that under the leadership of Bose, who was, at that time, the Congress President, an armed resistance on a grand scale was to be organized. Bhulabhai Desai in a statement in London said that the Congress wanted a compromise with the Government. Against this, an anti-compromise movement was started with the initiative of Bose and at the same time, preparations were also going on for a massive armed resistance. The *Anushilan* leaders together with Bose decided that if Congress started a mass movement, then from the outset only, it would be converted into an armed struggle. When Bose was suspended from the INC for his uncompromising stance, his bond with the *Anushilan* grew stronger than before. He went on a north-India tour with Trailokya Chakrabarty and met several veteran revolutionaries there. Akbar Shah of the north-west frontier province, Bhai Paramananda of Hamirpore, and many other like-minded nationalists were inducted in the ensuing revolutionary venture. Through Akbar Shah, contacts were made with the Army, and Bose's plan of going out of the country with Ganguly was discussed at length. Help was sought from the frontier workers of the revolutionary groups regarding the escape. Maharaj went to Madhya Pradesh on the advice of Bose and met the leader of the *Rashtriya Svayam Sevak Sangh* called Keshav Hedgeware who promised to help them with his 60000 volunteers. Maharaj met also Ganesh Damodar Savarkar, the elder brother of Veer Savarkar who, along with Sachindra Sanyal agreed to join the revolutionaries in the armed resistance.

Bose left India in 1941 for the erstwhile Soviet Union but circumstances compelled him to go to Germany to have military assistance in his fight for freedom. While making preparations for leaving India to launch an armed attack on the British from outside, he was helped by the Bengal revolutionaries in more ways than one. He used also the Anushilan network extensively for the ground preparations before his departure and "it was the Bengal Volunteers who shouldered the major burden of the funds required for his escape from India to foreign lands."[7] The Bengal Volunteers, even after his escape, maintained contact with him on a regular basis through transmitters to keep him abreast of the prevailing political situation at home and to receive instructions from him regarding the next course of action.[8]

During the 1930's, there was a feeling of discomfort among the democratic public, writes N.C.Chowdhury in *Mainstream* dated 27th January 1996 that Bose might have had a soft corner for fascism because in his book he had concluded by saying that what India needed was a synthesis of fascism and socialism. This led many to fear that perhaps ultimately he might be attracted by the frenzied commitment to fascism. But Bose, as he saw the unfolding of Hitler's Nazism, realized the unreality of his hope for a synthesis between fascism and socialism. This was clear from an interview that he gave to the British communist newspaper *Daily Worker* in which he declared that there could be no room for fascism as providing a way out for a country like India. A question is often raised, as it used to be at the time that Bose had a sneaking admiration for Nazism and that is why he went to Germany for assistance in his fight for India's freedom. This is a wrong view of the reason for his flight to Germany. It needs to be recalled, says Chowdhury, that for every ardent nationalist in those days, the slogan was, 'enemy's enemy is a friend'. This was the tradition set before the Indian revolutionaries even during the First World War when a whole host of revolutionary leaders had gone to Germany and Russia. The well-known Berlin Committee was composed of young Indian revolutionaries. Besides, Raja Mahendra Pratap took the help of German authorities to set up his provisional government of India in Kabul. Apart from that, Bose in his negotiations with the German Foreign Office made it clear that his Azad Hind Fauj would not fight against the USSR. He never surrendered to the dictates of Germany or any other country for that matter.

It may be mentioned here that there are many source materials now available to the researchers after the collapse of the erstwhile Soviet Union which show that the entire escape plan of Bose was organized by G.M.Dimitrov the then secretary to the Comintern. The initial detailed plan of escape was discussed by Niranjan Talib, editor, *Desh Darpan* who was introduced by Sardar Baldev Singh to Achhar Singh Cheena of the former Ghadar party. The Executive Committee of the Communist Party of Lahore decided that Achhar Singh whose Russian name was Larkin and who was one of the organizers of the Kirti Kissan Party in the North-West Frontier Province, should meet Bose in order to chalk out the detailed escape plan. In June 1940, Singh met Bhagatram Talwar, a member of Forward Bloc and an organizer of the secret activities of the Kirti Kissan Party in his village in the North-West Frontier. Singh asked him to help Bose reach the border of the Soviet Union passing through the tribal belt in Afganistan. After working out the escape plan, Singh left for the Soviet Union and in December 1940, however, he submitted his thesis named '*The National Front in India*' to Stalin. From the Comintern Archives, a document reads like this:

"The Indian in Kabul receiving assistance from the Executive Committee of the Comintern is not Pogatram but Bhagatram who is living at the moment in the village Halladzhar near the town of Mardan in the North-West Frontier Province of India. Bhagatram is a co-worker of Abbas Khan who lives in Peshawar. Under orders from Abbas Khan, Bhagatram has organized the movement of Larkin to Kabul in 1940."

A letter from the Head of the Cadre Section, Gulyaev and senior referent Kozlov to G.M.Dimitrov, concerning Bose, confirms that the information received from Achhar Singh Cheena or Larkin coincides with the details. They write:

"Also under instruction of the Kirti Group which is referred to everywhere in the document as the Executive Committee of the Communist Party of Lahore, he arranged the move of Bose to Kabul and then in May 1941, he accompanied Shervan (i.e.Harminder Sodhi, the former student of the

Conclusion

University of the Toilers of the East) to Kabul and finally he himself came to Kabul to establish contact with us."(ASAN: RAR 345, Indo-Russian Relations 1917-1947).[8A]

"From information from Bhagatram, it is evident that one of the leaders of the Kirti Group—Shervan—together with Bhagatram established links with German Intelligence and received from them a large sum (in Indian terms) for the organization of diversionary activity together with a certain amount of arms.

"Shervan, together with Bhagatram attempts to represent the matter as if they have only been using German Intelligence in the interest of their own party, have given them only trumped up information and themselves remain loyal to the affairs of the Communist Party and expect instructions from the IKKI (Executive Committee of the Communist International) and also expect tactical instructions concerning the attack of fascist Germany on the USSR."

The above passage clearly shows that Bose's intention was to reach the Soviet Union via Kabul and his collaborators were all associated with and loyal to the CPSU, following instructions from it and acting accordingly.

The Soviet Union was eager to collect more information about Bose than any other leader of the Indian freedom struggle. From the Soviet diplomatic mission in Kabul, a detailed report on Bose was sent to the Soviet authorities by Gulyaev and Kozlov on the 5th of February 1941, it goes like this:

"From the very beginning of the war between USSR and Finland, Bose criticized the anti-Soviet campaign. It should be noted that Bose was the only INC leader who unconditionally supported the Soviet Union...he tried to enter the Soviet Union twice but could not succeed. Bose asked Achhar Singh to approach comrade Stalin to seek armed help for India's struggle for independence."

According to Yuri Tikhonov, a professor of the Lipetsk University and a well-known Indologist, the Soviet Government and the Comintern were in conflict with one another over the issue of the status of the Indian Communist Party. During the War period, the Kirti Kissan Party and the Ghadar Party were at daggers drawn with each other as a result of which the CPSU came to be focused more on the Communist Party of India than on Bose.

The USSR was, evidently, instrumental in emigrating Bose to Moscow and this may be corroborated by a document available in the National Archives, New Delhi, (ACC No.6757) which shows that Schmidt, the then Secretary of the German Mission in Kabul met Kozlov on the 15th of March 1941 in order to obtain a visa for an Italian citizen Orlando Mazzotta, the pseudo name of Bose at that time. Giles MacDonough in his book *A Good German* on Adam von Trott zu Solz wrote, "He (Bose) had now decided that the Russians would be most sympathetic to his interesting blend of totalitarian thinking. His chosen destination was Moscow".

It may be recalled that while in jail, Bose made a plan along with his co-prisoners, particularly Pratul Ganguly of the *Anushilan* Samity to come out of the jail and prepare for an escape from the country. He went on a hunger strike along with the Anushilanites and a few other revolutionaries with a few demands. The authorities decided to release him as he fell sick due to the fasting, and subsequently kept him and Pratul Ganguly under house arrest. Bela Mitra was the channel of communication between Bose and Ganguly at that time.

It was decided that they would cross the border, go to the Soviet Union and seek the Russian help in their struggle for independence. It was also decided by them that Ganguly would leave for the Soviet Union after the arrival of Bose in that country to assist him.(*Bharater Swadhinata Sangram O Anushilan Samity* by Kshirod Kumar Dutta). But it was not possible as Ganguly was arrested again as soon as the news

Conclusion

of Bose's escape from India reached the Government. When Bose left India surreptitiously in January 1941, some of the Bengal revolutionaries were already at work in Japan, Singapore, Java and Malay. Their main concern was how to utilize the war situation in favour of India's independence. Swami Satyananda Puri was assisting Rash Behari Basu along with others. In his pre-*Sanyas* life, Puri was a veteran *Anushilan* leader known as Prafulla Kumar Sen in Faridpore of East Bengal.

The revolutionary movement in Bengal was started and nurtured by the educated middle class Bengalees described by the British Raj as Bengalee *Bhadraloks*. But the revolutionary movements were never directed towards the goal of promoting their own class interests, the interests of the *Bhadraloks*. Liberation of the entire nation was their long-cherished goal. The areas with a prosperous middle class produced more revolutionary activists than the other areas. In East Bengal, the middle class was educated and generally prosperous and that was why this part of Bengal became a perennial source of danger to the alien rulers with young revolutionaries in almost every middle-class family. The rulers were desperate to suppress the Bengal revolutionary 'terrorists' with the help of repressive legislations like Bengal Regulation III of 1818 which did not require any trial on a definite charge or the formulation of such a charge, Rowlatt Act of 1919, Bengal Ordinance of 1924, the Bengal Criminal Law Amendment Act 1925, Indian Press Emergency Powers Act 1931, the Post Office Act, Bengal Suppression of Terrorist Outrages Act 1932 (Bengal Act XII of 1932), Bengal Emergency Powers Ordinance 1932, and a series of amendments of the existing laws to make them more repressive. Books with a patriotic fervour used to be proscribed every now and then on the pretext of 'incitement to violence', with the help of the Indian Press Emergency Powers Act 1931. Bose's *Indian Struggle,* published abroad, was prevented from entry into India under Section 19 of the Sea Customs Act.

There was no jury system at that time and these laws were used by the Government without any respect for the Rule of Law the cardinal principles of which constitute the outstanding characteristics of the British constitution.

The efforts of the Raj in Bengal to combat Bengali 'terrorism' were not limited to repressive legislations and proscription of literature alone. The Royal Irish Constabulary (RIC) also played an important role in the way the Government tried to crush the revolutionaries. RIC exerted a profound influence on the development of policing in India. RIC was regarded as an ideal of what colonial policing should be. After the disbandment of RIC in 1921, large number of its officers as well as auxiliary forces were recruited for service elsewhere in the Empire.[9] Malcolm Seton of the India Office once commented that the members of the RIC, "a semi-military force" were considered "tactful in handling crowds.... In a place like Calcutta, the men should do very well indeed after a short training."[10] When the British Government awarded them a lucrative pension, quite a few RIC members were drawn towards the Indian service.

Ireland was the role model for Bose and the Bengal revolutionaries and ironically it was the same Ireland that played a crucial role in the development of British ideas about how best to combat 'terrorism' in Bengal.

Before I conclude I would like to say that *Bande Mataram* as a *mantra* elevated patriotism to the level of spiritualism for the Bengal revolutionaries. Their nationalism was not based on any feeling of hatred towards any particular race or community. It was the philosophy of humanism which served as the basis of their ideology of revolutionism. Rash Behari Basu in 1922 and Subhas Bose in 1938 expressed the same idea when they said that Indian independence was essential for the liberation of the enslaved world as a whole and for this reason only, India had to achieve independence. To get rid of colonial subjugation was not only the goal, it was a means as well for achieving a

Conclusion

nobler mission, and that was to build up a world order where mankind as a whole would live a life of freedom abolishing all forms of imperialism and militarism from the face of the world.

NOTES AND REFERENCES

1. Ghosh, Ganesh, *Muktitirtha Andaman*, p. 137, cited by Amalendu Ghosh in his *Biplabider Smarane O Sanniddhye* (in Bengali) p. 212, Purna Prakashan, Calcutta, 1999.

2. Ray, Parimal, *Down Memory Lane*, pp. 152-153, cited by Amalendu Ghosh, Ibid, pp 212-213

3. Speech delivered by Trailokya Chakrabarty at a seminar organized by Netaji Research Bureau at Netaji Bhavan, Elgin Road, Kolkata, dated 19/7/1970.

4. In an interview with the author, Abinash Dasgupta of the Revolutionary Socialist Party, at Kranti Press, Kolkata, narrated it on 7/1/2003.

5. Guha, Nalini Kishore, *Banglaye Biplabbad*, (in Bengali), A.Mukherjee and Co. Kolkata, Revised 4th edition, 1969, pp. 336-337.

6. Ibid, pp. 320-321.

6A. Ibid. p. 338

6B. Townshend, Charles, "The IRA and the Development of Guerilla Warfare," 1916-21, English Historical Review 94, No. 371, (April 1979).

7. Speech delivered by Prof. Uma Mukherjee, a veteran historian, at the Institute of Historical Studies, Kolkata, dated 29/7/2000.

8. Author's interview with Jyotish Chandra Bose of the Bengal Volunteers, at his Calcutta residence on 16th August 1997.

8A. Roy, Vasudevan, Duttagupta (ed.), Indo-Russian Relations 1917-1947, Vol. 2, Asiatic Society, Calcutta, 1997.

8B. Roy, Purabi, "New Findings on Subhas Chandra Bose : Russian, British and Indian Archives," Mainstream (XLIV. 33), August 5, 2006, New Delhi.

9. Fedorowich, Kent, "The Problems of Disbandment : The Royal Irish Constabulary," Irish Historical Studies 30, No. 117 (May 1996).

10. Seton to W.H. Vincent, Home Dept. Govt. of India, 13/4/1922, National Archives of India, Govt. of India, Home (Poll), No. 627 of 1922.

BIBLIOGRAPHY

PRIMARY SOURCES :

National Archives, New Delhi:
File Nos.
I.B. 379(24)
I.B. 61 (24)
27/5/37- Poll
41/7/37-Poll
27/13/36-Poll
22/92/36-Poll
24/22/35-Poll
39/15/35-Poll
8/5/35-Poll
22/29/35-Poll
22/64/35-Poll
22/63/35-Poll
43/30/35-Poll
32/2/38
8/18/38-Poll
Ibid. 233/28, Home Poll
37/1934, Home, Poll
Private Papers of Woods
Private Papers of Subhas Chandra Bose, Sl. No 10, 11, 13,

15. 15.2

22/92/1936-Home Poll

History Sheet of 1932, Home Poll 1932, IB Report dated 24/6 1930,

32/2/38 Poll.

45/42/34 Political.

44/56/34, Home Poll.

Micro-film — Accession No. 2728 (Oct. 1939 – Jan. 1940)

West Bengal State Archives :

File Nos.

I.R.C.I.D. Bengal, 39/25, serial no. 97/1925

Confidential 26/32, Part I: Introductory, IB, Calcutta

Confidential 90/1928, IB

80V/28,IB

562/32, Sl. No. 55

Intelligence Report on the political situation in Bengal during the second half of March, 1st half of May, 1931, WB State Archives

80C/27, Part I

35/8 of 1934, Home Poll

850/1930

840/32, Home Poll

41/7/37-Home Poll.,

223/1929, Home Poll,

749/1930, Home Poll,

50/31 (Sl. No. 1-2),

775/1930,

613/34,

524/39,

19/39, Home (Poll),
427/39, Home (Poll),
V596/40, Home (Poll),
572/31,
580/31
57(3-5)/31
66/31,
85/31
748/1931,
562/32,
872/32
1004 (1-2) /32,
1009/32,
701@/32(l-29),
459/32 (1)
582/32
688/32,
404(1-5) 1 32,
505/32
75/43,
345/43

Special Branch Calcutta Police, Govt. of West Bengal File Nos.
C 616/40,
PM 522/38,
CM 525/42,
700/40,
PM 511/38.
PM 805/42.

PM891/47.
M 598/39.
516/40.
PM 757/42
PM 806/42-C
CM 563/41
700/42
MacArthur Archives, Norfolk, Virginia, USA File No. R6-9, B. 158 F. "SACSEA, 1945–1946".

SECONDARY SOURCES

A Bunch of Old Letters, written mostly to Jawaharlal Nehru, Asia Publishing House, Bombay, 1960

Adhikari, Gangadhar, (ed.), *Documents of the History of the Communist Party of India,* Vol.2, People's Publishing House, New Delhi.

Azad, M.A.K., India Wins Freedom, Orient Longman, Calcutta, 1959.

Basu, Nimai Sadhan, *Desh Nayak Subhas Chandra,* (in Bengali), Ananda Publishers Pvt. Ltd. 1997.

Basu, Krishna, *Prasanga Subhas Chandra,* (in Bengali), Ananda Publishers, Calcutta, 1997.

Basu, Shankari Prasad, *Samakalin Bharate Subhas Chandra,* Vol. 1 & 2, (in Bengali), Mandal Book House, Calcutta, 1998.

Bell, David, *The End of Ideology,* Free Press, New York, 1965.

Bhattacharya, Siddhartha, *Bharatiya Rashtradarshan O Jatiya Andolan,* (in Bengali), Bharati Sahitya Prakashani, Calcutta, 2003.

Birla, G.D., *Bapu: A Unique Association,* Vol. 2, Bharatiya Bidya Bhavan, Bombay, 1977.

Bose, Asoke Nath, *My Uncle Netaji,* Bharatiya Bidya Bhavan, Bombay, 1989.

Bose, Sisir Kumar and Sugata, (ed.), *Netaji: Collected Works*, Vol. 1-8, Oxford University Press, New Delhi, 1995.

Bose, Mihir, *The Lost Hero*, Quartet Books, London, 1982.

Bose, Subhas Chandra, *Correspondences 1924-1932*, Netaji Research Bureau, Oxford Book and Stationary Co., Calcutta. 1967.

Bose, Subhas Chandra, *Selected Speeches*, with a biographical introduction by S. A. Ayer, Publications Division, Govt. of India, 1962.

Bose, Subhas Chandra, *The Indian Struggle 1920-1942*, Oxford University Press, New Delhi, 1997.

Broomfield, J. H., *Elite Conflict in Plural Society - 20th Century Bengal*, California, 1968.

Buddhadev Bhattacharya, (ed.), *Freedom Struggle and Anushilan Samity*, Vol. 1, Anushilan Samity 75th Anniversary Celebration Committee, Calcutta, 1979.

Chattopadhyay, Enakshi & Shantiranjan, *Bharatiya Bijnaner Uttaraner Kaal*, Cambridge India, Calcutta, 2003.

Calcutta Municipal Gazette, Netaji Centenary Volume, Kranti Press, Calcutta, 1997.

Chatterjee, Jogesh Chandra, *In Search of Freedom*, Firma K. L. Mukhopadhyay, Calcutta, 1967.

Chakrabarty, Radharaman, (ed.), *Netaji & India's Freedom, A Centenary Tribute*, Netaji Institute For Asian Studies, Calcutta, 1997.

Chakrabarty Bidyut, *Subhas Chandra Bose & Middle Class Radicalism*, St. Martin's Press, 1990.

Chakrabarty, Narendra Narayan, *Netaji Sanga O Prasanga* (in Bengali), Sundar Prakashan, 1370 BS.

Chakrabarty, Trailokya Nath, *Jele Trish Bachhar O Bharater Biplab Sangram* (in Bengali), Presidency Library, Calcutta, 1369 BS.

Chatterjee, Reva, *Netaji Subhas Bose, Bengal, Revolution & Independence,* Ocean Books Pvt. Ltd., New Delhi, 2000.

Chattopadhyay, Sabitri Prasanna, *Subhas Chandra O Netaji Subhas Chandra,* (in Bengali), Jaysree Prakashan, Calcutta, 1986.

Das, Naren, *Biplabi Andolaner Jijnasha* (in Bengali), Sujan Publications, Calcutta, 1983.

Dasgupta, Hemendra Nath, *Subhas Chandra,* Bharat Book Agency, Calcutta, 2005.

Dasgupta, Hemendra Nath, *Bharater Biplab Kahini* (in Bengali), Jyoti Prakashalay, Calcutta, 1948.

Dasgupta, Mrinal Kanti, *Biplab Sadhanay Nivedita* (in Bengali), Published by Uma Chakrabarty, Calcutta, 1377 BS.

Das, Sitanshu, *Subhas: A Political Biography,* Rupa &Co., New Delhi, 2001.

Dhar, Ira & Subal Samanta (ed.), *Agniyuger Dui Sainik: Shaheed Prodyot Kumar O Biplabi Prabhanshu Shekhar* (in Bengali), Anima Pal on behalf of Shaheed Prodyot Smriti Samiti, Midnapore, 1996.

Gandhi, Rajmohan, *Patel, A Life,* Navajivan Publishing House, Ahmedabad, 1990.

Gandhi M.K. and G.D.Birla, *A Bridge of Words* [letters exchanged], G.D.Birla Centenary Publications, Calcutta, 1994.

Gandhi, Collected Works, Volumes LXI, LXV, XXXVIII, Publications Division of the Government of India, Navajivan Trust, Ahmedabad 1970.

Gangopadhyay, Dwijen, *Biplab Banhi* (in Bengali), General Printers & Publishers Pvt. Ltd., Calcutta, 1385 BS.

Ghosh, Amalendu, *Biplabider Smarane O Sanniddhye,* (in Bengali), Purna Prakashan, Calcutta, 1999.

Ghosh, Amalendu, *Bharate Communism,* (in Bengali), Purna Prakashan, 1987.

Ghosh, Kalicharan, *The Footprints,* Sahitya Samsad, Calcutta, 1975.

Gopal, S., (ed.), *Selected Works of Jawaharlal Nehru,* Vol. 7, Orient Longman, New Delhi, 1974.

Gordon, Leonard, *Brothers Against Raj,* Penguin Books Ltd., India, 1990.

Guha, Samar, (ed.), *Jayasree: Netaji Subhas Chandra Basu Janmashatabarshiki Grantha,* (in Bengali), Jayasree Patrika Trust, Calcutta, 1999.

Guha, Nalini Kishor, *Banglaye Biplabbaad* (in Bengali), A.Mukherjee And Co. Pvt. Ltd., Calcutta, 1376 BS.

Gupta, Arun Kumar, (ed.), *Desh Nayak Subhas Chandra,* Vols. 1& 2, (in Bengali), National Council of Education Bengal, Calcutta, 1998.

Hale, H.W., *Terrorism in India 1917-1936,* compiled in the IB, Govt of India, Publications Division, 1937.

Haithcox, John Patrick, *Communism & Nationalism in India,* Princeton University Press, 1971.

Hees, Peter, *The Bomb in Bengal,* Oxford University Press, Delhi, 1993.

Holt, Thaddeus, The Deceivers, Skyhorse, New York, 2007.

John Jacob & Harindra Srivastava, *Netaji Subhas: The Tallest of the Titans, (But Betrayed and Belittled),* Ess Ess Publications, New Delhi, 2000.

Kumar, Ravindra, (ed.), *Selected Works of Subhas Chandra Bose (1936-1946),* Vols. 2 & 3, Atlantic Publishers & Distributors, New Delhi, 1992.

Kurti, Kitty, *Subhas Chandra Bose as I knew him,* Firma KLM Pvt. Ltd., Calcutta, 2000.

Lahiri, Tarapada, *Mahabiplabi Rash Behari Basu* (in Bengali), Pratyay, Calcutta, 1986.

Lahiri, Agamani & Bijoy Nag, *Shikhamoyee Lila Ray* (in Bengali), Jayasree Prakashan, Calcutta, 1999.

Laushey, David M. *Bengal Terrorism & the Marxists Left,* Firma K.L.Mukhopadhyay Pvt. Ltd, Calcutta, 1975.

Lytton, Earl of, *Pundits & Elephants,* Peter Davies, London, 1942.

MacDonogh, Giles, A Good German, Quartet Books Ltd., London, 1994.

Maikap, Satish Chandra, *Banhiman Netaji Subhas,* (in Bengali), Naya Prakash, Calcutta, 1987.

Markandeya, Subodh, *Subhas Chandra Bose: Netaji's Passage to Immortality,* Arnold Associates, New Delhi, 1990.

Majumdar,A.K., *Advent of Independence,* Bharatiya Vidya Bhavan, Bombay, 1963.

Majumdar, Nepal, *Rabindranath O Subhas Chandra,* (in Bengali), Saraswat Library, Calcutta, 1375 BS.

Majumdar, Ramesh Chandra, *Bangla Desher Itihaas* (in Bengali), Vol. 4, General Printers & Publishers Pvt. Ltd., Calcutta, 1982.

Mitra, Amal Kumar, (ed.), *Rashbeharir Atmakatha O Dushprapya Rachana* (in Bengali), Rick Prakashani, Calcutta, 1985.

Mitra, Sukumar, *Gandhiji, Subhas Chandra O Banglar Biplabira,* (in Bengali), Firma K.L.Mukhopadhyay Pvt. Ltd., Calcutta, 1998.

Mosley, Sir Oswald, *My Life,* Thomas Nelson & Sons Ltd., Britain, 1970.

Mukherjee, Amitabha, (ed.), *Netaji Subhas Chandra Bose in Historical Perspective,* The Institute of Historical Studies, Calcutta, 1999.

Mukherjee, Hiren, *Bow of Burning Gold,* New Delhi, 1977.

Mukherjee, Nanda, *Subhas Chandra Bose: British Press, Intelligence & Parliament,* Jayasree Prakashan, Calcutta, 1981.

Mukhopadhyay, Ashutosh, *Swadhinata Sangramer Abarte* (in Bengali), Barishal Seba Samity, Calcutta, 1987.

Mukhopadhyay, Jadugopal, *Biplabi Jibaner Smriti* (in Bengali), Academic Publishers, Calcutta, 1982.

Mukhopadhyay, Nanda, *Vivekanander Aloye Subhas* (in Bengali), Modern Column, Calcutta, 1983.

Nag, Hiten, *Anya Netaji* (in Bengali), Prakash Bhavan, Calcutta, 1996.

Nehru, Jawaharlal, *An Autobiography*, John Lane, The Bodley Head, London, 1947.

Neruda, Publo, *Memoirs*, translated from Spanish by Hardie St. Martin, A Condor Book, Souvenir Press, London, 1977.

Netaji Subhas Chandra Bose Birth Anniversary Number, Jayasree Patrika Trust, Calcutta, 1999.

Netaji Subhas Chandra Bose Commemoration Volume, edited by Alok Ray, Scottish Church College, Calcutta, 1998.

Netaji Subhas Chandra Bose: Relevance to Contemporary World, edited by S.R.Chakravarty and Madan C. Paul, Har-Anand Publications Pvt. Ltd. New Delhi, 2000.

Netaji Janma Shatabarsha Smarak Sangraha, edited by Rathin Chakraborty, Lokmat Prakashani, Calcutta.

Netaji Speaks, (a compilation of speeches), Vols. 1-10, Research Publishing & Printing Foundation, Calcutta, 1999.

Overstreet, Gene D. & Marshall Windmiller, *Communism in India*, University of California Press, Berkeley, 1959.

Parikh, Narahari D., *Sardar Ballabhbhai Patel* (original in Gujrati), Navajivan Publishing House, Ahmedabad, 1956.

Pakrashi, Satish, *Agnidiner Katha* (in Bengali) National Book Agency Ltd., Calcutta 1947.

Pundit, Vijaylakshmi, *The Scope of Happiness,* Vikas Publishing House, New Delhi

Ray, Dipti Kumar, *Biplabi Andolane Medinipur,* (in Bengali), Sujan Publications, Calcutta, 1997,

Roy, Vasudevan, Duttagupta (ed.), *Indo-Russian Relations,* Vol. 1& 2, Asiatic Society, Calcutta, 1997.

Saggi, P.D.(ed.), *A Nation's Homage: Life & Work of Netaji Subhas Chandra Bose,* Overseas Publishing House, Bombay.

Sareen, T.R. (ed.), *Forgotten Images, Reflections & Reminiscences of Subhas Chandra Bose,* S. S. Publishers, Delhi, 1997.

Samanta, Amiya, *Terrorism in Bengal,* Vol. 1-3, Govt of West Bengal, Calcutta, 1995.

Sarat Bose Commemoration Volume, Sarat Bose Academy, Calcutta, 1982.

Sarkar, Kalipada, *Itihaas Purush Netaji* (in Bengali), Rupa & Company, Calcutta, 1980.

Sanyal, Gopal Lal, *Je Kathar Shesh Nei* (in Bengali), Jayasree Prakashan, Calcutta, 1985.

Sehanabish, Chinmohan, *Roosh Biplab O Prabashi Bharatiya Biplabi* (in Bengali), Manisha Granthalaya, Calcutta, 1973.

Sedition Committee Report, Govt. of India, 1918, New Age Publishers Pvt. Ltd., Calcutta & Delhi, 1973, also cited in *The Indian Revolutionaries Abroad 1905-1922,* by A.C.Bose, Bharti Bhavan, Patna, 1971.

Silvestri, Michael, "The Sinn Fein of India," Article published in the Journal of British Studies, Vol. 39, No. 4, Oct. 200.

Singh, Durlabh, *The Rebel President,* Lahore, 1941.

Smith, Sir Dunlop, Private Secretary to Viceroy Lord Minto, *The Servant of India,* Longmans, London, 1966.

Sree Subhas Chandra Basu Samagra Rachanabali (in Bengali), Vol. 1, Ananda Publishers Pvt. Ltd., Calcutta, 1980.

Stenton, Michael, Stephen Less (ed.), *Who's Who in British Parliament, A Biographical Dictionary of the House of Commons,* Vol. 4, The Harvester Press, Sussex, 1981.

Subhas Chandra Bose—Facets Of A Great Patriot, Director, Netaji Institute for Asian Studies, Calcutta, 1996-'97.

The Glory of Bondage, Sarat Chandra Bose's Letters to Daughter Gita, 1942-45, Bharatiya Vidya Bhavan, Bombay, 1994.

Toye, Hugh, *Subhas Chandra Bose: The Springing Tiger,* Jaico Publishing House, Bombay, 2004.

ARTICLES:

Maity, Girish Chandra, 'Decisive Role of the INA in India's Freedom', published in The Asian Studies, (Calcutta), XXI, (I&2), Jan-Dec. 2003.

Chattopadhyay, Gautam, '*Subhas Chandra O Bharater Communist Andolan,*" published in Parichaya (Bengali periodical, Calcutta), June-July, 1996.

Devitkin, T.F., 'The socio-political views of Subhas Chandra Bose', published in the periodical "Past & Present", issued by the Academy of Sciences, Oriental Studies Institute, Moscow.

Limaye, Madhu, *'Netaji: The Legendary Seagull',* published in The Telegraph, Calcutta, dated 23/1/1984.

Mustafi, Ashoke, *'Jugantar, Anushilan O Subhas Chandra',* in Parichaya, op. cit.

Yasin, Madhavi, *'Gandhi- Subhas Controversy*' in the Quarterly Review of the Historical Studies, Vol. XLII, Calcutta, April-Sept. 2002.

Borra, Ranjan, 'Subhas Chandra Bose, The INA and The War of India's Liberation' in IHR The Journal of Historical Review, San Diego, CA 92143, 1999.

SEMINAR PRESENTATIONS:

'The Role of Bengal Volunteers in India's Freedom Movement", presentation by Prof. Uma Mukherjee under the auspices of the Institute Of Historical Studies, Calcutta, on 29/7/2000.

Biplabi Nagendra Shekhar Chakrabarty Annual Memorial Lecture delivered by Haridas Mukherjee on *"India's militant nationalism"*, dated 1/8/1998 at the Institute of Historical Studies, Calcutta.

Lecture delivered by Amitabha Mukherjee on *Subhas Chandra Bose* at the Ramakrishna Mission Institute of Culture, Calcutta, dated 27/6/1998.

Lecture delivered by Sukumar Bhattacharya at the Ramakrishna Mission Institute of Culture on *Partition of Bengal*, dated 6/9/2005.

NEWSPAPERS AND PERIODICALS

Advance

Anandabazar Patrika

Amrita Bazar Patrika

Banglar Katha

Bangabani

Bijoli

Basumati

Chaturanga

Daily News

Desh

Hak Katha

Hindustan Times

Hindustan Standard

Jayasree Patrika

Kalantar

Mainstream
Modern Review
Narayan
Parichaya
Prabasi
Rakhal Benu
Shankha
Soviet Land
Statesman
Telegraph
Times of India
The Quarterly Review of Historical Studies
Young India (journal for Indian youths in East Asia)

LIST OF PERSONS INTERVIEWED

1. Amalendu Ghosh, (Bengal Volunteers)
2. Helena Dutta (Dacca Sri Sangha)
3. Jyotish Chandra Bose (BV)
4. Lokendra Kumar Sengupta of Jugantar (Lalit Burman Group in Kumilla district).
5. Kamala Dasgupta (1) [BV]
6. Kamala Dasgupta (2) [Jugantar]
7. Prabhanshu Pal, (BV)
8. Samarendra Basu Thakur, (Jugantar)
9. Manohar Mukherjee, (Jugantar)
10. Amar Chatterjee, (BV)
11. Satyabrata Majumdar, (BV)
12. Sneha Ganguli, widow of Shantimoy Ganguli of BV
13. Lily Ganguli, (BV)
14. Abinash Dasgupta of Kranti Press (Revolutionary Socialist

Party, an offshoot of Anushilan Samiti)
15. Ashok Ghosh, (Veteran leader of the All India Forward Bloc)
16. Subir Bakshi, son of Satya Ranjan Bakshi
17. Shekhar Sen, (Bhabanipore Group)
18. Biswajit Dutta (BV)
19. Uma Devi (Sri Sangha)
20. Sunil Baran Gupta
21. Sukumar Bhattacharya
22. Pabitra Kumar Ghosh.
23. Shankariprasad Basu,
24. Nimai Sadhan Basu
25. Amitabha Mukherjee
26. Leonard Gordon
27. Uma Mukherjee

Party, an offshoot of Anushilan Samiti)
15. Ashok Ghosh, (Veteran leader of the All India Forward Bloc)
16. Subir Bakshi, son of Satya Ranjan Bakshi
17. Shekhar Sen, (Bhabanipore Group)
18. Biswajit Dutta (BV)
19. Uma Devi (Sri Sangha)
20. Sunil Baran Gupta
21. Sukumar Bhattacharya
22. Pabitra Kumar Ghosh.
23. Shankariprasad Basu,
24. Nimai Sadhan Basu
25. Amitabha Mukherjee
26. Leonard Gordon
27. Uma Mukherjee

APPENDICES

APPENDIX - I

File No. 32/2/38 Poll (Secret)
National Archives, New Delhi
CRIMINAL INVESTIGATION DEPARTMENT
Special Branch, Lucknow, U.P.
Dated the 12th February 1938

Extract from the interception diary of an officer of this department dated 11.2.38 page 68.

8. Mr. Subhas Chandra Bose, President-elect, Indian National Congress, Swaraj Bhawan, Allahabad, received a Registered cover (P.O. Mark Tokyo, Nippon, 24-1-38) R-No.914 containing a typed letter in English dated 25.1.38), from Rash Behari Bose, Tokyo, Japan, Copy of the letter is as follows :

I am glad to learn from a press despatch from India that you have been elected as the President of the next session of the Congress. I offer you my hearty congratulations. I am, as a Bengalee, proud of you. Bengalees were partly responsible for the British occupation of India, and it is, in my opinion, the primary duty of the Bengalees to make more sacrifices to recover the freedom of India. Bengalees by their sacrifices and sufferings are destined to lead India in the battle of freedom. This is my conviction, and hence I expect you to give a definite lead to the Congress for the attainment of our goal.

At present the Congress is passing through a crisis. It is now a constitutional organization and cooperating with the

Government. In a subject country no constitutional and legal organization can ever secure freedom, because the constitution or law is framed by the rulers for their own benefit and interest. Only unconstitutional or illegal organization from the British point of view can only lead the country to independence. The Congress became an unconstitutional body at the time of the civil disobedience movement, and hence it could do immense work. But at present it has reverted to its past position of a harmless body. There is practically speaking no difference between the Congress and other Moderate parties. I do not understand why Congressmen in the past criticized Sir Surendranath Bannerji when he accepted office. Congressmen are at present doing exactly what Sir Suren and other Moderates did at the time of the last so-called Reforms. Rather credit should be given to the Moderates of that time for their demand for a general amnesty to all political prisoners. Now only a limited number of political prisoners have been released, at that time all the political prisoners were immediately pardoned and released. What is now wanted for the Congress to lead the country correctly is to have a revolutionary mentality. It is now an evolutionary body. It must be made a pure revolutionary body. When the whole body is poisoned, applying medicine on certain parts will be of no use.

The fetish of non-violence should be discarded, and the creed should be changed. Let us attain our goal "through all possible means" : violence or non-violence. The non-violence atmosphere is simply making Indians womanly men. No nation in the present world should think of non-violence, if it wants to exist as a self-respecting member of the world. Our difficulty had been the "other worldliness" dinned into our ears for such a long period. The idea should be completely removed. Instead of "other worldliness" we must have "this worldliness" first as Swami Vivekananda preached. *Daridra Narayans* should be fed, clothed and sheltered first. Let them have the enjoyment of the world first. Then we can talk of heaven. The Muslims say : Pir, Amir e Fakir. Be a Fakir, so that one can defy the world. If you cannot be a Fakir, be an Amir, and enjoy life. If you cannot become an Amir, be a Pir. That means kill a Kafir, and your tomb or you in the other world will be worshipped by the people as a God. The Gita also says so. Let us sacrifice ourselves, so that the future generations may enjoy.

The Congress should devote attention to only one point, i.e. military preparedness. Might is still the right. This we must remember. It is no use deceiving ourselves by sanctimonious phrases. The Congress should agitate for control of the army first, all branches of the army. Education, Sanitation, etc. can never make us free. Strength is the real need. You should concentrate your whole energy on this point. I think, Dr. Moonji has done much more than the Congress by establishing his military school. Indians should first of all be the masters of the army. They must secure the right to bear arms.

Next important thing is the Hindu solidarity. The Muslims are Hindus too, when they are born in India and when their religious practices differ from those of the Muslims of Turkey, Persia, Afghanistan, etc. Hinduism is catholic enough to give a place to Islam within the Hindu fold, as it has done in the past. All Indians are Hindus, though they may believe in different religions, as all Japanese are Japanese though they may be Buddhists, Christians, etc.

The Congress should support the Pan-Asia movement. It should not condemn Japan without understanding her motive in the Sino-Japanese conflict. Japan is a friend of India and other Asiatic countries. Her chief motive is to destroy British influence in Asia. She has begun with China.

The Congress ought to have a world outlook. International situation should be studied and utilized for India's benefit and interests. We should make friends with Britain's enemies. This should be our foreign policy. Sentiments should find no place in actual politics. Interest is always the basis.

Japan is at present the eye-sore of England, Russia and America for obvious reasons. They want to down Japan by hook or crook. Japan's fall will vanish the hope of a regenerated and free Asia. The Congress had made a great mistake by carrying on anti-Japanese movements. We should remember that a time may come when England will shake hands with Japan, and control India pointing to Japan the anti-Japanese activities of the Indians in Japan's hour of trial. It is now the best policy for the Indians to support Japan and utilize this opportunity to increase their influence in world-politics and extract as much concessions from Britain now as possible.

For a subject country, dictatorship is absolutely necessary in a freedom movement. As in time of war, dictatorship is indispensable, at present in India's struggle for freedom dictatorship is equally indispensable. At the time of the civil disobedience movement, dictatorship came into being to a certain extent, and hence the movement achieved so much success.

APPENDIX - II

From : The Private Papers of S. C. Bose
National Archives, New Delhi
DOCUMENT No.4
ABSTRACTS FROM INDIAN PRESS 1938-1941
(Items on Bose)
Bose's proposals on United Front rejected by Gandhi

In *"Tribune" 23 February.* The correspondence between Gandhi and the leader of "Forward Bloc" before Bose's disappearance was published. It is evident from Bose's letter sent to Gandhi on December 23 1941 that Bose was not religious and mystical as it was depicted in newspapers after his disappearance. In two of Bose's letters sent to Gandhi he offered the United Front and participation of "Forward Bloc" members in the Satyagraha campaign. At the same time he indicated that this movement (Satyagraha) was limited and thought that only mass struggle could result in victory. "I thought he wrote, "that you would declare a mass movement as you did in 1921, 30 and 32 though I knew that you allow only personal disobedience. It is quite evident now that the movement organized by you does not pursue objects of national liberation struggle. This movement is not a mass struggle to such an extent. If the government should have agreed to allow anti-war military speeches the movement would be dismissed by you. Nevertheless we would like within the framework of our programme to unite with you in this movement in spite of limited character.

Ignoring our disagreement with the Congress high leadership we propose unity without demanding any special conditions. Simultaneously we of course don't shut our eyes on more wider tasks that our country should settle. Please accept our proposals regarding our joint actions".

Gandhi rejected these proposals saying that the trends of movement headed by these leaders are quite opposite.

APPENDIX III

Nov. 15, 1946,

Dinner Hotel Pierre.

Pietro Quaroni.

In 1933 Subash Chandra Bose came to Rome and saw Mussolini. B.asked that some Italian official to be sent to India to keep in touch with their movement. That is when Q. first met B. in Rome. In 1936 Q. was sent to Kabul as Minister (he was opposed to the Abyasinian campaign and was sent to Kabul as punishment). Q.visited India in 1936, 1937 and 1938. Each time he saw Gandhi, Nehru, Bose, Jinnah, Patel, Rajaji and other Indians. After Bose was was arrested by the British in Calcutta in 1939 his friends wrote to Q. in Kabul saying that B.wanted to go to Russia, Germany and Italy, and asked for help. An Indian doctor who was a member of the Forward Bloe, but whom the British did not know as such, examined Boss in prison and reported that B.was too sick to stay in Jail. He was released on parole, and plans were made for his escape. Q.arranged with Afjans and were friendly to him. The tribesmen used were Mohmands. B.had grown a beard and mutaohe. He arrived in Kabul in February 1940, and stayed secretly in Q's house for more than a month until he left for Russia. B.had read "Mein Kampt" but he did not understand Hitler. He accepted at face value what Hitler had written about the liberation of colonies. He thought there was real friendship between Stalin and Hitler and that they would agree to liberate Asiatic countries on Lanininst Lines. He wanted to create a free Indian government in Berlin and wanted to unite in it all Indians who were abroad and some who who might be smuggled out of India. He expected to get into touch with the Indians prisoners in Italy and to form a Free India army. B.was anxious to get a joint public declaration signed by the German, Italian, Russian and Japanese governments in favour of full independence for India... Bose waited more than a month in

Kabul for his Soviet visa. The Russians could not make up their minds to admit him. Finally the German minister in Kabul asked Berlin to intercede in Moscow. The Russians did not want him in Russia. After Bose passed throw for a few hours between trains. He travelled from Termez to Moscow by train and then from Moscow to Berlin by train. In Moscow Bose met somebody from the Italian embassy. While Bose was in Kabul his idea was to establish contact between Q.and the Forward Bloc in Calcutta. He expected that after he had set up his Free India government in Berlin or Rome it would send messages to Kabul and Q.would then get them in to India. But in Berlin B.got a flat refusal from Hitler. Q. believes that Hitler hoped until the end to come to an understanding with England and to neutralize England in the war ... Q.was told that B.got to Japan by German submarine. But, he says, it is also possible that he flew from Rohdes to Burma in 1943 by Itallian Plane. I remarked that it was a very long distance but he said that he had heard that ten such flights wer made ... Q.thinks that it is possible that B.is still alive. He was friendly to Chiang Kai-shek. The report was that he was killed flying from japan to Formosa. But Q.says that B.might have been on his way to China and might have got there but did not want the British to look for him so the false rumor of his death was circulated. Q.says Bose may be biding his time for a return to India (In Kabul Q.s wife took photographs of Q. and B. which he has in Moscow. He may send them to me.)

APPENDIX IV

Soviet Land, Dec. 1990

SUBHAS CHANDRA BOSE AND SOVIET RUSSIA

Editor : L.V. Mitrokhin

Mahatma Gandhi, Bal Gangadhar Tilak, Bhagat Singh, Jawaharlal Nehru, Indira Gandhi, and other leaders, heroes and martyrs of the Indian national liberation movement are well known to the Soviet people. Strange as it may seem, few of them have till now known Subhas Chandra Bose. For a long time Soviet researchers were not allowed even to mention this passionate patriot and staunch freedom fighter because of the complexity of his destiny, his controversial political moves, and his relationship with Nazi Germany and collaboration with imperialist Japan.

Glasnost is removing many blank spaces in Soviet history and in the USSR's relations with foreign countries and restoring the truth about various events and personalities. Thus, quite a few complicated episodes in Soviet-Polish relations have been brought to light. Soviet researchers are now also revising their attitudes towards Subhas Chandra Bose.

APPENDIX V

OPERATIONAL PRIORITY - SECRET

OPERATIONAL PRIORITY   C/S   RJM/jrf

17 OCTOBER 1945

FROM : CINCAFPAC ADV

TO : SACSEA

REFERENCE FOUR THREE FIVE OF ONE ONE OCTOBER PD CA. 53440) MISTER SHIGEMITSU IS STILL ALIVE BUT IS PHYSICALLY UNABLE TO MAKE THE TRIP TO DELHI AT THIS TIME PD MISTER MATSUMOTO CMA VICE MINISTER OF FOREIGN AFFAIRS FROM NOVEMBER ONE NINE FOUR TWO TO OCTOBER ONE NINE FOUR FOUR AND MISTER SAWADA CMA VICE MINISTER OF FOREIGN AFFAIRS FROM OCTOBER ONE NINE FOUR FOUR TO MAY ONE NINE FOUR FIVE CMA ARE AVAILABLE PD THEY WOULD PROBABLY BE THE BEST SUBSTITUTES FOR MR. SHIGEMITSU PD REPRESENTATIVES OF THE FOREIGN OFFICE HAVE SUGGESTED THAT THIS TRIAL IS POSSIBLY IN CONNECTION WITH RELATIONSHIPS WITH CHANDRA BOSE PD FURTHER THAT THE INDIAN ARMY AFFAIRS IN CONNECTION WITH CHANDRA BOSE ACTIVITIES WERE HANDLED BY THE IMPERIAL GENERAL HEADQUARTERS FD MISTER HACHIYA CMA WHO WAS JAPANESE MINISTER TO CHANDRA BOSE CMA IS NOW SUPPOSED TO BE IN SAIGON OR BANKOK PD HE WOULD HAVE MOST INTIMATE KNOWLEDGE OF ANY MATTERS HANDLED BY THE JAPANESE GOVERNMENT AND CHANDRA BOSE PD THE TWO VICE MINISTERS WILL BE SENT TO DELHI IF YOU SO DESIRE PD WILL AWAIT

FURTHER WORD FROM YOU ~~SECRET~~

OFFICIAL :

    N. W. ALLEN
    Colonel, A.G.D.,
    Asst Adjutant General

DISTRIBUTION

C/S (2)
Legal Section
G-2
CIO
British Staff Section

435 - 11 Oct 45

Appendices

COPY   COPY

~~SECRET~~   OPERATIONAL PRIORITY

11 October 1945

Supreme Commander Allied Powers

TO : SCAP, R, ALFSEA C IN C INDIA
FROM: SACSEA
NR : 435

DECLASSIFIED PER EO 11652

Joint trial by General Court Martial of 3 officers of the Indian Army commences in Delhi 5 November. These charged with traitorous conduct and murder and or brutal treatment.

CINC INDIA has asked whether Mr Mamoru Shigam Itsu, Foreign Minister, is still alive or a senior member of the Japanese Foreign Office who could give information regarding Indian affairs could be made available as witness. He would be witness for the defence but in view of importance of trial and publicity being given to it by many political leaders in India request such official be made available if reasonably possible.

Grateful you signal soonest whether witness can be sent and if so proposals regarding his despatch.

No Sig

TOO : 101425 Z
MCN : YFA 26

DISTRIBUTION:

    ACTION COPY TO:

       LEGAL SECTION

    INFORMATION COPIES TO:

       COMMANDER-IN-CHIEF
       CHIEF OF STAFF
       G-2
       C CI O
       BRITISH STAFF SECTION

OPERATIONAL PRIORITY

7649
COPY   COPY

APPENDIX VI
Pramode Sengupta C/O Dr. H. N. Sen Krishnanagar, Bengal

When the Germans occupied Paris in June 1941. I joined from Indian Students and set out for the South. After a lot of adventures we reached Toulouse where we settled down with our studies at the University.

In next year as the war was entering a decisive phase, I felt very restless. It was about this time that we began to hear all sorts of rumours about Netaji. We all knew that he had escaped from India but what happened to him after that? According to one Reuter message appearing in all French papers, Subhas Chandra Bose died in a plane crash while he was flying to Japan. After a few days, however. I read in a Swiss paper. Journal de Geneve, that he was living in Germany. Then for a long time there was no news about him at all. It was all very confusing.

Again in the months of May and June, more rumours began to spread among the Indian colony in the South of France. Some said Netaji had been to Paris. Soon afterwards I came to know that some of my friends had "disappeared", nobody could say where. Was it the work of the Gestapo or was it an escape from blockaded France? Naturally I was very much perturbed.

However I was not to remain in darkness for a long time. One day as I was about to leave for the University, one of those "disappeared" friends emerged before me. It was Dr. J. K. Banerjee the former correspondent of the Hindustan Standard. We sat down in a Cafe and there I heard from him the whole story of Netaji's activity in Germany. Banerjee came from Netaji with a message inviting me to go to Berlin in order to discuss with him if I would like to collaborate in his movement which he just initiated. I was also told that I would be given a return ticket and if I did not agree to work with Netaji, I could come back whenever I liked.

It was not easy for me to accept Netaji's invitation. My greatest difficulty was that I have been an active anti-fascist and therefore to go to Germany in the midst of the War appeared to me betraying my own cause. But then we saw that the War had created a new situation which gave us many opportunities for furthering the cause of Indian Independence. The other alternative was to sit quiet and rot in France until the end of the War. I discussed the problem with Banerjee for three days from all angles and then finally decided to meet Netaji in Berlin.

When I reached the German capital, I was taken to Netaji's residence...at the end of the Tiergarten in Sophien Strasse which formerly belonged to the Press Attache of the British Embassy. After a prolonged discussion with Netaji. I agreed to join his movement and start my work at once.

I came to know from Netaji and from others that he had to overcome immense difficulties before he could have his own way. Netaji succeeded in reaching Germany after a long and risky journey through Afghanistan and the Soviet Union just before Germany made that fatal decision of invading Russia. He was so run down by the journey that he had to spend several months in a sanatorium to recover his health. After coming back from the sanatorium Netaji began to negotiate with the German Foreign Office in order to establish an Indian organization in Berlin and to organize INA.

But some of the high Nazi officials were hard nut to crack. They were not waging the war for philanthropic motives. Some of the German militarists had even plans of conquering India after defeating the British. There was also a powerful section of aristocratic officials, who imbued with Nazi racial doctrine, were attached to their cousins on the other side of the Channel and equally hostile to any colonial struggle for independence. The object of these hard-headed Nazis was to exploit Netaji and the Indian movement by setting up a special India

Department under the German Foreign Office. Netaji naturally flatly refused to cooperate with the German Government unless India was recognized as a free nation and he was allowed to form his own independent organization. Netaji was, however, fortunate in having the support of some important Foreign Office men like State Minister Keppler and Dr. von Trott zu Solz. Keppler, like many Germans, had a sort of mystic reverence for India genuinely believing in India's cause. Later on it was he who brought Netaji into contact with Ribbentrop and Hitler.

Dr. von Trott was a different type of person. He was only in his thirties and formerly a member of the German Social Democratic Party and had traveled widely in Asia. For sometime he studied at Oxford and there formed an intimate friendship with Prof. Humayun Kabir. A genuine believer in Indian and Chinese revolution, he subsequently became one of the leading members of the anti-Hitler conspiracy -and after the attempt on Hitler in July 1944 failed, he was hanged together with hundreds of other high-ranking officers.

Finally the German Government agreed to accept Netaji's proposal and in March 1942, the Zentrate Freie Indien (Azad Hind Sangh) was established in Berlin. It was given a diplomatic status and even though India was not a de facto independent state. Netaji was given all the privileges of an ambassador. In all official communications, he was called His Excellency Mazotta which was an Italian name he used in his passport while traveling to Germany.

Netaji also told me that apart from recognizing the Azad Hind Sangh as an independent body, the agreement with the Government was based only on common fight -against British imperialism; regarding the war against the Soviet Union, the Azad Hind Sangh will remain neutral; and Germany will lend to the Azad Hind Sangh a definite sum every month which will be paid back after India was free.

I had still one more question—on what basic principle

the Azad Hind Sangh and the INA will be organized? Netaji replied that he was there as the representative of the whole of India, not as the leader of a group. His object was to unite all the anti-imperialist forces in India against the British Government. Netaji was firmly convinced that unless all the revolutionary forces were united for the common cause, India could not be liberated. He did not believe that India could be freed by foreign intervention. The main revolutionary upsurge must come from within, from the masses of the people and the AHS and the INA are only part of that broader struggle. Netaji emphasized not only on the need for Hindu-Muslim unity but also stressed upon the urgency of building up a united anti-imperialist struggle consisting of all the revolutionary parties of India.

That was the spirit which prevailed in the AHS office at 2, Lichtenstein Alley situated in the midst of the diplomatic quarters of Tiergarten which before the War used to be the Luxemburg Embassy. The activities of the AHS consisted of broadcasting through the Azad Hind Radio in English and in all the important languages of India; supplying news and articles to the German Press; bringing out a German-English bi-monthly magazine called Azad Hind etc. I was not long in Berlin when Netaji was invited by Hitler for an interview. In course of the conversation Netaji asked Hitler whether he really believed what he wrote about India in Mein Kampf. Hitler said that at that time it was necessary for Germany to be on friendly terms with England and he would delete those passages from the next edition.

The most important work of Netaji in Germany was the creation of the INA. He was convinced that without an army of her own, India would not be able to win and retain her independence. Soon after my arrival in Berlin, I was taken by Netaji to visit the INA training centre Frankenberg near Dresden. There we found that tremendous enthusiasm prevailed among men. They all had a profound faith in Netaji and were prepared to die for him and for the cause. Another aspect which impressed me very much was their extraordinary sense of solidarity. There was no difference between Hindus, Moslems, Sikhs and Christians. We all dined together around the same table and ate food prepared by Moslems. An expert German officer Major Krappe was in charge of the military training of the INA. Major Krappe who had a profound respect for Netaji, treated the INA men as his own children and took a keen interest in their training.

None of us had ever suspected that Netaji's stay in Germany would be so short. As the developments in South-East Asia offered him better chance for materializing his dreams, he arranged with General Oshima, the Japanese Ambassador in Berlin for a submarine trip to Shonan (Singapore). In the beginning of February 1943, he left us saying that he was going for a long inspection tour. We all believed him and waited for his return. Then one day in June, it was announced in the newspapers that Netaji had safely reached Shonan.

Pramode Sengupta

INDEX

Anandamath, 7, 266, 269

Anderson, John, 105, 106,107,108,111, 170, 171, 273

Anushilan Samity, 1, 18, 22, 23, 24, 26, 27, 28, 33, 41, 51, 52, 53, 55, 91, 204, 222, 223, 226, 227, 228, 230, 241, 245, 249, 250, 265, 268, 270, 271, 275, 276, 281, 285, 286, 290, 291

Anandabazar Patrika, 111, 172, 209, 236

Army, Hindustan Socialist Republican, 53

Association, Hindustan Republican, 54

Ataturk, Kamal, 154, 208,

Atmashakti, 18

Bakshi, Satyaranjan, 48, 64, 84, 202, 213, 215, 256, 257, 259

Banerjee, J.K., 117

Banerjee, Madhu, 107,108

Banerjee, Manoranjan, 108,109

Banerjee, Rabi, 108, 109

Bank, Mahalakshmi, 60

Bari, Abdul, 97

Barret, Tufnell, 103

Barisal, 77, 82

Basu, Rash Behari, 21, 22, 23, 25, 60, 125, 267, 275, 291, 292

Basu, Satish, 265

Bengal Chemicals, 54

Bengal Renaissance, 51

Bengal Volunteers, 1, 19, 29, 41, 44, 52, 55, 56, 59, 61,62, 69,76, 91, 108, 204, 211, 213, 223, 224, 243, 255, 258, 259, 274, 281, 282, 286

Bengal Regulation III of 1818, 16, 134, 129, 133, 137, 139, 143, 149, 150, 162

Bengal Emergency Powers Ordinance, 291

Benu, 66, 71

Bernherdi, Friedrich von, 22

Bhowmik, Ramen, 87

Bhabani Mandir, 269

Bhabanipore Group, 89

Bhattacharya, Bhabani, 108,109,110

Bhattacharya, Narendra, 23, 26

Bhattacharya, Pratul, 57

Bijoli, 18,

Birla, G.D., 110, 190, 196,
Black and Tans, 105, 106, 107
Bose, Janakinath, 132
Bose, Jyotish, 259, 260
Bose, Satyen, 27
Bose, Sarat, 65, 79, 102, 103, 167,168, 212, 241, 245, 246, 247, 280
Bose, Binay, 86, 67
Breen, Dan, 103, 104, 284
CPGB, 156, 179, 180, 198, 207, 218
CPSU, 180
Calcutta Congress, 28, 29, 30, 33, 41, 42, 43, 45, 47, 49, 55, 82
Cama, Madame, 22, 125, 127,128, 173, 174, 175
Camp, Hijli, 85
Case, Lahore Conspiracy, 55, 52
Chakrabarty, Ambika Charan, 244, 247
Chakrabarty, Narendra Narayan, 87, 214
Chakrabarty, Binod, 57
Chakrabarty, Trailokya, 227, 228, 275
Chatterjee, Jogesh, 52, 53
Chattopadhyay, Bankim Chandra, 172, 266, 269, 276
Chattopadhyay, Ramananda, 169
Chattopadhyay, Sarat Chandra, 68, 90
Chattopadhyay, Suniti Kumar, 26
Chattopadhyay, Virendranath, 116,125,128, 174, 175
Chaudhury, Suniti, 69
Chittagong Armoury Raid, 59, 60, 98, 104, 111, 112,144, 221, 240, 244
Chokkalingam, T.S., 82
Chowdhury, Ashrafuddin Ahmad, 275
Comintern, 8, 27,116, 288, 290
Commission, Simon. 35, 38
Dakshin Kolikata Sevak Samity, 53
Das, Anil, 69
Das, Bina, 69
Das, C.R., 8, 9, 10,11,12, 13, 14,15,17,18,19,20,40,42,45,46, 64, 92, 114,163, 165,167,237, 255, 265, 268, 271, 284
Dasgupta, Sasanka (Comet), 257, 259
Das, Jatin, 52, 53, 54, 55, 56, 75, 80, 103, 214, 282
Das, Pulin, 52
Das, Purna, 13, 28, 51, 70, 83, 232
Despard, Madame Charlotte, 100, 101, 123
Devi, Basanti, 40, 42
Devi, Sarala, 249
Dimitrov, G.M., 288
Dipali Sangha, 29, 64
Dutt, Rajni Palme, 178, 218
Dutta, Bhupendra Nath, 270
Gandhi, M.K., 2, 3, 9, 11, 21, 29, 39, 40, 41, 45, 46, 47, 48, 51, 56, 57, 65, 72, 73, 75, 78, 81, 90, 92, 111, 112, 113, 114, 118, 119, 144, 164, 165, 166, 167, 182, 188, 189, 192,193, 195, 197, 199, 203, 208, 212, 224, 225, 234, 235, 254, 255, 260, 274, 283
Ganguli, Bipin, 70

Index 327

Ganguli, Pratul, 28,52,53, 83, 228, 241, 249, 275, 277, 290
Ganguli, Shantimoy, 258
Garibaldi, 40, 240
Gaya Congress, 284
Ghadar Party, 21, 22, 60,125, 290
Ghosh, Amalendu, 259
Ghosh, Aurobindo, 20,126,152, 236, 239, 240, 265, 267, 268, 271, 276
Ghosh, Atul Krishna, 23
Ghosh, Ganesh, 58, 60, 273
Ghosh, Hem Chandra, 19, 39,52, 61, 62, 64, 66,69, 70,71, 257
Ghosh, Shanti, 69
Ghosh, Sukumar, 107, 108, 110
Ghosh, Suren, 28
Greenwood, Arthur, 176
Guha, Arun, 28,84
Guha, Jatish, 107, 212, 257, 259
Gupta, Badal, 70
Gupta, Dinesh, 29, 39, 40, 67, 69, 70, 71, 73, 246
Gupta, Satya, 30, 52, 57, 62, 63, 67
Hashmi, Jalaluddin, 83
Huxley, Aldus, 145
Irwin, Lord, 48, 72, 97
Jinnah, M.A., 196, 234
Joardar, Jyotish, 67
Jugantar, 1, 20, 23, 28, 29, 32, 34, 41, 51, 89, 90, 91, 111,112, 152, 222, 223, 224, 271, 274, 281, 284
Krishnavarma, Shyamji, 22, 125, 173
Lahore Congress of 1929, 33, 48
Lahore Conspiracy Case, 74
Lala Hardayal, 22, 60, 125,128
Lala Lajpat Rai, 127,128, 237, 239
Lotus and Dragon society, 268

Lowman, 69, 70
Mallik, Mati, 108, 109
Majumdar, Bhupati, 21, 22, 26
Majumdar, Hemaprova, 210
Majumdar, Ujjala, 69,108,109
McBride, Madame Maud Gonne, 100,102, 123
McSwiney, Terence, 56, 103, 156, 214
Maw, Ba, 201, 202
Maxton, James, 160,161
Mein Kampf, 115
Midnapore College, 70
Mitra, P.N.,265, 267
Mitra, Santosh, 81
Modern Review, 169
Mosley,Oswald, 107
Mukherjee, Abani, 22, 25, 26, 27
Mukherjee, Jatindra Nath, 23, 240, 270
Mukhopadhyay, Jadu Gopal, 21, 240
Mukti Sangha, 19, 39, 51, 52, 61, 63, 64, 69, 91
Mulgand, Narsingh, 121
Nag, Lila, 29, 64
Nambiar, A.C.N., 116,117
Nehru, Jawaharlal, 2, 28, 33, 47, 99, 100, 158, 159, 164,165,172, 174, 177, 191, 192, 197, 198, 224, 230
Nehru, Motilal, 11, 40, 41, 42, 45, 56, 57, 165, 237
Neruda, Pablo, 57
Pal, Bipin Chandra, 126, 173, 174, 236, 237, 276
Patel, Vallavbhai, 11, 46, 76, 78, 118,119,120, 165
Patel,V.J., 101, 103, 104, 113, 114, 118, 119, 120, 121, 193

Pather Dabi, 66
Prabasi, 145
Pundit, Vijaylakshmi, 41, 217
Punjab Nau Jawan Bharat Sabha, 67, 75
Rahman, Habib-ur, 117
Rajguru, 73, 79
Ray, Anil, 232
Ray, Kiran Shankar, 83
Ray, Bhupendra Kishore Rakshit, 63, 68, 76
Ray, Kamakshya, 257, 258
Ray, Manindra Kishore, 256
Ray, R.E.A., 32, 90
Ray, Rammohan, 265, 266
Roy, M.N., 197, 200
Rodda Arms Raid, 61
Roy, Dilip Kumar, 96
Roy, Krishnadas, 163, 164, 165, 166, 167, 182
Royal Irish Constabulary, 292
Saha, Meghnad, 54
Sanyal, Sachin, 24, 25, 54
Sen, Keshab Chandra, 266
Sen, Narendra Mohan, 52
Sen, Satindra Nath, 77, 84
Sen, Surya, 41, 51, 58, 59, 60, 221, 281
Sengupta, Binay, 257
Sengupta, J.M., 33, 40, 41, 44, 76, 79
Sengupta, Subodh Chandra, 66, 266
Sengupta, Sunil, 71
Sengupta, Tarakeshwar, 81
Shankha, 18
Shaw, George Bernard, 145
Shri Sangha, 63, 112
Simpson, 85
Singh, Bhagat, 2, 52, 55, 56, 73, 74, 75, 76, 77, 79, 92, 125, 282
Singh, Kripal, 24
Singha, Ananta, 60
Sinn Fein, 74, 96, 97, 104, 157, 177, 220, 284, 285
Sister Nivedita, 265, 268
Sorensen, 161
South Calcutta Youth Association, 67
Sukhdev, 73, 79
Swami Vivekananda, 7, 62, 179, 222, 223, 264, 265, 277
Swarajya Party, 11, 13, 15, 20, 27, 40, 46, 64, 65, 104, 114, 165, 237, 187, 284
Tagore, Rabindra Nath, 24, 66, 145, 172, 197, 241, 255, 276
Tagore, Suren, 265, 269
Talwar, Bhagatram, 257, 288, 289
TASS, 116
Tegart, Charles, 11, 13, 14, 246
Thurtle, Ernest, 135, 161
Tilak, Lokmanya, 2, 126, 152, 236, 237, 269, 282
Triple Crown, 65
Valera, de, 100, 104, 113, 153, 154, 155, 156, 157, 177, 216, 220, 284
Vidyasagar, Ishwar Chandra, 266, 276
Waddedar, Pritilata, 68
Wells, H.G., 145
Wilkinson, Ellen, Cicely, 160
Woods, Mrs., 100, 101, 105, 122, 123, 153
Zetland, Lord, 157, 187, 192.